Silence, Feminism, Power

Also by Aimee Carrillo Rowe

POWER LINES: ON THE SUBJECT OF FEMINIST ALLIANCES

Silence, Feminism, Power

Reflections at the Edges of Sound

Edited by

Sheena Malhotra and Aimee Carrillo Rowe
California State University, Northridge, USA

First published 2013 by
PALGRAVE MACMILLAN

Palgrave Macmillan in the UK is an imprint of Macmillan Publishers Limited,
registered in England, company number 785998, of Houndmills, Basingstoke,
Hampshire RG21 6XS.

Palgrave Macmillan in the US is a division of St Martin's Press LLC,
175 Fifth Avenue, New York, NY 10010.

Palgrave Macmillan is the global academic imprint of the above companies
and has companies and representatives throughout the world.

Palgrave® and Macmillan® are registered trademarks in the United States,
the United Kingdom, Europe and other countries.

ISBN 978–1–137–00236–5

This book is printed on paper suitable for recycling and made from fully
managed and sustained forest sources. Logging, pulping and manufacturing
processes are expected to conform to the environmental regulations of the
country of origin.

A catalogue record for this book is available from the British Library.

A catalog record for this book is available from the Library of Congress.

Transferred to Digital Printing in 2013

For Audre and Gloria,
in whose voices our silences reside

Contents

Acknowledgments

This project was birthed in community, in the spaces between silence and voice. It has been carried by the enthusiastic resonance it found in the audiences who were present in the first conference sessions in which we participated on the subject. We thank those audiences for encouraging its potential in the very beginning. *Silence, Feminism, Power* got molded and took its shape through the work of the writing circle to which we belong, which includes many contributors to the volume. We give our thanks to Laila Farah, Cricket Keating, Kimberlee Pérez, Francesca Royster, Ann Russo, and Kathryn Sorrells for the many readings and the feedback throughout the various incarnations of the project. To the writers who have stayed with us along the way, and to those who helped shape the project, we give thanks.

Silence, Feminism, Power found a home and really came into being at Palgrave Macmillan, and we are especially grateful to the editorial staff there. In particular, we appreciate the work and support of Felicity Plester, who believed in the present vision for the project even before we did, and of Catherine Mitchell, who has been invaluable in manifesting the minute details that turned the vision into a book. We thank Cherline Daniel and Adele Cole for their fine copy-editing of our manuscript.

Finally, we are always and ever grateful to our moms, Jamila Malhotra and Alicia Rowe, who believed in our work; their graceful embodiment of the possibilities within silence has inspired us.

Contributors

Kris Acheson-Clair, PhD, is Director of Undergraduate Studies and a lecturer in intercultural communication in the Department of Applied Linguistics at Georgia State University, USA. She studies communicative silences and communication across race and class, and is also interested in the relationship between ethnocentrism and language learning, use, and attrition.

Bryant Keith Alexander, PhD, is Professor of Communication Studies and Dean, College of Communication and Fine Arts at Loyola Marymount University, Arlington, Virginia, USA. He is coeditor of *Performance Theories in Education* (2005), and author of *Performing Black Masculinity: Race, Culture, and Queer Identity* (2006) and *The Performative Sustainability of Race* (2012).

Jeffrey T. Bile received his PhD in communication studies from Ohio University, USA. He is an associate professor in the School of Communication at Spalding University in Louisville, Kentucky, USA. His work is carried out at the intersection of critical cultural studies, feminist theory, social ecology, and critical rhetoric.

Aimee Carrillo Rowe, PhD, is Associate Professor of Communication Studies at California State University, Northridge, USA. She teaches and writes in the areas of rhetoric, feminist theory, and cultural studies. Her book, *Power Lines: On the Subject of Feminist Alliances* (2008), explores subjectivity as relational, generating possibilities for transracial feminist alliances.

Robin Patric Clair, PhD, is a full professor in the Brian Lamb School of Communication, Purdue University, West Lafayette, Indiana, USA. She teaches courses in organizational communication, ethnography, and rhetoric. She is the author of *Organizing Silence: A World of Possibilities* (1998) and has won the Outstanding Book of the Year award as well as the Golden Anniversary Award from the National Communication Association.

Laila Farah, PhD, is a Lebanese-American feminist performer-scholar. She is an associate professor and graduate director in the Department of Women's and Gender Studies at DePaul University, Chicago, Illinois, USA. She continues to work on future performances, and tours with her production of *Living in the Hyphen-Nation*. Her creative scholarship includes publications of postcolonial identities and "alien-nation," ethnographic, and autoethnographic performance.

Alexandra Fidyk, PhD, is an assistant professor in the Department of Secondary Education, University of Alberta, Canada, and adjunct faculty at Pacifica Graduate Institute, California, USA. Her work draws from process philosophy, depth psychology, Buddhist thought, curriculum theory, and poetic inquiry. She is a certified Jungian psychotherapist.

Sarah Amira de la Garza, PhD, is a Southwest Borderlands Scholar at Arizona State University, USA. A performance ethnographer and postcolonial methodologist, her work interrogates culture, spirituality, and gender through performance and autoethnographic writing. She is the author of *Maria Speaks: Journeys into the Mystery of the Mother in My Life as a Chicana* (2004).

Julia R. Johnson, PhD, is faculty and an associate dean at University of Wisconsin-La Crosse, USA. She is a critical intercultural communication scholar. Some of her recent publications have appeared in the *Journal of International and Intercultural Communication* and edited volumes such as *Border Rhetorics: Charting Enactments of Citizenship and Identity on the U.S.–Mexico Frontier* (2012).

Christine (Cricket) Keating, PhD, is an associate professor in the Department of Women's, Gender, and Sexuality Studies at Ohio State University, USA, and is a codirector of la Escuela Popular Norteña, a popular education center based in Valdez, New Mexico, USA.

Rachel Levitt is a graduate student of American studies and a teaching assistant for the Women Studies Program at the University of New Mexico, USA. Her research interests include postcolonial queer studies, feminist theories, comparative settler colonialisms, and legal theories of identity.

Cheryl Lossie, PhD, is faculty at Fayetteville Technical Community College, North Carolina, USA and teaches public speaking for the US Army

John F. Kennedy Special Warfare Center and School at Fort Bragg, North Carolina, USA. She has been fascinated by the silence heard through listening ever since her first community building experience with the Foundation for Community Encouragement.

Sheena Malhotra, PhD, is Professor and Chair of Gender and Women's Studies at California State University, Northridge, USA. Her research focuses on media in India and the Indian diaspora, drawing on feminist media studies and transnational/postcolonial feminism. She is coauthor of *Answer The Call: Virtual Migration in Indian Call Centers* (2013).

Kimberlee Perez is currently finishing her dissertation at Arizona State University, USA. She writes, performs, and teaches at the intersections of performance, culture, and queerness.

Della Pollock, PhD, is Professor of Communication Studies at the University of North Carolina (UNC) at Chapel Hill, USA, specializing in performance and cultural studies. She is the author of *Telling Bodies Performing Birth* (1999), editor of *Remembering: Oral History Performance and Exceptional Spaces: Essays in Performance and History* (2005), and coeditor of the journal *Cultural Studies*. She is Acting Director of the Southern Oral History Program at UNC and Executive Director of the non-profit Jackson Center for Saving and Making History.

Francesca T. Royster, PhD, is Professor of English at DePaul University, Chicago, Illinois, USA. Her publications include two books, *Sounding Like a No-No: Queer Sounds and Eccentric Acts in the Post-Soul Era* (2012) and *Becoming Cleopatra: The Shifting Image of an Icon* (2003), as well as numerous essays.

Ann Russo, PhD, teaches women's and gender studies at DePaul University, Chicago, Illinois, USA. Her books include *Taking Back Our Lives* (2001), *Talking Back, Acting Out* (2002), and *Third World Women and the Politics of Feminism* (1990). Her current project is *Cultivating Accountability: Transformative Practices to End Everyday Oppression and Violence*.

Susan B. Shimanoff, PhD, is Associate Dean of the College of Liberal and Creative Arts and Professor of Communication Studies at San Francisco State University, USA. Her research interests include communication rules, emotional expressiveness, gendered perspectives on communication, facework, and lesbian, gay, bisexual, transgender, and queer representations in children's picture books.

Gust A. Yep, PhD, is Professor of Communication Studies and core graduate faculty of sexuality studies at San Francisco State University, USA. He has authored over 60 articles in interdisciplinary journals and anthologies and is the lead editor of *Queer Theory and Communication: From Disciplining Queers to Queering the Discipline(s)* (2004).

1
Still the Silence: Feminist Reflections at the Edges of Sound

Aimee Carrillo Rowe and Sheena Malhotra

Reflections on silence

This book provides a series of reflections on the paradoxes and transformative possibilities of silence. Our title, *Silence, Feminism, Power: Reflections at the Edges of Sound,* evokes the paradoxical relationship between sound and silence that is obscured when we assume an equation between voice and agency, and its inverse equation—silence and oppression. Our impulse is to challenge the binaristic relationship that has been assigned since antiquity to voice vis-à-vis silence. We seek to break with the Western tradition, reiterated from Aristotle to Audre Lorde, that locates silence as a site of reform and privileges voice as the ultimate goal of and means to achieve empowerment. If one of the major interventions we have inherited from Lorde (1984b) is that the "master's tools will never dismantle the master's house" (110), our work seeks out new tools of speaking, listening, and wading into the fullness of silence.

The articulation between silence and powerlessness is almost common sense within Western culture, an assumption that is reified across literary, progressive academic, and activist contexts. Its equation presumes a political imperative: for an individual or group who is silenced to gain power, they must activate *voice* in order to resist and transform the conditions of their oppression. Sometimes an intermediary (a more powerful representative) can "speak for" the subaltern or marginalized classes.[1] The lacuna within this formulation is that the burden of social change is placed upon those *least* empowered to intervene in the conditions of their oppression. The figure of the subaltern gaining voice captures the political imaginary, shifting the focus away from the labor that might be demanded of those in positions of power to learn to listen

1

to subaltern inscriptions—those modes of expression that are often interpreted as "silence." This anthology interrupts this dynamic, providing a new imaginary for how the spaces between silence and voice might be traversed. It opens up space between transnational feminist work on subalternity and US third world feminist calls for women of color to come to voice. As such it functions as a bridge piece, joining women of color and their white allies—and various groups who are unevenly empowered—at the edges of sound.

Silence, Feminism, Power builds on the ironic relationship between voice, silence, and power to reveal the complexities that lie within these often-obscured interconnections. Authors engage questions like: What forms of resistance and healing does silence make possible? What nuances, strategic forms of engagement and ways of navigating or resisting power are made possible through silence? What alliances might be enabled as we learn to read silences? Under what conditions is it productive to move between voice and silence? How might the binaristic construction of voice and silence be reconfigured and with what political effects? What *is* silence?

Silence, Feminism, Power examines silence as a space of possibility. The authors argue that in entering the stillness of silence we might communicate deeply at the edges of sound. Silence allows us the space to breathe. It allows us the freedom of not having to exist constantly in reaction to what is said. Standing in silence allows for that breath, for that reflection that can create a space of great healing. We theorize silence as a space of fluidity, non-linearity, and as a sacred, internal space that provides a refuge—especially for nondominant peoples. Silence is a process that allows one to go within before one has to speak or act. This is crucial if our work as activists, writers, and creative artists is to come from a grounded place that connects the spiritual with the political.

In what follows we detail the various literature on silence and voice. We begin with a discussion of disciplinary and interdisciplinary treatments of silence, exploring the ways in which disciplinarity can enable, but also constrain, how silence is theorized. Next, we provide a more detailed account of feminist treatments of silence. Finally, we trace a genealogy of feminist treatments of silence as a political and intellectual point of departure for this volume.

Disciplinary and interdisciplinary treatments of silence

The authors featured here draw on a host of academic disciplines and interdisciplinary fields with a history of theorizing silence, primarily rhetoric and communication studies, postcolonial studies, anthropology, and critical pedagogy. This chapter traces a body of related research to excavate a genealogy of silence as it has emerged as an object of intellectual inquiry. It focuses primarily on critical and feminist perspectives, especially those critics and theorists who have examined the relationships between silence, voice, and power. We note the disciplinary frames in which silence has emerged and consider what's gained and lost through previous discipline-based investigations of silence. We also consider the importance of interdisciplinary approaches to silences, like the one we employ in this volume.

While the literature on silence crosses various fields that are beyond the scope of the project at hand, we have limited our review of the literature to the disciplines from which the scholars and writers included here draw their insights and expertise. Silence, for instance, has a long tradition that is associated with Buddhist meditative practices. Buddhist practitioner Thich Nhat Hanh explains that silence is not an external but an internal state that is achieved through mindful living: "Silence comes from our heart and not from the absence of talk" (2009, p. 76). Silence has also been associated with yoga as a means to achieve deep reflection and meditation. Yogic practitioner Steven Cope describes the ways in which his energy shifts when he engages in "restraint" from speaking: "My energy is clear. It's powerful. It's focused, and quiet all at the same time" (Cope, 2006, p. 163). While many of our authors are inspired by the teachings of Buddhists like Thich Nhat Hanh and Pema Chodron and engage in yogic practices, the expansive scholarship that surrounds their texts is beyond the scope of this book.

Rhetoric and communication studies

The relationship between silence and voice has emerged as an important topic of investigation in the fields of rhetoric and communication studies. Heavily influenced by Western understandings of communication practices, voice has traditionally been elevated as a privileged object of study within these fields (Tannen and Saville-Troike, 1985). Deborah Tannen and Muriel Saville-Troike challenge traditional treatments of silence and voice, drawing on close readings of conversations to render silence as a "valid object of investigation, bounded by stretches of verbal material which provide boundary marking for its identification" (1985, p. 4). Their work seeks to provide a fuller description of communication processes that are erased through the assumption that silence is absence. In her essay "Silence: Anything But," Tannen[2] (1985) employs conversational analysis to demarcate the distinction between a conversational pause and a silence. She finds that a pause tips into a silence when it is "too long," thus while silence "communicates" for Tannen, it remains negatively valenced within her analysis.

Feminist communication studies scholars such as Karlyn Kohrs Campbell (1989), Lana F. Rakow and Laura A. Wackwitz (2005), and Karen and Sonja Foss (1991) have undertaken important work to uncover women's silences and the patriarchal conditions that produce them, as well as the vital ways in which women leverage voice to resist silence. Campbell (1989) has worked over the long trajectory of her career to recover women's rhetoric by tracing the history of early women's rights movement that focused primarily on women's suffrage. While vital to the field of feminist rhetoric, her work remains bound within a frame that valorizes voice against a backdrop of silence, in which silence is equated with oppression. The work of Rakow and Wackwitz is compelled by this tradition as well, exploring the ways in which "women are either denied access to communication forms...or admitted to them only to have their ideas dismissed out of hand as deviant or irrelevant." Silence for Rakow and Wackwitz is a devastating condition of women's lives to be overcome, for "to have voice is to possess both the opportunity to speak and the respect to be heard" (2005, p. 9). Karen A. Foss and Sonja K. Foss (1991) expand the archive of what constitutes women's voices, exploring the various ways in which women's lives and their art becomes acts of "speaking." Centering women as communicators, their project explores the "eloquence" of women's lives in diverse forms of expression: gardening, graffiti, jewelry design, motherhood, needlework, painting, quilting, photography, and rituals.

Other communication studies scholars have begun to question the equation of silence with absence. Robin Clair and Kris Acheson, whose current work on silences is featured in this volume (chapters 6 and 14), have been at the forefront of this intervention, pushing the field to rethink the assumption that silence is somehow opposed to and distinct from communication. In her important book *Organizing Silence: A World of Possibilities* (1998), Clair argues that silence is both an aesthetic and a political practice that can be traced to the origins of language. She believes that "exploring silence as a fundamental part of communication, culture and conflict may illuminate the complex nature of social relations" (1998, p. 4). Her work looks at the ways in which silence is structured into language and, by extension, "interests, issues, and identities of marginalized people," who are "silenced and how those silenced voices can be heard" (Clair, 2012). Drawing on a rich archive of philosophical treatments of silences within communication, she excavates the often-overlooked silences that constitute language, institutions, and society. Her feminist treatment of silences situates silencing practices as embedded in and cross-cut by relations of power. In "Silence is a Gesture: Rethinking the Nature of Communicative Silences" (2008), Acheson argues that silence and speech are often defined as binaristically opposed to one another, obscuring the multiple meanings of silence as a form of human expression. Following the phenomenological work of Merleau-Ponty, Kris Acheson suggests that silence is "as like speech as it is different," thus is a "gesture," enacted by bodies in a physical world. This means, for Acheson, that silence is not secondary to expressed thought but rather is essential to embodied life.

Rhetoric and communication studies scholars have also focused on the relationship between silence, speaking, and listening. Krista Ratcliffe's (2006) *Rhetorical Listening: Identification, Gender, Whiteness* argues that listening is under-examined in both pedagogy and communication theory, while Cheryl Glenn (2004) explores silence as a subordinated term within the rhetorical canon. Ratcliffe (2006) affirms the notion in her observation that "Listening is rarely theorized or taught" (2006, p. 18). She theorizes rhetorical listening as an interpretive invention, and as a code of cross-cultural conduct, as she points out the gendered and raced[3] dimensions of listening, which is a function of power differentials in society, proposing *rhetorical listening* as a practice to bridge these gaps. Glenns' project argues that silence is a "rhetorical art" that has been ignored in the rhetorical tradition due to the elevation of speech as a "gift of the gods" in ancient times (2004, p. 3). Alternately, she proposes that silence "reveals speech," even as it "enacts its own sometimes complementary rhetoric" (2004, p. 3). *Unspoken: A Rhetoric of Silence* is an explicitly feminist project that underscores the importance of choice in assessing the quality of silence. Glenn's opening lines signal the feminist impulse that drives the project as she observes the deeply gendered nature of silence that brought her to the writing: in her efforts to write women into the field of rhetoric, she observes "pockets of female rhetorical activity that punctuated those long stretches of silence" (2004, p. 1).

The work on silence in rhetoric and communication studies has been influenced by philosophical treatments of silence in communication. Clair credits Max Picard as being the first Western philosopher to offer "a full treatment of silence that asserts that *speech and silence exist simultaneously*" (1998, p. 25). Picard personifies silence, characterizing it as "always present" during human communication: "Silence is listening. That is what gives breath to a conversation" (1948, p. 25). Silence has a rhetorical force in Picard's writing, a quasi-spiritual essence that "comes from afar" to "give words a new fullness" (1948, p. 25). While these works productively bring silence more fully into focus by challenging the epistemological conditions of its annihilation, they remain bound to Western and modernist assumptions about completeness of understanding. Our volume addresses this gap, providing perspectives on silence from a host of diverse positionalities and inter/disciplinary perspectives. As silences are embedded and performed in specific contexts, silence emerges in multiple manifestations in relation to voice and power.

Anthropology

Silences have also been taken up—as a marker or manifestation of cultural difference and as a category deployed to challenge power relations—in the field of anthropology. Keith Basso's early work on silence within Western Apache culture (1970) was foundational to the theorizing of silence, voice, and culture in the field of anthropology and beyond. His linguistic studies explored the six conditions under which the Western Apache deployed silence: meeting strangers, early courting, children returning home after a long absence, encountering an angry person, and dealing with people in mourning or participants in healing ceremonies. His findings suggest that the Western Apache use silence in situations in which the social status of participants is ambiguous, unsettling expectations for social roles and thus deploying silence to *respectfully* allow for uncertainty to play out. Following Basso's early mapping of Native American silences, Lawrence Gross has conducted a series of studies on the relationship between Anishinaabe uses of silence, open-mindedness, and senses of humor. "I see silence and humor as sharing an attitude of open-mindedness that allows the individual to experience the world as it is and to appreciate the world for what it is, complete with all the contradictions and incongruities that lead to humor," he writes (2007, p. 70). He underscores the importance of silence to what he calls the "comic mind": "the ability to observe the world keenly" (2007, p. 70). Gross is interested in the ways in which silence generates an "openness" of perception among Native Americans, which engenders the capacity to see oneself as flawed and stricken with contradictions—as fragmented, imperfect subjects who can laugh at these incongruities.

Maria-Luisa Achino-Loeb's edited volume titled *Silence: The Currency of Power* argues that studying silence is central to understanding the more elusive aspects of power and identity within anthropological contexts as it enables us to "trust that our categories of experience are discrete, as opposed to arbitrary bindings of fluidity" (Achino-Loeb, 2005, p. 36). Because she situates practices of silence "at the heart of the very experience of any identity as a discrete entity," (p. 3) silence becomes an active and dynamic host of *practices* that anthropologists might excavate to more deeply understand identity formation. Trinh T. Minh-Ha (1989) calls attention to the "suspension of language" as the precondition to knowing the other, a paradoxical voyage through which one arrives only to realize that she has never taken a step. As she poetically writes, "Silence as a will not to say or a will to unsay and as a language of its own has barely been explored" (1990, p. 373). Silence emerges as a threshold between presence and absence, and as intimately tied to agency and resistance. Kamala Visweswaran signals the importance of learning to read silences in ethnographic settings to explore the resistive strategies through which activist women cultivate their identities, such as utilizing strategic omissions that rewrite the 'script' of the ethnographic encounter. She observes that "'Lies, secrets, and silence' are frequently strategies of resistance. Yet the ethnographer's task is often to break such resistance" (1994, p. 60). Visweswaran draws on an ethnographic encounter with a woman she calls "M" to unpack multiple and contradictory uses of silence as resistance. Through various evasions of speech and detours into silence, M refuses to be subjected to the author's anthropological inquiry. Reading M's silences, Visweswaran underscores the importance of how anthropologists construct meaning around silences and how they might be held accountable to subjects' *strategic* uses of silence. "For the story I give you is not exactly about this woman," she says. "...It is rather more about how I negotiate and understand the construction of a silence, how I seek to be accountable to it" (1994, p. 60).

Visweswaran's theatrical reading of M's silences makes her reader aware of the responsibility and accountability that we must undertake when we encounter silence in an/other, and the ways in which we become implicated in the silences of others. Every act of inscription, or assertion of voice, is simultaneously an act of omission. Each time we speak, something is said and so much more is not said. Visweswaran calls these moments "situational knowledges" in the ethnographic contexts. She writes that such "situated accounts by definition exclude some analytic elements from their purview while focusing intensely on others," concluding that "Acts of omission are as important to read as acts of commission in constructing the analysis" (1994, p. 48). This argument

complicates contexts in which feminists of privilege seek to break previous speaking patterns. While it is productive, for instance, for white
antiracist allies to name the specificities of white privilege, it is also
useful to recognize that whiteness continually *speaks over and through*
silence. If every act of commission is contingent upon countless omissions, then voice functions through silence. This means that we can and
should analyze uses of silence within the context of who is speaking,
what is being said, and—especially our concern here—what is *not* being
said within each oration. These texts prompt us to question prevailing
cultural norms around interpretations of silences.

Postcolonial studies

Silence, Feminism, Power builds on the work of the Subaltern Studies
Group (Guha, 1997) to pose processes of subalternity as *relational*—not
as a condition residing within an individual or group but rather as a
relational dynamic that gets played out among differently located social
actors (Carrillo Rowe, 2008). Such a view places responsibility—not only
for silencing processes but also for decoding or reading silences—on
those who hold power and have access to public voice. Thus we take
seriously the challenge put forth by Gayatri Spivak (1998) and others (e.g. Glenn, 2004; Ratcliffe, 2006) that the work of the academic
and political left is to learn to listen to and decode subaltern inscriptions. In her famous essay "Can the Subaltern Speak?", Spivak challenges
critical theorists Michel Foucault and Felix Delueze, who seek to trans-
parently represent subaltern groups. In their efforts to liberate them,
Spivak argues, academic left scholars may unwittingly end up reinscrib-
ing subaltern silences, while gaining value as Western scholars on the
backs of the oppressed. She concludes the essay with a reading of the suicide of a Bengali woman, Bhuvaneswari Bhaduri. The dominant reading
of the suicide would suggest that Bhaduri took her life as an "outcome
of illegitimate passion" (1998, p. 103). So Bhaduri, aware of this diagnosis, "had waited for the onset of menstruation," potentially rewriting
the "social text of sati-suicide in an interventionist way" (1998, p. 103).
In taking the "immense trouble to displace (not merely deny) the physiological inscription of her body," Bhaduri challenges its "imprisonment
within legitimate passion by a single male" (1998, p. 104). While her
act was read as a "case of delirium rather than sanity," it challenges the
male ownership of her body, as well as the edict that the widow should
wait until she is "clean" (no longer menstruating) before she asserts her
"right to immolate herself" (1998, p. 104). Spivak's reading of Bhaduri's
silent inscription is as inspiring as it is politically astute. She interprets
the gesture through a close reading of the various social cues through

which the act of desperation might be reread as an act of resistance. In this way, the subaltern *speaks*, if those in positions of privilege could learn to *listen*—and learn to decode the silences that inscribe resistive meanings to potentially rewrite the social text.

Placing silence and voice, speaker and listener, in relation to one another shifts the responsibility for silencing processes to those who hold power. For instance, King-Kok Cheung's (1993) insightful literary analysis of Asian American women writers decenters the logocentric tendency to privilege voice over silence. She thus invites her readers to become literate in the multiple tongues through which Asian (American) women speak. Her work aims to "explode" the stereotype of passive Asian (American) women, inviting us to become fluent in the strategic and culturally specific uses of silence through which alternative historiographies of Asian America might be decoded. Cheung and others teach us that as cultural workers we must become fluent in reading what is not said, or what is actively omitted, to unravel the imperative to domination embedded within any efforts to represent or know "others."

Critical pedagogy

Critical pedagogy is another site of emerging theories that unearth the binary between silence and voice, centering strategies of silence within the classroom. Alexandra Fidyk, whose work is featured in our volume (Chapter 9), has argued for the centrality of uses of silence in the classroom and in creative, poetic, and scholarly writing. Her (2011) work resituates "knowing and not-knowing" within an alternate epistemic framework: one that privileges contemplative and imaginative ways of knowing in the classroom. Fidyk and others making this move draw upon the work of Parker Palmer, one of the founding critical scholars of engaging contemplative practices in the classroom. In *The Courage to Teach: Exploring the Inner Landscape of a Teacher's Life*, Palmer unpacks the "simple premise: *good teaching cannot be reduced to technique; good teaching comes from the identity and integrity of the teacher*" (1998, p. 10). To do so entails making the teacher "available and vulnerable in the service of learning" (11), a "presence" enabled through practices of mindfulness, such as silence. Working in this tradition, Mary O'Reilly (1984) approaches teaching as a space-clearing activity in a departure from the compulsion to constantly fill the classroom with our voices. She argues that silence creates the classroom as an expansive space in which students can explore their own relationships with the course materials. Tobin Hart (2011) speaks of the deeper nuances of knowing that might be accessed through silence, "Silence also provides access to the streaming depths." He notes that poetry, and Sufi poetry like Jalaluddin Rumi's, has recognized the ways in which in stillness and in breath we are able to access a deeper place and become a conduit for the information we find there. Rumi (1995) writes:

> There is a way between voice and presence where information flows.
> In disciplined silence it opens.
> With wandering talk it closes. (p. 109)

What are the depths of knowing and wisdom we might be able to access through a pedagogy that includes silence as an integral part of its practice?

Other critical pedagogy scholars have situated uses of silence in the classroom in relation to questions of power, identity, and culture. Barbara J. Boseker and Sandra L. Gordon (1983) describe the importance of inverting the traditional frame of indigenous education in the USA. Whereas the traditional model underscores what Native American people need to know "in order to survive in today's world," Boeseker and Gordon argue that educators have much to learn from Native American people: cooperation over competition, collectivity over individualism, consensus over majority rule, the importance of privately attending to the body, and uses of silence. They note that the Native American students and community members with whom they have worked demonstrated a "tolerance for silence" that allows for a "wait-time" following a question, which enables students to engage in "speculative thinking" as opposed to rote memorization. Third world feminist scholar Sherene Razack (1998) interrogates her own complicity with the story-telling imperative within contemporary critical pedagogy when a white woman seeks to draw a story from a black woman, and all the people of color in the room feel that it is not a "safe space." Razack gestures toward the necessity of respecting the "right to silence" but acknowledges that, as an educator, she finds the "idea of silence extremely unsettling" (1998, p. 53). As these examples demonstrate, critical pedagogy scholars excavate their own teaching practices to help students and readers come to a fuller understanding of the importance of silences in the classroom.

A genealogy of feminist treatments of silence

Early second-wave feminist movement writers Adrienne Rich and Tillie Olsen have passionately attended to the politics of women's writing. Their narratives, poetry, and theorizing reveal the often-obscured politics of labor, marginality, and privilege entailed in the production of knowledge—in writing itself. Attending to the gendered and classed restrictions imposed on (white) women writers—on their time, on their labor, on their bodies, on the male reception of their words—Rich and Olsen analyze the texts of their own lives to render palpable the struggle involved in "coming to voice" as women. Rich's work outlines a complex relationship between voice, gender, and silence. Several of her essays address the material conditions that produce women's silences: a lack of time, privacy, and space; the compulsion to serve men and care for children; the exclusion of women from higher education; and men's domination of public spheres of knowledge production. Her book *On Lies, Secrets, and Silence* (1979) traces the struggles of women— particularly feminists of the second-wave historical context in which she writes—to speak and be heard. Rich's tone exudes a sense of urgency as she maps out the stakes for "re-visioning": it is the "act of looking back, of seeing with fresh eyes, of entering an old text from a new critical direction" (1979, p. 35). Re-visioning becomes possible as women break the isolation of domestic life to find each other through writing and speaking. Rich stresses that re-visioning is "an act of survival" for women. "In a world where language and naming are power," she writes, "silence is oppression, is violence" (1979, p. 204). Here Rich underscores in stark terms the equation of silence with oppression. Yet elsewhere, especially in her poetry, silence takes on a surprisingly rich and resistive form:

> Silence can be a plan
> rigorously executed
> the blueprint of a life
> It is a presence
> it has a history a form
> Do not confuse it
> with any kind of absence. (1978, p. 5)

Here silence is expressed as agentive: at once surreptitiously resistive (a plan rigorously executed) and an historical presence. Rich's work, then, points to the complexities and contradictions of silence as both a form of violence that must be rigorously rejected *and* a form of resistance in and of itself.

Rich's contemporary, Olsen, was one of the first feminist writers to highlight the relationship between silence and power. Her work sought to render visible the erasure of countless, overlooked creative processes undertaken by those marginalized by gender, race, and class. Like Rich, Olsen underscores the conditions of women's silences in the male-dominated public sphere. "Literary history and the present are dark with silences," she writes. "Some the silences for years by our acknowledged greats; some silences hidden; some the ceasing to publish after one work appears; some the never coming to book form at all" (1978, p. 6). Also like Rich, Olsen distinguishes between different forms and valences of silence: some are "natural silences" that allow "necessary time for renewal, lying fallow, gestation, in the natural cycle of creation," while others are "unnatural"—the "thwarting of what struggles to come into being, but cannot" (1978, p. 6). Elaine Hedge and Shelly Fisher Fishkin trace a compelling genealogy of Olsen's work, arguing for its continued relevance through their collection. *Listening to Silences: New Essays in Feminist Criticism* investigates the "simultaneously paradigmatic and problematic" components of Oslen's work.[4]

While early (white) feminist writers like Rich and Olsen leveraged their writing and organizing to break silences, their efforts did not necessarily empower all women to speak. Indeed, feminists of color often found white women's efforts to speak for "women" served to reinscribe the very silences that white feminists sought to remedy. The tradition of US third world feminism is forged within a (post)civil-rights context in which women of color challenged oppressions imposed on them by calling for visibility and voice in various cultural and political contexts. Feminists of color writing in the 1970s and 1980s theorized the importance of accounting for the intersections of gender, race, class, and sexuality. Nonetheless, feminists of color did not challenge the basic premise of the political imperative to break silences. From Audre Lorde (1984a) ("your silence will not protect you") to Cherríe Moraga (1981/1983) ("Silence *is* like starvation"), radical feminists of color write about the importance of coming to voice, of overcoming their silences, in order to liberate themselves and others.

Many US feminists of color have palpably interrogated the embodied conditions of their own silences. Gloria Anzaldúa, in her open letter to third world women, encourages women of color writers to write and to speak their truths. "The act of writing is the act of making soul, alchemy," she charges. "It is the quest for the self, for the center of the self, which we women of color have come to think as 'other' – the dark, the feminine. Didn't we start writing to reconcile this other within us?" (Anzaldúa, 1981/1983, p. 169). Her call to expression through writing evokes the importance of finding voice and therefore finding "self" in previously silenced lives. Feminist writers of color have struggled to

break the silences constituted by multiple and intersecting displacements: to speak to the shame of poverty, racism, homophobia, and
gender subordination in their own lives and in the cultural landscapes
in which they are embedded. In this vein, bell hooks echoes Anzaldúa's
call in *Talking Back* (1989) through her vivid critique, which exposes the
lack of cultural spaces for African American women to be heard.

Looking back at this important work, we see a struggle in these
feminist interventions to break free from a purely oppositional stance
in which silence emerges as an unexamined force of oppression that
must be thrown off. We see this dynamic in the generative exchange
between critical race feminist scholars Margaret Montoya and Dorothy
Roberts on the ambiguous nature of women of color silences in the
courtroom and the classroom. Montoya's treatment of silence in the
courtroom attends to the difficulties of distinguishing between silence
that is repressive and silence that is resistive. On the one hand, Montoya
finds that Latin@ silences reinscribe dominant power relations. For
instance, during jury selection processes, silences were misread within
the white courtroom, resulting in Latin@ jurors being dismissed and,
by extension, Latin@ defendants losing the right to be judged by their
peers. Yet Montoya is reticent about dismissing the resistive possibilities of silence out of hand. She concludes her essay by contemplating
her own silence in response to an incident of hate speech on her campus. While she wrote a letter condemning the act, she never sent the
letter. She seems reluctant to settle the score for her readers, yet she
ends her story by noting: "It is hard to know what gives me greater
power—holding silence or breaking silence [...] Finally I have decided
that this incident silenced me, that my silence has not been volitional.
Perhaps that was its purpose" (2000, p. 324). While Montoya ultimately
falls in line with a traditional feminist treatment of silence, reasserting
the equation between silence and oppression, her meditations and critical analyses reveal a host of resistive moments in her own and others'
silences. She seems to relish the possibility that her silence might be
the stance that "gives [her] the greatest power." This moment of possibility is one we seek to tease out more fully in this volume, as well
as the vexed movements between silence and voice we see at work in
her piece. Dorothy Roberts' reading of Montoya's essay seeks to parse
out the conditions under which silences might be oppressive or liberating. She highlights an important point, noting that the task at hand
is not ultimately to figure out the theoretical distinction between subjugation and resistance but "to listen to those who have been silenced
so that we might learn how to work toward a more just society" (2000,

p. 347). Yet Roberts ultimately comes down firmly on the side of the argument that people of color—students in particular—need to break silences: "Our goal for these students of color should be to help them speak up more rather than to encourage them to remain silent" (Roberts, p. 354). Like Montoya, she opens up alternative spaces for readers to decode the silences of people of color, yet she reverts to the logic that we seek to disrupt in this volume: that the burden of speech should fall on those most marginalized. While we affirm the importance of breaking silences, we also want to underscore an alternative path: that those in positions of privilege learn to *read* and *respect* the silences of marginalized people. Montoya and Roberts' essays both *perform* this critical reading practice—they demand that dominant readers decode the silences of people of color in the courtroom and the classroom—even if their arguments ultimately undercut this political possibility.

Taking the impulse to liberate silences a step further, Veena Das' (1997) article, which interrogates the feminist imperative to "break silences," underscores the violence embedded in the relationship between language and pain within imperial contexts. Writing in a philosophical tradition, Gemma Fiumara's work (1990) on a "listening silence" has also informed our conceptualization of how silence works. She critiques Western philosophies for privileging expressive language, while reducing everything else that surrounds language to a void. Drawing on the insights of Ludwig Wittgenstein, Martin Heidegger, and Han Georg Gadamer, among others, she argues for us to develop an authentic listening to silence.

Interrogating the Western compulsion to speak entails that we learn to read silences. Joanna Kadi is a working-class Arab Canadian radical queer woman. The refrain of her piece, "Speaking (About) Silence," is: "If there is a hesitation with which I speak, it is because I am surrounded by spaces filled with my silences. If you want to hear me, listen to my silences as well as my words" (2002, p. 541). Like the spaces between footfalls, or the breath within the breath, there is a deep and abiding kind of knowledge that arises from the spaces *between* words, from the spaces *between* silences. The spaces filled with silences that surround Kadi are those of marginality, of non-belonging. She argues that spaces speak to us, or are spoken by us, telling us who belongs and who does not. "If you feel comfortable and speak easily, it's because those spaces have been set up for and by your own particular group of people" (2002, p. 541). The construction of these spaces is a collective process, then, that takes place through communication practices through which "comfort" is produced through a set of mutually constitutive silences and orations. The "spaces filled with silences" might productively be understood, then, as the silences not of the marginalized but of the privileged—or better, as constitutive of both a process of marginalizing and of privileging.

Mab Segrest writes of the psyche and the soul of the oppressor as functioning through a deep investment in individuality, a sense that we are born to domination, isolation, and separation. Her theory of the souls of white folks offers a chilling account of the Western compulsion to speak. The will to voice and imperative to fill space with words are animated both by a fear of invisibility and a fear of visibility in more full form. To tell the story of hegemony, to tell stories of belonging, requires voice. But the "community of the lie"[5] also functions through a set of strategic omissions, continually (re)staged within our own and our students' communication practices (2002, p. 248). We inherit this story and keep it alive through our spoken silences. Gloria Akasha Hull, in her study of black feminist spirituality, *Soul Talk*, recognizes the relationship between creativity, inspiration, stillness, and silence. Quoting the poet Carolyn Forché ("The language of God is silence"), she equates the "absolutely stunning and sacred sound of silence" with "the space of the all-creative" (Hull, 2001, p. 140).

Silence, Feminism, Power honors the multiplicity of views and struggles of our feminist forerunners; it is inspired by the politics and poetics of their texts. However, we take third world feminist critiques of white women's struggles, which underscore the power imbalances among differently located women, as a point of departure for our text. *Silence, Feminism, Power* works within and against US third world feminist traditions. We recognize that it is the voices and activism of feminists of color from the 1970s and 1980s that have created the space for our explorations today. Without their work to make visible the lives and stories of women of color, racial politics would have continued to oppressively silence and invisibilize us. Just as many feminists of color in this particular historical moment are complicating and further nuancing their arguments about race, identity, and the politics of location, we hope to build on their insights around voice by grappling with notions of silence within feminist praxis. The authors assembled in *Silence, Feminism, Power* are inspired by the political fire of US women of color feminism, but we seek to recuperate the abjection of silence from within these texts. Rather, we consider how feminists (white and of color) deploy, rewrite, and move through silences in multiple and often productive ways. Thus silence is inscribed through diverse tones and textures to reveal how women can be multiply positioned vis-à-vis silence, not always already subjected by it. Some 30 years later, we stand on the shoulders of these women, empowered by the force of their words of fire to carry their political vision to another horizon. Here at the edges of sound we might cultivate a host of silent practices: we might dwell within the possibilities of silence; we might use our silences as a weapon; we might rest; we might meet one another; we might encounter our shadow and our light within its expansive embrace.

Origins and organization of *Silence, Feminism, Power*

Silence, Feminism, Power is an interdisciplinary edited collection from cultural critics on the paradoxes and possibilities of silence. The initial conversations that inspired this book originated at three conference panels in which the editors participated and which they helped to organize: the National Communication Association (2003), the National Women's Studies Association Annual Conference (2004), and the Western States Communication Association Conference (2005). The conversations these panels generated were invigorating. Audiences and panelists alike were eager to rethink and engage the possibilities of silence. Several authors featured in the book participated in those early conversations. We followed this enthusiasm for the topic by collecting work that engaged the silence/voice binary and imagined strategic possibilities for silence in a host of interdisciplinary and activist contexts. We have arranged the essays into the following parts:

- I: Transformative Silences: Intersectionality, Privilege, Alliances;
- II: Learning to Listen: Academia, Silence, Resistance;
- III: Recovering Silences: Community, Family, Intimacy;
- IV: Legacies of Silence: Memory, Healing, Power.

The authors in Part I: "Transformative Silences: Intersectionality, Privilege, Alliances," explore alternate strategies through which we might organize and imagine feminist politics that push up against the voice = empowerment/silence = oppression binary. Exploring what Adrienne Rich calls "cartographies of silence," the authors create new political maps through which to navigate political alliances across power lines. We open with Cricket Keating's essay, "Resistant Silences" (Chapter 2), which argues that in addition to not confusing silence with absence it is vital to distinguish between different forms of silence. Drawing on democratic social theory and transnational feminist theory, Keating maps distinctions between "enforced" silences and "engaged

and oppositional" silences: "silent refusal," "silent witness," and "deliberative silence." Ann Russo's contribution, "Between Speech and Silence:
Reflections on Accountability" (Chapter 3), explores her experience
in a host of feminist organizing contexts. This auto-critique excavates white women's strategic "uses of silence, speech and privilege"
for purposes of empowerment and domination. These insights are, in
turn, extended and recast in queer and multiracial settings in Julia
Johnson's "Qwe're Performances of Silence: Many Ways to Live 'Out
Loud'" (Chapter 4). She explores the possibilities and political stakes
in "qwe'reing silence" to ask how silence can be used to contain
and control resistance within lesbian and gay communities, as well as
how multiracial alliances circulate through silences to disrupt white
supremacy. In "Silence Speaks Volumes: Counter-Hegemonic Silences,
Deafness, and Alliance Work" (Chapter 5), Rachel Levitt interrogates her
hearing privilege in her alliances with members of the deaf community.
She mobilizes silence in its political multiplicity "as resistance to hearing
norms, an act of solidarity, a pedagogical tool, and a counter-hegemonic
strategy."

In Part II: "Learning to Listen: Academia, Silence, Resistance," the
authors explore the multiple roles that silence might play in knowledge
production, progressive pedagogy, and campus activism—creating space
for transformation within academia. In "*Imposed Silence* and the Story of
the Warramunga Woman: Alternative Interpretations and Possibilities"
(Chapter 6), Robin Clair traces a genealogy of scholarly representations of Warramunga women to reconsider the presumption that the
women's silences were necessarily imposed. Alternately, Clair argues,
their silences have been "used, and at times abused, by scholars, for
purposes of theoretical and ideological commentary." Jeff Bile theorizes
the role of silence in human communications with the extra-human
world in "Silence and Voice in a More-than-Human World" (Chapter 7).
The academy's investment in logocentrism, he argues, deafens us to the
sounds of nature and reinscribes the human in an anthropomorphic
world. Sarah Amira de la Garza meditates on the uses of silence and
the ethics of research she conducted in the Navajo nation. Her essay,
"*Inila*: An Account of Opening to Sacred Knowing" (Chapter 8), reflects
on her identity as a woman of indigenous descent and ethnographic
researcher as she excavates the place of "Inila," the Lakota word for
silence, in indigenous solidarity and ethnographic research methods.
Alexandra Fidyk theorizes what she calls a "pedagogy of presence" in her
classroom and her writing (Chapter 9: "Attuned to Silence: A Pedagogy
of Presence"), seeking to cultivate the active, generative, creative, and

meditative qualities of silence within the academic context. Extending the convergence between silence and "presence," Cheryl Lossie's essay, "Hear I Meet the Silence: The Wise Pedagogue" (Chapter 10), works to "hear" silence—to create a space to "meet the silence" within the chaos of the end of the semester. She utilizes critical pedagogical practices to bring out the voices of students to ensure that there is sufficient space for both students and professor to deeply hear themselves, each other, and the voices of those whose work they've studied. Analyzing the structural and historical force of their particular social locations, Gust Yep and Susan Shimanoff theorize the political potential of silence and solidarity in LGBTQ politics on the USA's "Day of Silence" (Chapter 11: "The US Day of Silence: Sexualities, Silences and the Will to Unsay in the Age of Empire").

Part III: "Recovering Silences: Community, Family, Intimacy" rethinks the assumption that recovery is equated with coming to voice in order to theorize the role of silence in processes of healing. It opens with Della Pollock's "Keeping Quiet: Performing Pain" (Chapter 12) to theorize the relationship between pain, silence, and dignity. As with Keating's essay, Pollock distinguishes between forms of silence, considering the importance of "tending silence" as a process that enables a relational approach to pain—one that extends beyond the individual body in pain. In "3210 S. Indiana: Silence and the Meanings of Home" (Chapter 13), Francesca Royster uses memoir to explore the silences of her ancestral home to intervene in the grand narratives of the Great Migration in Chicago. She reads the stories held in her growing-up home, where her mother was the silent center of the family, to cultivate a "theory in the flesh" of silence, memory, and black female respectability. Cultivating a critical poetic ethnographic methodology, Kris Acheson takes readers into the "home of addiction" in "Fences, Weapons, Gifts: Silences in the Context of Addiction" (Chapter 14). There she finds the unexpected silences that mark the speech of the "tongueless," who name the edges of sound at the interface between addiction, intimacy, and recovery. Kimberlee Pérez's essay "My Monster and My Muse: Re-Writing the Colonial Hangover" (Chapter 15) utilizes silence as a meditative methodology to theorize white heteropatriarchal temporality, producing an important political, cultural, and historical critique.

In Part IV: "Legacies of Silence: Memory, Healing, Power," the authors stretch back into unspoken realms, reclaiming legacies and learning through embodied silences to reach a place of healing and power. In "The Silence in My Belly" (Chapter 16), Sheena Malhotra reads her own experience as a cancer survivor in conversation with Audre Lorde's

Cancer Journals to theorize agency within silence and the paradox of needing silence *and* needing voice to create a space for healing. Bryant Alexander reads the silences surrounding his father's passing to theorize intergenerational questions of genealogy and sexuality, masculinity, and blackness in "Standing in the Wake of My Father's Silence (An Alternative Eulogy)" (Chapter 17). Next is Laila Farah's essay, "Stitching Survival: Re-visioning Silence and Expression" (Chapter 18), in which she travels to the Palestinian refugee camps in Lebanon to learn about the role of silence in women's efforts to recover and "perform" a nation without territory. This final part (and the book) concludes with Aimee Carrillo Rowe's "Sun Moon Silence" (Chapter 19), which draws on the sensual experience of her participation in sun moon dances to highlight the importance of silence in allowing dreams and visions to manifest. Her reflections reveal how holding sacred experiences, which would be lost through speaking, generates an expansive silence. Navigating between archive and repertoire, memory and healing, the essay points to an ontology that allows for uncertainty as part and parcel of spiritual design.

Notes

1. This move has been productively problematized by feminist and cultural critics, who point out that there is no transparent, innocent, or apolitical way to represent others (see Roof and Wiegman, 1995).
2. Deborah Tannen outlined the difference in listening and speech patterns between men and women in her 1991 bestseller *You Just Don't Understand: Women and Men in Conversation*, which created much debate and drew attention to different communication styles between men and women (Tannen, 1991).
3. Ratcliffe (2006) demonstrates that listening often has racial dimensions, in the sense that those in positions of lesser power are more inclined to listen than those in positions of greater power.
4. Hegde and Fishkin's volume offers a textual analysis of "feminist critical treatments of the idea of 'silence' itself," (1994, p. 6) examining the potentially empowering aspects of silence in feminist literary texts, as well as offering a discussion of silencing practices within the academy. While the volume opens up the space for examining silence as empowering, several essays that are highly evocative and important critical interventions nonetheless revert to the assumption that silence is oppressive.
5. Segrest writes in her piece "On Being White and Other Lies" of the "community of the lie" white folks inherit as a colonial legacy,

> When the exploring party of Cabeza de Vaca lost three of its men in an accident, the survivors were amazed when the Indians who discovered them sat down among them and expressed a loud and earnest grief,

feelings that the Spanish had not been able to muster for their own people. It is this failure to feel the communal bonds between humans, I think, and the punishment that undoubtedly came to those Europeans who did, that allowed the 'community of the lie' to grow so genocidally in the soil of the "new world". (2002, p. 248)

Works Cited

Achino-Loeb, Maria-Luisa (Ed.). 2005. *Silence: The Currency of Power*. Oxford & New York: Berghahn Books.
Anzaldúa, Gloria. 1981/1983. "Speaking in Tongues: A Letter to Third World Women Writers." In C. Moraga and G. Anzaldúa (Eds), *This Bridge Called My Back: Writings by Radical Women of Color*. New York: Kitchen Table, Women of Color Press. pp. 165–174.
Anzaldúa, Gloria. 1987. *Borderlands/La Frontera: The New Mestiza*. San Francisco, CA: Spinsters/Aunt Lute.
Basso, Keith H. 1970. "To Give Up on Words: Silence in Western Apache Culture." *Southwestern Journal of Anthropology*, 26(3): 213–230.
Boseker, Barbara J. and Gordon, Sandra L. 1983. "What Native Americans Have Taught Us as Teacher Educators." *Journal of American Indian Education*, 22(3): 20–24.
Campbell, Karlyn Kohrs. 1989. *Man Cannot Speak for Her: Volume II, Key Texts of the Early Feminists*. Westport, CT: Praeger Paperback.
Carrillo Rowe, Aimee. 2008. *Power Lines: On the Subject of Feminist Alliances*. Durham, NC: Duke University Press.
Cheung, King-Kok. 1993. *Articulate Silences: Hisaye Yamamoto, Maxine Hong Kingston, Joy Kogawa*. Ithaca, NY: Cornell University Press.
Clair, Robin. 1998. *Organizing Silence: A World of Possibilities*. Albany, NY: SUNY.
Clair, Robin. 2012. "Organizing Silence: Silence as Voice and Voice as Silence in the Narrative Exploration of the Treaty of New Exhota." *Western Journal of Communication*, 61(3) (Summer 1997), 315–337.
Cope, Stephan. 2006. *The Wisdom of Yoga: A Seeker's Guide to Extraordinary Living*. New York: Random House Digital.
Das, Veena. 1997. "Language and Body: Transactions in the Construction of Pain." In Arthur Kleinman, Veena Das, and Margaret Lock (Eds). *Social Suffering*. Berkeley, CA: University of California Press. pp. 67–92.
Fidyk, A. (2011). "Suffering within: Seven Moments of Ignorance." In E. Malewski and N. Jaramillo (Eds). *Epistemologies of Ignorance and Studies of Limits in Education*. Charlotte, NC: Information Age Publishing. pp. 129–165.
Fiumara, Gemma C. 1990. *The Other Side of Language: A Philosophy of Listening*. London & New York, Routledge.
Foss, Karen and Foss, Sonja. 1991. *Women's Speak: The Eloquence of Women's Lives*. Long Grove, IL: Waveland Press.
Glenn, Cheryl. 2004. *Unspoken: A Rhetoric of Silence*. Carbondale, IL: Southern Illinois University Press.
Gross, Lawrence W. 2007. "Silence as the Root of American Indian Humor: Further Meditations on the Comic Vision of Anishinaabe Culture and Religion." *American Indian Culture and Research Journal*, 31(2): 69–85

Guha, Ranajit. 1997. *A Subaltern Studies Reader, 1986–1995*. Minneapolis, MN: University of Minnesota.

Hanh, Thich Nat. 2009. *Answers from the Heart: Practical Responses to Life's Burning Questions*. Berkeley, CA: Parallax.

Hart, Tobin. 2011. "Supporting Inner Wisdom in Public Schools." In Aostre Johnson and Marilyn Neagley (Eds). *Educating from the Heart: Theoretical and Practical Approaches to Transforming Education*. Lanham, MD: Rowman & Littlefield Education. pp. 13–24.

Hedges, E. and Fishkin, S.F. 1994. *Listening to Silences: New Essays in Feminist Criticism*. New York & Oxford: Oxford University Press.

hooks, bell. 1989. *Talking Back: Thinking Feminist, Thinking Black*. New York: South End.

Hull, Akasha Gloria. 2001. *Soul Talk: The New Spirituality of African American Women*. Rochester, VT: Inner Traditions/ Bear & Co.

Kadi, Joanna. 2002. "Speaking (About) Silence." In M.J. Alexander, L. Albrecht, S. Day and M. Segrest (Eds). *Sing, Whisper, Shout, Pray! Feminist Visions for a Just World*. Fort Bragg, CA: Edgework Press. pp. 539–545.

Lorde, Audre. 1984a. *Sister Outsider: Essays and Speeches by Audre Lorde*. Freedom, CA: The Crossing Press.

Lorde, Audre. 1984b. "The Master's Tools Will Never Dismantle the Master's House." In *Sister Outsider: Essays and Speeches by Audre Lorde*. Freedom, CA: The Crossing Press. pp. 110–113.

Moraga, Cherríe. 1981/1983. "La Guera." In C. Moraga and G. Anzaldúa (Eds), *This Bridge called my Back: Writings by Radical Women of Color*. New York: Kitchen Table: Women of Color Press. pp. 27–34.

Olsen, Tillie. 1978. *Silences*. New York: Delta/Seymour Lawrence.

O'Reilly, Mary. 1984. "The Peaceable Classroom." *College English*, 46(2): 103–112.

Palmer, Parker. 1998. *The Courage to Teach: Exploring the Inner Landscape of a Teacher's Life*. Ann Arbor, MI: University of Michigan.

Picard, Max. 1963. *Man and Language*. Chicago, IL: H. Regnery Co.

Rakow, Lana F. and Wackwitz, Laura A. 2005. *Feminist Communication Theory: Selections in Context*. Thousand Oaks, CA: Sage.

Ratcliffe, Krista. 2006. *Rhetorical Listening: Identification, Gender, Whiteness*. Carbondale, IL: Southern Illinois University Press.

Razack, Sherene H. 1998. *Looking White People in the Eye: Gender, Race, and Cultural in Courtrooms and Classrooms*. Toronto: University of Toronto Press.

Rich, Adrienne. 1978. *The Dream of a Common Language: Poems, 1974–1977*. New York: W.W. Norton.

Rich, Adrienne. 1979. *On Lies, Secrets and Silence*. New York: W.W. Norton.

Roof, Judith and Wiegman, Robyn (Eds). (1995). *Who Can Speak? Authority and Critical Identity*. Chicago, IL: University of Illinois.

Rumi, J. 1995. *The Essential Rumi* (C. Barks Trans. With J. Moyne, A.J. Arberry and R. Nicholson). San Francisco, CA: HarperSanFrancisco.

Segrest, Mab. 2002. "On Being White and Other Lies: A History of Racism in the United States." In M.J. Alexander, L. Albrecht, S. Day, and M. Segrest (Eds). *Sing, Whisper, Shout, Pray! Feminist Visions for a Just World*. Fort Bragg, CA: Edgework Press. pp. 243–285.

Spivak, Gayatri. 1988. "Can the Subaltern Speak?" In Cary Nelson and Lawrence Grossberg (Eds). *Marxism and the Interpretation of Culture*. Chicago, IL: University of Illinois Press. pp. 271–315.

Tannen, Deborah. 1985. "Silence: Anything But" In D. Tannen and M. Saville-Troike (Eds). *Perspectives on Silence*. Norwood, NJ: Ablex.

Tannen, Deborah. 1991. *You Just Don't Understand: Women and Men in Conversation*. New York: Ballantine Books.

Tannen, Deborah and Muriel Saville-Troike (Eds). 1985. *Perspectives on Silence*. Norwood, NJ: Ablex.

Trinh, Minh-ha T. 1989. *Woman, Native, Other*. Indianapolis, IN: Indiana University Press.

Trinh, Minh-ha T. 1990. "Not You/Like You: Post-Colonial Women and the Interlocking Questions of Identity and Difference." In Gloria Anzaldúa (Ed.) *Making Face, Making Soul: Creative and Critical Perspectives of Women of color*. San Francisco, CA: Aunt Lute. pp. 371–375.

Visweswaran, Kamala. 1994. *Fictions of Feminist Ethnography*. Minneapolis, MN: University of Minnesota Press.

Part I

Transformative Silences: Intersectionality, Privilege, Alliances

2
Resistant Silences

Christine (Cricket) Keating

In her poem "Cartographies of Silence," Adrienne Rich (1978) urges her readers to remember that silence "has a presence." She writes that

> It has a history a form
> Do not confuse it
> With any kind of absence (p. 17)

Like Rich, feminist and critical race theorists and activists have worked hard to document and challenge the many concrete ways that marginalized and oppressed groups have been forced to be silent. In this chapter, I argue that in addition to not confusing silence with absence, it is also important to be able to distinguish *between* different forms of silence. Since silence and force have been so closely linked in our histories, it is tempting to collapse the two and focus on silence, instead of its enforcement, as what must be overcome. In this essay, I distinguish enforced silences—often the ones that progressive theorists and activists have in mind—from three kinds of engaged and oppositional silences: silent refusal, silent witness, and deliberative silence. Far from marking a capitulation to power, these modes of silence can be important techniques or technologies of resistance. I argue that these forms of silent engagement can be important tools for political struggle, and pay particular attention to the ways that these modes of silence might be useful for those occupying positions of hegemonic power, privilege, and dominance to challenge or reject such positions. Further, I suggest that a theoretical attention to modes of resistant silence, as well as to voice in dialogue, can be useful in theorizing deliberative democratic approaches to social critique.

Like silence, voice can also be enforced. Instead of a demand for silence, speech is often enlisted to back up or support hegemonic power. "Silent refusal" is a mode of being silent that aims to resist these coercions to speak in the service of power and that seeks to challenge enticements to voice in a hegemonic vein. In *Fictions of Feminist Ethnography,* Kamala Visweswaran (1994) gives examples of silent refusal as resistant engagement. She notes that in much feminist theory "speech has been seen as the privileged catalyst of agency; lack of speech as the absence of agency" (p. 68). In her self-reflective account of her experiences interviewing women involved in the Indian Independence movement, however, she encountered "a kind of agency in which resistance [was] framed by silence, a refusal to speak" (p. 51). For example, one woman Visweswaran attempted to interview, a leader in the nationalist movement whom she refers to as "M," refused to speak about her own role in the Indian freedom struggle. After a year of putting Visweswaran off, M finally consented to an interview. In their conversation, M evaded questioning about the independence movement and emphasized instead her contemporary social work with orphans. To account for this emphasis, M explained that "so many people come and want to give this award or that award, but Gandhiji said that the work itself is its own reward" (p. 66). Visweswaran interprets M's silence as an example of a subject who "refused to historicize herself, who repudiated not only the telling of her own history, but that of the nation's as well" (p. 66). She explains that in doing so, M resists a particular narrative about both herself and the nation.

> Like many freedom fighters, she is keenly aware of the uses to which her subjectivity may be put [and] the fame and glory of continual press coverage which old freedom fighters are honored by being asked to inaugurate or preside over various state functions, perhaps legitimating in M's eyes, a vision struggled for and not won. For to participate in the nation's newly won status was to confirm that the nation had already arrived and was not still in the process of arrival. (p. 67)

In contrast to an enforced silence, M's silence in this example is chosen. Indeed, disentangling force and silence allows us to see the particular ways that it is voice not silence that is enticed in this situation. In refusing the narrative of the nationalist hero, she must resist accolades and pressure by the interviewer and presumably others to tell her story. Rather than marking a disengagement, M's silent refusal signals a desire for more complex stories and ongoing accounts of the struggles for social justice in India, accounts that the hegemonic nationalist narrative foreclose.[1]

As Visweswaran's discussion of M's silence suggests, among the interventions that silent refusal can make is that it can enable those located in subject positions, who are in some ways privileged, to work against the narratives of self or conversational patterns that support hegemonic discourses. Sometimes resisting the pull to domination requires speech (e.g. interrupting racist or sexist jokes) but sometimes this work might also necessitate silence, a rejection of a narrative that celebrates one's insertion in relations of power and/or the speech practices that support that power.

Another mode of silent resistance might be called "silent witness." This form of silence is often—though it doesn't have to be—organized and collective and is used as a marker of respect, of mourning, of protest, and of defiance. Whereas silent refusal highlights the ways that *voice* is enforced, silent witness underscores the way that *silence* is enforced. An example of such silent witness is the Day of Silence sponsored by the Gay and Lesbian and Straight Education Network (GLSEN) and organized by students in middle schools, high schools, and universities across the USA. For one day, usually in April, participants remain silent in order to protest discrimination against lesbian, gay, bisexual, and transgender people. This protest replaces an enforced silence with a chosen, commemorative silence.

As opposed to detaching and isolating the participants from collective deliberation, the students' silence is geared to instigating thought and engagement. As one participant observed "in my first period English class (all seniors), half the students were silent. No one in school that day could have missed it...I think the Day really made people think" (GLSEN Accessed on 8/25/12). This student's observation underscores that students participating in the day both have company in their silence and hope to elicit company through their silence. Although silence is usually associated with solitude, this form of silence takes on its resistant edge in part because of the alternative sociality that the students create through their action.

While the exercise of silent witness on the Day of Silence is an important form of resistance and solidarity for those in the LGBTQ community, here I will focus on ways that silent witnessing can serve the project of crafting an anti-dominant self for those who identify as straight. Indeed, the Day of Silence gives those who are heterosexually identified the opportunity to experience in a visceral way the enforced silencing involved in heteronormative figurations of high school life in the

USA. As such, it exposes the cost of such enforced silencing both to the one silenced and to those around her or him. One student who participated in the day explained "being silent not only allows you to feel how someone who is oppressed feels, but it allows others to see what they are missing when they oppress others so they cannot speak" (GLSEN Accessed on 8/25/12). Further, the practice of silent witnessing can play a role in interrupting the configurations of heteronormative sociality upon which the practice of heterosexist domination often depends. For example, one student recalled an incident in which "a straight guy who WAS NOT a part of our Gay Straight Alliance [GSA], held strong even when his other guy friends were making fun of him and trying to make him talk. It just goes to show you that not speaking at all is sometimes stronger than speaking many words" (GLSEN Accessed 8/25/12).

The ability to be silent is a valuable skill that subordinate groups have too often been forced to develop, and one that dominant groups have often had little practice with. The Day of Silence gives the straight students an opportunity to develop this skill in the practice of resistant solidarity.

A third form of resistant silence is one that Tony Lynch dubs "deliberative silence" (Lynch, 2001). What deliberative silence requires, according to Lynch, is that one tempers one's own desires or thoughts that one considers problematic or, in his words "repugnant" by not giving voice to them. He argues for the practice of deliberative silence as "an important technique of virtue," one that is often lost sight of in contemporary philosophy with its emphasis on what he calls "radical truthfulness" (p. 251). He suggests that such a radical truthfulness may see us being, or becoming, untrue to ourselves ... it insists that whatever is there now, within us, come into the light and ignores the foundations in virtue in a concern that we be, and be truly, a certain kind of person. It is this concern which opens the strategy for dealing with temptation through the practice of renunciation. Such a practice aims at temperance, a temperance realized in the attainment of deliberative silence before the otherwise, the previously attractive (p. 269).

As an example of the deleterious effects of failing to exercise deliberative silence in public life, Lynch recounts the decision of the then Prime Minister of Australia John Howard to raise the question of introducing a racialist immigration policy in 1988. With this decision, Howard broke the "political and community silence" about such measures (p. 265). Howard justified his public broaching of this heretofore taboo topic by saying that he had only "brought out in the open" what people were thinking privately (p. 265). Lynch condemns this move, arguing that by giving voice to racialism, Howard was guilty of intemperance.

While Lynch is interested in making room for silence alongside the imperatives of radical truthfulness in moral theory, I am interested in making room for silence alongside the imperative of voice in political theories of race, class, and gender justice. Given that part of learning to be a member of a dominant or a subordinate group entails a schooling in desires, opinions, and understandings that often do oneself or others harm; part of resisting one's own positioning as dominant or as subordinate is learning how to restrain, reject, or temper those sorts of desires, opinions, or understandings.

Deliberative silence is a risky kind of resistant silence, and is one that I feel two minds about given that sometimes desires that can seem problematic or even repugnant can be ones that can hold keys to different possibilities of living. In her book *At the Heart of Freedom*, for example, Drucilla Cornell (1998) writes specifically about the process of freeing what she calls our "sexuate beings." Cornell writes that "the effort to challenge, engage with, and imagine who we are sexually demands that we have the courage to look into the crevices in ourselves to see things frightening indeed. We need to sink ourselves into our dreams" (p. 24). I agree with Cornell that excavating, recognizing, and exploring one's desires—sexual or otherwise—are crucial to the project of freedom. All too often, we are pressured to temper or ignore the desires that might motivate and move us toward freer or fuller lives. Not all of these desires that we have, however, lead down roads of liberation: some of them lead down roads of oppression, despair, and harm. While excavating and exploring desires—especially those that feel risky—is an important process in the project of liberation, another step is to interrogate those desires, either collectively or individually. What desires are forbidden to us along the axes of domination and subordination that we inhabit? What desires are we encouraged to have or are fostered in us? Whom do these desires serve? As we identify desires that serve oppression rather than liberation, learning to "temper" them, in Lynch's words, is an important task. This is often difficult work, because desire can be insistent, compelling. The notion of deliberative silence in a radical vein can help to valorize the "silence" work that is sometimes necessary in transforming oppressive desires.

An example from the work of the popular education collective La Escuela Popular Norteña (EPN) illustrates the possibilities of the use of deliberative silence in feminist and anti-racist work. In the late 1990s, on the invitation from sororities of color at a college campus, members of the collective held a workshop which had as its aim the generation of dialogue between men and women of color on issues of violence. During the first half of the day, the men and women met separately to discuss questions related to the topic of violence against women of color. In this half of the workshop, both the men and women of color had the opportunity to explore their interactions and give voice to their own desires, opinions, and understandings of relationality.

The second half of the workshop brought the whole group together. In this large group, the men had the task of listening silently to the women's reflections on their morning conversation. In withholding their comments, and in particular in remaining silent about desires, opinions, or understandings that the women of color might find demeaning or offensive, the men of color were being asked to listen closely to women of color. In this sense, the men of color were asked to be "true" to themselves in the sense of a self that works as an ally, even if it meant quieting the impulse that they might have had to defend or justify ways of being that the women of color were describing as harmful. This was not easy work for the men to do, in part because in contemporary feminist and critical race praxis to be asked to exercise silence means to be oppressed. In a world that denigrates silence, it is tremendously difficult to ask people to exercise silence as a radical practice. Validating deliberative silence as an important tool of social transformation could help to provide both a context and a motivation for this work.

Resistant silences and deliberative democratic theory

As an approach to democracy, deliberative democratic theorists argue that we need to expand participation in contemporary democracies and to make that participation more meaningful by creating more opportunities for public deliberation. These public deliberations will result, optimally, in a more informed populace and better public policy, and thus lead to democratic renewal. At the heart of the logic of deliberative democratic theory is the notion of an inclusive conversation in which people can have a voice in the decisions that affect their lives.

In *Political Theory and Feminist Social Criticism*, Brooke Ackerly (2000) points out, however, that power inequalities among groups prevent equal participation in conversations. To illustrate this point, she points to a Bengali proverb that holds that "when you live in the water, you don't argue with the crocodiles" (p. 1). Without an account of a deliberative democratic social critique that can identify and challenge power inequalities, she suggests, deliberative democratic theory will fall short of its goal of including everyone in the conversation. To address this issue, Ackerly analyzes the real world deliberations and activism of third world feminists to describe a deliberative democratic approach to social criticism that can serve to challenge power. Below, I suggest that the three modes of resistant silence that I outlined above all play or could play a critical role in this mode of social criticism.

Ackerly's account of a model deliberative democratic approach to social criticism pivots on an exchange that took place in Bangladesh in September 1993 as Ackerly and a group of rural Bangladeshi women activists walked to and from meetings on women's legal rights. On their walk, they heard shrieks of terror from a household on the other side of the field. Ackerly describes the exchange:

> "What's going on?" I asked. Sahara, a Tangail woman turned to me with anger and a memory of terror in her eyes and hit her right fist into her cupped left hand. She had experienced domestic violence and recognized the sounds from across the field. After a time, Sahara asked, "Do husbands beat their wives in your country?" "Some do," I answered, "even though it is illegal." We all laughed at the irony, having just learned about women's legal rights in Bangladesh and noting how they differed from local practice.
>
> "Why do men hit their wives?" I asked. "Because they had a bad day. Because they are poor," answered Sahara. "Because the rice is too hot or there is not enough rice, said Apfza, a woman from Kustia. Then she added, "A good husband does not hit his wife even when they are poor."
>
> Then Jahanara, another Tangaila woman overhearing our conversations told the story of her women's group which went as a group to the house of a member who was being abused and asked her husband to stop beating her. This reminded another Tangail woman walking ahead of us of another group's effort to get a member's husband to allow their daughter to continue in school even though he was ready to arrange a marriage. They staged a sit-in at the member's home (2000, pp. 1–2).

According to Ackerly, this exchange illustrates a deliberative approach to social criticism that can enable those that are living in the water to "argue with the crocodile." She notes that "these women live under familial, social, political, and economic values, practices, and norms that enforce women's silence. However, they have identified a way to break that silence with each other and to force their husbands to hear them" (2000, p. 4). In particular, in the scenario that she describes the different women promote inquiry, deliberation, and institutional change in ways that make their exchange effective as social critique. By asking the women what was going on, for example, Ackerly promoted inquiry; by discussing the different reasons for domestic violence in Bangladesh, the Bangladeshi activists were promoting deliberation; by bringing up examples of the confrontations and the sit-in, the Bangladeshi women were pointing to the possibility as well as promoting institutional change. By engaging in this process, these third world feminist critics illustrated the ways in which deliberative democracy can be effective in challenging power.

It is not only the activists' exercise of voice in the interchange that is instructive in signaling the possibilities of deliberative democratic social critic, however, but also the exercise of different forms of resistant silence. Indeed, the conversation among the women in Bangladesh with an ear for silence as well as an ear for voice, for example, all three forms of silence discussed in this chapter come into play. For example, in promoting inquiry, Ackerly exercised silent refusal as well as voice. In particular, she refused a particular mode of hegemonic speech that would position her, as a feminist from the global north, as the one in the "know" about questions related to violence against women. In order to refuse this subject position, Ackerly asked a question, and then remained silent while the Bangladeshi women themselves discussed reasons for violence against women in Bangladesh, and only entered the dialogue again when asked about the situation in the USA. Further, the women in the scenario that Ackerly describes point to the exercise of silent witness—the sit-in in front of the house of the man who was going to refuse his daughter's attendance at school—as an effective strategy of protest, alongside their descriptions of examples of voiced protest (such as the group of women that intervened and asked a husband to stop beating his wife). Finally, in order for the critiques to be successful in promoting social change and transformation, the abusers described in the scenario would have to learn to temper their violent impulses and desires: a goal that the exercise of deliberative silence can be useful in achieving.

The central argument of this essay is that while silence has been a tool of marginalization and exclusion, certain forms of silence can be important and sometimes indispensable for social change. Silence can be used to reject, to witness against, and to temper modes of domination so that we can not only articulate but also forge new truths about ourselves and our relations. Instead of imagining domination and silence to be inextricably linked, we must work to free silence from domination's grip to help work toward this possibility.

Note

1. In everyday life in the USA, an example of this form of silent refusal that comes to mind is refusing to stand and sing the national anthem or recite the pledge of allegiance in school. I was reminded of this form of silence when my young daughter came home from one of her first days of school complaining about having to recite the pledge of allegiance. She eventually reached a compromise with her teacher in which she would stand with the other children but would not have to recite the pledge. In this case, it is voice that is enforced—overtly or more subtly—such that remaining silent can be understood as an act of resistant agency.

References

Ackerly, Brooke. *Political Theory and Feminist Social Criticism.* Cambridge: Cambridge University Press, 2000.

Cornell, Drucilla. *At the Heart of Freedom.* Princeton, NJ: Princeton University Press, 1998.

Gay and Lesbian and Straight Education Network. http://www.dayofsilence.org/content/gi_testimonials.html, 2012.

Lynch, Tony. "Temperance, Temptation, and Silence," *Philosophy* (2001), 76: 251–269.

Rich, Adrienne. *The Dream of the Common Language.* New York: Norton, 1978.

Visweswaran, Kamala. *Fictions of Feminist Ethnography.* Minnesota: University of Minnesota Press, 1994.

3

Between Speech and Silence: Reflections on Accountability

Ann Russo

In the 1970s, when I first got involved in the feminist movement, I felt compelled to speak to everything and everybody. Speaking was my resistance. I had started speaking out as a kid in my white middle- to upper-middle-class Catholic family in Central Illinois. I was mad at the injustices I experienced and observed that were perpetrated by my father, by the Catholic Church, by the schools, and by people within my communities. I was one of those white middle-class girls who sometimes talked back and often got punished for it. But that didn't stop me from speaking. I was ecstatic to discover feminism when I was a college student. The white middle-class liberal, socialist, radical, and lesbian feminisms I found on campus validated my anger at the everyday patriarchy, homophobia, racism, and classism I either experienced and/or observed in my family and in my community. Feminisms provided me with the social theories and critical analyses that helped me to name and understand the systems and practices that I found oppressive and unjust, and with the relationships and activist communities where I found support, encouragement, and courage to develop ideas, strategies, and visions for change. In many ways, these feminist, socialist, and lesbian communities provided me with spaces from which to collectively organize and talk back to power.

As I came into feminist speech, I equated silence with oppression, and speech with liberation. I came to assume that my socialist, radical, and lesbian feminist politics, in combination with my experiences with oppression and violence, gave me a kind of authority to speak out in whatever contexts I chose. It didn't occur to me at the time that my taking up space, my sense of "authority," and my comfort with speaking in generalities could be connected with my race, class, able-bodied, and citizenship privileges located in the predominantly white middle-class university setting, or could serve to marginalize and/or silence women of color, working class, poor, and/or immigrant women, and/or women with disabilities. Nor did I realize how the unspoken *privileges* of my identity and location were implicated in and serving to reproduce the very systems and relationships of power that I thought I was combating.

It has been through my experiences of intentionally building relationships and alliances across "power lines" (Carrillo Rowe, 2008), that I continue to build critical consciousness about how the praxis of speech and silence are intricately connected with the power systems we are working to dismantle and transform. In the context of building alliances across power lines, I must remind myself to critically interrogate both my compulsion to speak as well as my compulsion to be silent, particularly in terms of how my actions may reinscribe unequal power lines. In multiracial and transnational feminist communities, I've come to rethink the call to speech as *the* primary method for transformative change, to no longer assume that speaking up is necessarily *the path* to liberation and freedom. And I have come to be more critical of my presumption of feminist "authority." Through dialogue and reflection with others, I have come to recognize how my sense of entitlement to speech is intricately connected with my simultaneously privileged location as a white and middle-class feminist scholar in the university. As importantly, however, I also must be attentive to my "inhabited silences," particularly in relationship to dynamics of privilege and power, which may serve to reinscribe, rather than disrupt, the unequal power lines that continually structure our relationships to one another. In this essay, I reflect on the practices of speech and silence as they relate to cultivating accountability across the power lines embedded in feminist movement building.

Disrupting speech as entitlement: The practice of listening and embodied silence

Talking, speaking out, demonstrating your knowledge, and making yourself known are often taken as the signs of "real" engagement, leadership, and contribution in many middle-class feminist, queer, and/or social justice organizations. The cultures created within these groups often privilege those most able to demonstrate their powers of knowledge and expertise, and those who are able to command the authority called for in any given situation. The power lines produced within these organizations often follow along the preexisting lines formed by structural and systemic oppression and privilege in terms of race, class, education, language, and so on, even when the stated goal is to dismantle and transform these structures of oppression.

In speaking of the importance of shifting power dynamics among feminists, María Lugones and Elizabeth Spelman (1983) offer white feminists with locational privilege suggestions for theorizing with women of color in ways that do not reinscribe asymmetrical power relations; they write,

> So you need to learn to become unintrusive, unimportant, patient to the point of tears, while at the same time open to learning any possible lessons. You will also have to come to terms with the sense of alienation, of not belonging, of having your world thoroughly disrupted, having it criticized and scrutinized from the point of view of those who have been harmed by it, having important concepts central to it dismissed, being viewed with mistrust, being seen as of no consequence except as an object of mistrust. (p. 580)

The cultivation of such practices to shift one's own sense of self in relation to consciousness building and knowledge production has the potential to shift feminist spaces. The practices disrupt the hegemony of white privileged power and the relational dynamics it produces.

One of the simplest, most profound, and yet consistently difficult practices that disrupts the automatic entitlement to hegemonic speech is active listening. Stepping back from speaking and stepping up to active listening is one method of undermining the presumed entitlement to be at the center of the conversation, to speak in universals, and to determine the direction of the conversation and agenda. Active listening implies an openness to a more collective process, one in which those most privileged are not at the center, and one in which our ideas and our selves are open to modification, change, and transformation. This is not simply about the physical act of hearing without speaking, or making space for "others" without real engagement. As Lynet Uttal (1990) laments about her experience as a woman of color speaking in white-dominant feminist spaces, "I am tired of feeling that my words were given space, but they might as well have not been said because they didn't get built upon or incorporated into the conversation" (p. 319). Active listening, to me, implies a willingness for our identities, ideas, theories, and actions to be transformed in the process of dialogue. Megan Boler's (1999) distinction between "passive empathy" and "testimonial reading" is instructive here. She writes, "The primary difference between passive empathy and testimonial reading [listening] is the responsibility borne by the reader [listener]. Instead of a consumptive focus on the other, the reader [listener] accepts a commitment to rethink her own assumptions, and to confront the internal obstacles encountered as one's views are challenged" (Boler, 1999, p. 164). For Boler, this includes the willingness to "recognize oneself as implicated in the social forces that create the climate of obstacles the other must confront" (p. 166).

Engaging in active listening, however, does not necessarily mean power dynamics have shifted. Audrey Thompson (2003), in reflecting on the asymmetries of listening, writes, "we [white people] have a hard time finding ways to listen that do not simply reinscribe our sense of entitlement" (p. 86). One of the manifestations of such entitlement is the conditions placed on our willingness to listen; for instance, saying that we will listen as long as we do not feel bad, or excluded, or blamed (p. 86). Thompson suggests that this form of listening is based on the idea of "formal reciprocity" where "everyone is to be treated identically" (p. 86). It doesn't consider the differential stakes in conversations about race, class, and public policy. By way of example, Thompson offers the story of a white student who "once protested that her concerns were not being given the same validation as black peoples" in the class (p. 86). This student struggled with the Black students in class who argued that, for them, it was a priority to increase the number of Black teachers in schools with predominantly Black populations; the white student felt that her desire for racial integration was necessary *for her* to unlearn racism, and so it was *as important* to the desire of the Black students for Black teachers. She resisted the idea that there were different stakes involved. It was through a subsequent commitment to deep active listening that "she came to appreciate the differences in power and privilege at stake." Through the process, she came to understand that accountability to the African American students was more important than her own needs and desires (Thompson, 2003, pp. 86–87). In reflecting on her process, she shared with Thompson: "All I could see at first...was what *I* needed and wanted" (quoted by Thompson, 2003, p. 86).

These practices of listening, decentering, minimizing intrusiveness, and stepping back often create discomfort, particularly for those with structural advantage in such contexts. In my own experience with such practices in feminist spaces, I often feel "less important" as a participant as defined by the standards of normative power relations. For instance, when Incite! Women of Color Against Violence organized a national conference in Chicago in 2002, I volunteered to be a white ally volunteer. Incite!'s goal was to create a women of color-centered space for the event. This decision, while controversial to some, was an important intervention given the history of white middle-class dominance in feminist antiviolence work, including the marginalization of the identities, experiences, perspectives, and approaches of women, lesbian, queer, gender queer, and trans people of color, poor people, women from the global south, among many other groups. In order to interrupt these power relations, Incite! organizers decided that white women and male-identified allies would contribute to some aspects of planning (e.g. fundraising and logistical support) and would deliberately withhold from participating in others (e.g. substance of the program). During the conference, those of us who were white women and male-identified allies agreed not to attend workshop sessions except those designated for allies and also to support the logistical issues (e.g. registration). Some of us stepped up to talk with white women and men of all colors who were uncomfortable with or in opposition to the centering of women of color. The experience of participating from the margins was a very good one, even though at times I struggled with my feelings of being an "outsider" to the conference. I respected the space being created, I understood its significance within the broader movement, and I felt honored to contribute in the ways mentioned. It also was uncomfortable, in part, because I wanted to be in sessions to listen, to learn, and to participate. In this process, I came to recognize that this de-centering did not necessarily mean non-participation. Instead, it meant another kind of belonging, a belonging not conditioned by my own sense of centrality, and yet nonetheless a deeply connected belonging, contingent on a practice of accountability to the work of transforming, rather than reproducing, deeply entrenched power relations.

These transformational moments in my life have mostly occurred when I am intentional about how much space I take up and how much space I give to listening; when I stop myself from thinking only about what I have to say, or assuming that what's most important in this moment is for me to reveal myself as knowledgeable. It happens when I listen with curiosity rather than simply for confirmation of what I think I already know. Cynthia Enloe talks about this disposition in terms of "being open to surprise" which she says "may be among the most useful attitudes to adopt to prepare one's feminist self for what lies ahead" (Enloe, 2004, p. 2).

Through active listening and learning, and striving to shed a teacher and know-it-all feminist persona, I am reminded of how much I do not know and how much I do not understand. This is a most humbling experience. It consistently deepens my awareness of how much a privileged location in the university has propped me up to be "all-knowing." It also provides me with opportunities to consider how distorted my race and class-bound consciousness can be when left on its own, isolated from multiracial and transnational social justice and feminist relationships and communities.

This shifting of locations of "authority" and "knowledges" (my own included), in many ways, is just as central as speaking to power for re-making the world. As M. Jacqui Alexander (2005) writes,

> There is something quite profound about not knowing, claiming not to know, or not gaining access to knowledge that enables us to know that we are not the sole (re)producers of our lives. But we would have to apprehend the loss that comes from not knowing and feel its absence in an immediate and palpable way in order to remake ourselves enough, so that our analyses might change. We have to learn how to intuit the consequences of not knowing, to experience their effects in order to reverse some of the deeply embedded deposits on which an imperial psyche rests—a psyche that still holds on to the idea of manifest destiny and the fiction of protection and safety from an enemy, who is either calculating on the borders outside or hovering on the margins within. We would have to visit the devastation of living segregated lives... (2005, pp. 109–110)

The practices of being aware of not knowing, of stepping back, of committing to being "in conversation, not domination, with a range of relational knowledges" (Alexander, 2005, p. 109), create new possibilities for transforming feminist movement building that undermine, rather than entrench, existing power lines.

Interrupting the "inhabited silences" of whiteness

Reflecting on the spaces between speech and silence and their relationship to power, I have also come to be more attentive to the spaces of "inhabited silences" that may be implicated in my complicity with whiteness (Mazzei, 2008). Here I am thinking about how keeping whiteness an invisible and unscrutinized presence reproduces unequal power lines rather than disrupting them. White middle- and upper-middle-class feminists, like me, have often premised building solidarity on shared experiences of oppression and/or resistance, with less attention to the unequal power lines that separate and divide people. There seems to be an active investment in sameness as evident in the "me too" that we may insert into this or that conversation as a way of commiserating, creating common cause, and building an alliance. While on the one hand the "me too" can be a way of creating connection, it also may serve to obscure the ways our experiences, perspectives, and actions are differentiated and fractured because of where we are located within these hierarchical structures of oppression and privilege. In addition, the "me too" may deflect attention from our complicity with the systems that shape our differential experiences, and therefore from becoming accountable to one another in struggling against these unequal divides (see Keating, 2005). By way of example, I remember being in a discussion focused on the dearth of leadership of faculty of color at the university, when a white woman faculty member, with significant institutional power relative to most faculty of color in the room, commiserated. She asserted a "me too" in response to the issue of institutional racism, by identifying herself as one of the "outsiders" in the academy (i.e. shared positionality of oppression). She went on to narrate a story about how despite her "outsider" identity, she had ascended through the ranks of power through her own individual persistence and with good mentoring. And it's true that she has been treated as an "outsider" at times given her gender, sexuality, and class identifications. And yet what was missing from her narrative was how her growing status as an insider has been, in part, contingent on the structural privileges she gained through relations of white heterosocial belonging.[1] These privileges are related to the networks of power she has been able to access through personal and then institutional relationships with white men in leadership positions in the university; relationships in part made possible because of whiteness and heterosociality.

This experience led me to deeper reflection on the politics of claiming oneself an "outsider" in any given context, and the ways it might serve to evade and/or resist oppressive power dynamics and our complicity with them. The claim to be an outsider and to have the "me too" experience does not necessarily lead to collective solidarity, nor to a commitment to identify and dismantle the varied multiple structures of institutionalized oppression and privilege that shape our differentiated experiences. Instead, it may function to evade reflection on our participation and complicity in unequal and unjust systems. Ultimately, a discourse of shared oppression, in this case through shared "outsider" identity, maintains the "inhabited silences" around the specificities of white racial heterosexual privilege, and the power lines that are integral to faculty's differentiated experiences within the academy.

Alternatively, breaking the "inhabited silences" by explicitly naming whiteness and white supremacy as a systemic hierarchy might create possibilities for strategic alliance building for change. Such naming would shift the dynamics of what is being said and not said, examined and not examined. In the context of faculty of color and leadership at the university, it would shift the focus of scrutiny from faculty of color who are told that they just "need mentorship" to become an "insider" to a critical examination of the practices and processes by which white faculty ascend into leadership through their mostly white heterosocial networks. Aimee Carrillo Rowe's interviews with white feminist academics reveal the workings of power lines and alliances in the academy (2008). The stories the white women tell reveal explicitly how whiteness shaped their differentiated experiences based on white heterosocial belonging, and ultimately their complicity in the systems of race-based privilege for their individual gain. Most significantly, her analysis reveals the different goals underlying the decision making of white women and women of color around alliance formation in the university. While most of the white women were interested in individual gain, women of color felt more accountable to their broader communities in terms of expanding opportunities, including leadership. For white feminists with similar commitments to accountability, she found that their commitments were often connected to their relationships and communities of belonging with women of color.

"Outsiders" and relations of belonging

Returning to the question of identification as "outsiders," I'm interested in what it looks like to shift the claim of "outsider" from an identity of shared oppression to an identity grounded in differential belonging with a commitment to coalition building. In other words, if we connect outsiderhood to a praxis of resistance and solidarity as well as accountability, then the possibilities expand for potential alliance for social change and collective liberation. In other words, we might intentionally coalesce around this "outsiderhood" and come together across power lines with the goal of collectively strategizing to deconstruct unequal structures and relations of power. Within a frame of multiracial alliances, an "outsider" identification becomes less about shared identity or oppression, and more about collective accountability. Such a shift might be akin to Cathy Cohen's transformative approach to *queer* politics; in her essay, "Punks, Bulldaggers and Welfare Queens," she envisions a radical and imaginative politics grounded in a space where queer becomes a signifier of non-conformity and resistance to white, middle-class, heteronormativity, rather than a static unidimensional identity which is always already implicated in existing power hierarchies (Cohen, 1997). Within this context, creating "outsider" communities might be built through "coalitional consciousness building" that recognizes the differential relations of power operating in the world as well as the ways in which we are differentially implicated in any given situation (Keating, 2005). Coalitional consciousness building would set the groundwork for developing collective strategies that are also grounded from differential positions and relations of power.[2] Coalitional consciousness would require that we break "inhabited silences" and make our differential relations to power explicit, rather than implicit, used rather than evaded, and yet still from within a place of collective movement building.

Breaking ranks with the whiteness of feminist belonging

When whiteness becomes subject to examination in the analysis of inequalities, the myths of meritocracy and individualism are diminished (McIntosh, 2003). In her essay, "Silence Speaks," Lisa Mazzei (2008), drawing on Elizabeth Ellsworth (1997), suggests that silence about whiteness as a system of power becomes "a means of 'fitting in,' remaining invisible, protecting the vulnerability to emotional/intellectual exposure, or simply avoiding calling attention to oneself" and is linked to a broader cultural system of whiteness (Mazzei, 2008, p. 1132). Based on her work with white students in the field of teacher education, she argues that the students resist the naming of whiteness because it "means they risk a loss of privilege, identity, and comfort... A loss of identity when an undoing of white privilege means that their unspoken, unacknowledged, unnoticed position of whiteness is suddenly called into question and redefined, reinscribed, or refuted" (pp. 1134–1135). By naming and owning white people's everyday implication in a broader system of racism and white supremacy, we lose our claims to innocence, ignorance, and distance from the problem (p. 1135). Such naming, then, is uncomfortable, causes distress, and demands accountability.

In Thandeka's book, *Learning to Be White* (2005), she argues that the investment white people have in deflecting conversations about race onto people of color and in evading explicit discussions of whiteness is that these are the conditions of belonging mandated by most white families and communities. She came to this conclusion through her experience of talking with white people about their white racial identities. Her investigation began in response to a query from a white colleague who asked her to talk about "what it felt like to be black," but who was then flustered when Thandeka responded to her colleague by asking her "what it felt like to be white." From this exchange, she invented what she came to call the "Race Game." She suggested that her colleague, over the course of one week, ascribe the term *"white* whenever she mentioned the name of one of her Euro-American cohorts." Thandeka instructed her friend, for instance, to say—" 'my white husband, Phil' or 'my white friend Julie,' or 'my lovely white child Jackie' " (p. 3). The colleague never met up with her to discuss the results. When Thandeka asked other white people to engage in the "Race Game," most could not or would not do it, and were equally unwilling to talk with her about why it was so difficult. She went on to write the book *Learning to Be White* in an effort to explore the "feelings [that] lay behind the word *white* that were too potent to be faced" (p. 4).

Thandeka (2005) finds that it is shame that underlies white people's discomfort with examining our white identities, a shame that does not preclude a comfort in talking about race in relation to people of color. She found that many whites have experienced rejection, discipline, and punishment from their white families and communities when they failed to follow the rules of whiteness. These rules include uncritically going along with the racist mistreatment of people of color as well as maintaining race-segregated relationships and communities. In order to avoid punishment and exile, white children and adults became complicit with these rules. To be accepted, many white people resist naming and exploring whiteness and avoid critically engaging other white folks in discussions of white entitlement, racism, and white supremacy. Adherence to these rules becomes the condition of acceptance in white families and communities. Thandeka also suggests that the cost of *becoming white* for white people is to live with the shame of this complicity.

Thandeka's analysis prompts the question: Are there conditions of belonging to white-dominant feminism? And I would say "yes!" I would suggest, in fact, that *silence* with regard to the practices and structures of racism are often a condition of membership in predominantly white feminist communities. If you want to be part of the group, it means you must not speak up about racism within feminism, you must not explicitly name whiteness or white supremacy in relation to feminist identities, and you must not align with women of color in critically engaging other white feminist women or organizations. I've certainly experienced such conditions when I've spoken up about racism within organizational contexts; for instance, when I have challenged feminist racism, I have often been accused of divisiveness and told that I'm not a real feminist, that I don't care about women's issues, and/or that I am a race traitor.

Additionally, the conditions of whiteness become evident when antiracist critique and/or women of color are centered within a feminist context, and white feminists complain that we feel "silenced" or "victimized," or that the event or activity is no longer feminist. I've been in situations where white women say that "they" (i.e.,—we) feel silenced, no longer feel "welcome," no longer "belong" or no longer have a place in feminism. Sometimes, such statements are made in response to programming and/or politics that highlight racism or multiple and interlocking systems of oppression, or that privilege particular groups of women of color, poor women, queer women, transgender people, among others. I feel that such statements reveal an anxiety as well as an anger at having whiteness made visible, open to scrutiny, no longer a stand-in for individualized universality. I think these claims around these feelings of being "silenced" must be interrogated in the context of white entitlement and dominance, particularly since silence is so often equated with oppression.

A very good friend of mine shared this story with me about an incident that occurred in a Women's Studies Program. This was a program whose faculty were predominantly white with very few faculty of color and a program that had not had any direct conversations about issues of race and racism. At a meeting of the broad interdisciplinary committee, a relatively new woman of color faculty member made the observation that there were very few faculty women of color involved in Women's Studies. She suggested that the committee reflect on the situation and strategize on how to broaden the involvement of more women faculty of color. In response, one of the white women faculty members began to cry, offering to drop out of the committee to make room for women of color. In response, all of the white faculty members' attention re-focused on the white woman in order to reassure her that her membership was very important and that there would be no way that she would be asked to step down. It should be noted that the woman faculty of color never asked the white faculty members to step off of the committee. The concerns that she, the faculty of color, brought to the table were dropped, and of course, there was no similar outpouring of concern about her sense of community within the program, nor those of other women of color. The emotional outburst served to deflect from the problem of exclusion and to focus instead on the identity, experience, and feelings of belonging of this white woman, and by extension all the other white women in the program. Rather than address why so few faculty of color are involved in women's studies, the focus became making sure that white women feel validated. Rather than consider the harm caused by institutional marginalization, it became more important to protect the speaker and her membership in the community from scrutiny, to retain her "innocence."

Sarita Srivastava (2006) explores similar situations in a variety of feminist organizations which she sees as governed by "therapeutic conventions" that uncritically privilege emotional expression over critical analysis. She suggests that there is a pattern of white feminists responding to antiracist critiques with hurt feelings and claims that such critiques make the space less "safe." In these instances, Srivastava argues, the white women in leadership label the women of color as "angry" while they perceive themselves and other white women as innocent victims of antiracist critique, represented by the image of a "tearful white woman" (Srivastava, 2006, p. 83). In these contexts, white women's expressions of vulnerability become more important than the antiracist critical analysis of women of color. Gail Griffin (1998) suggests that such dynamics simply perpetuate the "long, tiresome history of white middle-class women espousing 'weakness' as a buffer from consciousness, responsibility and struggle" (p. 12). What is left unsaid in such instances is how these emotional disclosures themselves are "shaped by the inequitable relations of race" (Srivastava, 2006, p. 83) and serve to maintain the status quo. They serve to deflect attention from white accountability for perpetrating in and/or being complicit with institutional racism. The uncritical, unreflective acceptance of white women's emotional outbursts in response to antiracist critique undermines efforts to engender structural shifts and changes in organizations.

What would it take to challenge and transform such dynamics? What would it look like to name the dynamics created by the "tearful white woman" (Srivastava 2006), and to interrogate the systems such tears serve in the face of antiracist critique? Srivastava (2006) argues that feminists must rethink the role of emotion in organizations and address "the historical relations of power that prompt emotional resistance to discussions of race, and that allow white participants to openly express their tears, anger, and despair in the face of anti-racism" (p. 85). This might include explicitly naming the segregated and white hegemonic belongings that are called up in the defenses of women's studies and/or feminist communities?

I've certainly experienced these conditions. Early on in my own trajectory of feminism in the early 1980s, I remember my shock at how quickly my white middle-class liberal and radical feminist peers in a graduate Feminist Theories class turned against me for simply naming feminist racism, following the lead of the radical women of color feminisms offered by Cherríe Moraga and Gloria Anzaldúa (1981), bell hooks (1981), Angela Davis (1981), among others. They accused me of being anti-feminist and homophobic for simply raising the questions. More recently, during the Democratic Primaries in 2008, I was surprised at how quickly white feminist leaders like Gloria Steinem and Robin Morgan, among others, questioned the feminism of so many of us for daring to support Obama rather than Clinton for president. Again, a litmus test for feminism—if you do not posit gender over race, then you're not a "real" feminist, and your status of belonging to feminism is made suspect. And yet this prompted many of us women of color and white allies to re-commit ourselves to a multiracial feminism that refuses such false oppositions. For instance, Melissa Spatz, Director of the Women and Girls Collective Action Network, and I issued a petition "Stop the False Gender/Race Divide: A Call to Action" that asked white allies to step up to refuse this divide and actively cultivate a broader intersectional and social justice politics.[3]

It seems that the rules of whiteness that Thandeka (2005) outlines apply within white feminist circles as much as they apply in other areas of life; if not challenged, they will continue to divide and immobilize broader coalition and alliance building. One question, then, is what would it take to expand a politics of disloyalty to whiteness with a simultaneous commitment to multiracial justice and community within and outside of feminism?

What might be the risks involved, given contexts of power and privilege, with calls for white feminists, for instance, to name whiteness? One of the risks might be that we re-center whiteness and re-appropriate the stage of authority and the space of all-knowing speaking-subject. Another risk might be that such naming is done in isolation from the relationship, coalition, and alliance building with women of color, and thus no accountability around the necessary practices of active listening. Our attentiveness to such risks must be at the center of our practice; we must recognize that the balance between speech and silence is always contextual, rather than presupposed. In "White Identities and the Search for Racial Justice," Jennifer Eichstedt (2001) explores the dilemma of "white antiracist activists" who "must undermine white identity and white supremacy while they simultaneously must embrace

their identification of themselves as white and unduly privileged...."
As we work to "deconstruct whiteness as a system of meanings and
power distributions," we are also working against the tendencies toward
denial and silence with regard to our implications in racism. She suggests that white antiracist activists "hold onto whiteness, not as a place
from which to act, but as a location of responsibility" (Eichstedt, 2001,
pp. 466–467).

In bell hooks (1996) essay "beloved community" she talks about the
importance of making visible and expanding multiracial communities
who share a commitment with one another to addressing everyday
white supremacy within and outside of the community. It is within
these communities that I continue to practice the negotiations of silence
and speech in relation to dynamics of power and privilege. What I've
come to realize is that it is not a speech or silence that are liberatory on
their own, but an awareness of how both can undermine or reproduce
the unequal divides that we are working to dismantle.

Conclusion

The question for me is how to critically interrogate the tensions between
speech and silence without making myself into the righteous one, the
all-knowing one, and the morally superior one. I believe strongly that
white people need to step up and speak out in the face of injustices, and
yet do so without making ourselves the center of power and knowledge.
This is the challenge. I continue to explore ways to speak out while
simultaneously implicating, rather than distancing, myself in the process. In other words, I am learning to speak not as an "authority," but
as a learner, and to speak with humility as someone also implicated in
the dynamics that I am simultaneously trying to undermine. All of this
is dependent and must be embedded within a commitment to silent
witnessing and active listening as practices necessary to changing these
deeply entrenched power relations and to transforming relationships
and alliances across power lines. This path of negotiating both silence
and speech must be one that undermines and resists rather than reproduces dynamics and structures of inequality. What I've learned is that I
must accept that there are no easy answers and that, in any case, I alone
will not be *the* one with the necessary "authority" or knowledge to offer
them. And most importantly, I have learned that it is through building
relationships and communities across unequal divides that we're able
to create the knowledge, strategies, and visions necessary for deep and
expansive social transformation.

Acknowledgments

A heartfelt thanks to Francesca Royster and Lourdes Torres for their support and guidance on this essay, and a very special thanks to my amazing writing circle of sister friends—Laila Farah, Cricket Keating, Sheena Malhotra, Kimberlee Perez, Aimee Carrillo Rowe, and Francesca Royster, for all of their ideas and for their unending generosity in reading earlier drafts.

Notes

1. See Aimee Carrillo Rowe's book, *Power Lines: On the Subject of Feminist Alliances* (2008), for an incisive analysis of how whiteness and heterosociality inform the alliances of a significant number of the white academic feminists she interviewed. In part, she found that white feminists tended to have a different approach to alliances from feminist academics of color. For many of the white feminists, though not all, they approached alliances as a method of advancing their own careers, including within women's studies; whereas alliances, for the feminists of color, were more about creating support as well as solidarity for change (Carrillo Rowe, 2008).
2. Cricket Keating (2005) offers a powerful methodology for what she calls coalitional consciousness building, which she distinguishes from "consciousness raising" which is built on a shared oppression model.
3. The text of this petition can be found on the Women & Girls Collective Action Network, http://www.womenandgirlscan.org.

References

Alexander, M. Jacqui. *Pedagogies of Crossing: Meditations on Feminism, Sexual Politics, Memory and the Sacred.* Durham, NC: Duke University Press, 2005.

Boler, Megan. *Feeling Power: Emotions and Education.* New York: Routledge, 1999.

Carrillo Rowe, Aimee. *Power Lines: On the Subject of Feminist Alliances.* Durham, NC: Duke University Press, 2008.

Cohen, Cathy. "Punks, Bulldaggers, and Welfare Queens: The Radical Potential of Queer Politics," *GLQ: A Journal of Lesbian and Gay Studies* 3:4 (1997): 437–465.

Davis, Angela. *Women, Race and Class.* New York: Random House, 1981.

Eichstedt, Jennifer L. "White Identities and the Search for Racial Justice." *Sociological Forum* 16:3 (September, 2001): 445–470.

Ellsworth, Elizabeth. "Double Binds of Whiteness." In *Off White: Readings on Race, Power, and Society,* edited by Michelle Fine, Lois Weis, Linda C. Powell, and L. Mun Wong, 259–269. New York, NY: Routledge, 1997.

Enloe, Cynthia. *The Curious Feminist: Searching for Women in a New Age of Empire.* University of California, 2004.

Griffin, Gail. "Speaking of Whiteness: Disrupting White Innocence." *The Journal of the Midwest Modern Language Association* 31:3 (1998): 3–14.

hooks, bell. *Ain't I a Woman: Black Women and Feminism.* Boston, MA: South End Press, 1981.

hooks, bell. *Killing Rage, Ending Racism.* New York: Holt, 1996.

Keating, Cricket. "Building Coalitional Consciousness." *NWSA Journal* 17:2 (2005): 86–103.

Lugones, Maria, and Elizabeth Spelman. "Have We Got a Theory for You! Feminist Theory, Cultural Imperialism and the Demand for 'The Woman's Voice.'" *Women's Studies International Forum* 6:6 (1983): 573–581.

Mazzei, Lisa A. "Silence Speaks: Whiteness Revealed in the Absence of Voice." *Teaching and Teacher Education* 24 (2008): 1125–1136.

McIntosh, Peggy. "White Privilege and Male Privilege." In *Privilege*, edited by Michael S. Kimmel and Abbey L. Ferber, 147–160. Boulder, CO: Westview Press, 2003.

Moraga, Cherríe, and Gloria Anzaldúa, eds. *This Bridge Called My Back: Writings by Radical Women of Color.* Watertown, MA: Persephone Press, 1981.

Srivastava, Sarita. "Tears, Fears, and Careers: Anti-racism and Emotion in Social Movement Organizations." *Canadian Journal of Sociology/Cahiers canadiens de sociologie* 31:1 (2006): 55–90.

Thandeka. *Learning to Be White.* New York: Continuum, 2005.

Thompson, Audrey. "Listening and Its Asymmetries." *Curriculum Inquiry* 33:1 (2003): 79–100.

Uttal, Lynet. "Nods that Silence." In *Making Face/Making Soul: Haciendo Caras*, edited by Gloria Anzaldúa, 317–320. San Francisco, CA: Aunt Lute Books, 1990.

4

Qwe're Performances of Silence: Many Ways to Live "Out Loud"

Julia R. Johnson

When I first considered the role of silence in forming alliances, the idea of writing about silence was intriguing and freeing. As I pondered silence, my body overtook my usual controlled, linear, and deliberate writing process. It had something to say about silence that my mind couldn't contain. The more I focused on thinking, the more belligerent my body became. I squirmed in my chair and my eyes glazed over as I stared at the computer screen. No matter how forcefully my academic mind struggled to identify the perfect theory or compelling moment that I might neatly insert into a linear essay, corporeality hounded me, pushing me into silence. Only through an unexpected blurring of boundaries brought on by the disruption of the Cartesian mind/body split, and after hours of sitting in the silence of my discomfort, did I realize that longings for silence and bringing silence into words is messy, confusing, contradictory. John R. Barrie (2008) states that "When all mental ruminations are at last exhausted, genuine silence emerges" (p. 10). So, after days and weeks of struggling through thoughts, I immersed myself in silence and turned to my body for the knowledge I sought. I closed my eyes, breathed deeply, and turned my attention to my physical and emotional bodies to learn what they might show me about the silence that resides there.

I catapulted out of the here and now into a conflated momentum where past, future, and present merged. Time shifted and I lost my "self"...floating between yesterday and today, here and there, wholeness and fragmentation. Feeling drove me. Rage and joy surged, washing over me, unexpectedly driving energy to the keyboard. Thoughts emerged: I found myself anxious that the privileged whining of a 40-something, middle-class, white academic would consume the coexisting cellular reality of a trans-[1] identified, gender queer, fat

50

pansexual, dyke with an "invisible" disability and working-class roots who has constantly been told to "lower her voice," professionally and personally. Working to contain myself at the intersections of privilege and oppression is both familiar and hopeless. My physical excess always pushes my sense of self b-e-y-o-n-d—beyond patience, propriety, and others' desire to contain me. My anxiety is desire—a desiring to challenge power and a desiring to resist the privileges that always already fill the corners of my house, body, and mind—a privilege that will always follow me out the door. My self is always stretching with contradictions, but to seek a coherent narrative of self will fail us as it closes us off to the people we most desire (as my friend Kimberlee reminded me). I desire connection within and through the contradictions.

Feelings emerged: The rage and joy mingling in my solar plexus—raw, visceral, uncontrollable feelings that override the social rules and consequences that use silence as a weapon of discipline and control. Silence *is* a weapon the privileged use to surveil, control, and dehumanize... Silence *is also* resistance (Clair, 1998; Lorde, 1984; Moraga, 1983; Rich, 1979). It is a tool of justice wielded to ensure survival and to create space within structures of domination. It can be a radical act of agency. Silence and voice are paradoxically one. Silence is part of all discourse, all communication (Foucault, 1990).

Thoughts and feelings converged: as I felt/considered the complimentary and contradictory nature of silence, I sensed a queer impulse toward it. Is silence queer? How might silence be queered? How might silence be done in a way that turns power on its head? Judith Halberstam (2005) defined queer as "nonnormative logics and organizations of community, sexual identity, embodiment, and activity in space and time" (p. 6). Initially, this definition moves me because it challenges dominant notions of what it means to be queer and who can be queer. Yet, the queerness I want to define is not the assimilation(ist), white supremacist, bourgeois, US nationalist, lesbian and gay occupation of the term queer. Rather, it is the queer born from the lives and work of radical intellectuals and activists. I mean an anti-assimilationist queerness and a queer figured by the explicit intention to combat oppression and injustice of all kinds, including racisms and transphobias *within* lesbian and gay communities. The queerness I'm imagining is a queerness that challenges complicit silences... such as the quare articulated by E. Patrick Johnson (2001) and the kuaer expressed by Wenshu Lee (2003). Quareness and kuaerness resist heteronormativity as well as the whiteness and bourgeois sensibilities upheld in many US lesbian and gay communities. Lee takes us even deeper into the erasures of queer theory as she presents "a transnational womanist quare theory and politics" (p. 162) that reconceptualizes queerness within and beyond the racialized borders of the US and global economies. Like Johnson and Lee, I also mean a queer that rejects capitalist consumption and bourgeois longings. This kind of queerness gives the finger to imperialism and does everything in its (our) power to stop war, stop violence, and stop the advancement of normative homo-ness built on the bodies, minds, and souls of the "queer terrorist of elsewhere" (Puar, 2007, p. xxv). I mean the queer that is engaged as a radical space of relational possibility in which the needs of trans-, poor, im/migrant, and/or people of color become the interests of us all—*on their/our terms*. I invoke the queer that disrupts a sense of normative embodiment (in all its constructions), that knows the intimate relation between sexuality and disability, and challenges the able-bodied heteronorms that pathologize physical multiplicity (Kafer, 2003).

This queerness I imagine is qwe'reness (we ARE together): a reflexive practice of solidarity built on radically intersectional relations that address our distinctions and separations as a basis for seeking commonality. Qwe'erness creates something contingent, messy, and complex—it is constantly moving and shifting, yet always aware of the power of dominance to define the corporeal in real (material and dehumanizing) ways. It operates as a "counter publicity" that "makes an intervention in public life that defies" all forms of ideological domination (Muñoz, 1999, p. 148) and it is a politic that acknowledges "the specificity of oppression" (Moraga, 1983, p. 29). Qwe'erness is embodied in the performance of collaborative resistance in which we work together to continually disrupt the rigid cultural norms and categories that oppress and dehumanize. It assumes no one can be fully human, or can "have rights," until the complexity of *all our* oppressions are transformed.

Time continues to shift and past becomes present: when I spend time with the queer words of others, my own words come and I find a way to live in silence, move with silence, and write about silence, which manifests in the power to be more fully in my fat, gender queer, disabled, white body, and to reorganize my body in time and space to write about the pedagogy of silence, or the ways silence teaches us how to *be*, how to *relate*, how to *ally* against power qwe'rely. This is a space of anti-essentialism and a radical possibility of alliance formation that speaks of embodiment as well as the kind of political belonging in which the "self" "is radically inclined toward others, toward communities to which we belong, with whom we long to be and to whom we feel accountable" (Carrillo Rowe, 2005, p. 18). It recognizes both the realities of privilege embodied and given to us as well as the possibility of "being together" and "structuring social relations" (p. 33) in acts of affiliation and shared resistance.

This is the kind of queer for which I long—a qwe're politic, ontology, and epistemology. This is a way of being that bends time, requiring us to stay in the moment as we reflect on the past, all of which always points beyond into unknown possibility. It is a doing that creates reality and binds us together in a social contract—a commitment to social justice and intersectional action. It is a way of knowing that is never complete, but requires constant vigilance and commitment to silence as an act of attending to others and to places of self knowing that cannot be accessed in the noise of speech. Narratives of progress have no place here. Time and space bend with possibility—as do bodies—even in the face of ideology's efforts to fix us all. In this state of flux and strategic essentialism, I came upon two (re)emerging moments from my life that offer examples of queer silence, time, and space.

In this essay, I unpack the idea of qwe'reing silence by exploring how silence is used to foreclose and enable the possibility of alliances within two different, diverse communities. In the first example, I explore how silence is used as a weapon of containment and control within lesbian and gay communities. In the second example, I explore how qwe're relations were made possible by allies of color as they used silence to show me my investment in white supremacy. Time bends across these examples and silence is enacted differently in each scenario. There is no linear logic to follow, only connections to be made between seemingly distinct moments in time. My physical and affective bodies took me on this journey. The writing followed.

Through these examples, I also explore the rhetorical and paradoxical nature of silence. Without words, silence would not exist. If not for silence, sound would have no meaning. As Cheryl Glenn (2004) states "Speech and silence depend upon each other: behind all speech is silence, and silence surrounds all speech" (p. 7). Silence is sound and rhetorical force—it echoes in its stillness and induces thought and action. "Each of these rhetorical arts carries with it a grammar, value, and most of all meaning" (p. 7). In what follows, I explore the rhetorics of silence and voice to discern their qwe're potential.

The silence Janice Raymond produces

Queering silence is not the sole domain of queers or gender benders, although sex, gender, and sexuality are primary sites of queer analysis. Some of the most unqueer behavior I have observed has come from lesbian and gay communities who use silence as a weapon against those who are transgender, people who are poor or working class, im/migrants, and/or people from historically oppressed racialized groups. Enacting silence within lesbian and gay contexts often means disrupting the oppressions we have internalized and use against each other to further isolate and divide.

Take the lesbian feminist Janice Raymond, for example. In 1979 Raymond argued in her now (in)famous text, *The Transsexual Empire: The Making of the She-male*, that gender is defined by biology and, as a result, transsexual women are predators who "infiltrate" lesbian spaces to "capture" "strong female energy" (Riddell, 2006, p. 137) and "to function as image-makers of the lesbian feminist—not only for the public-at-large, but also for the women's community" (p. 141). In spite of nuanced and righteous critiques of Raymond's position (see Hale, 1998; Riddell, 2006; or Stone, 1991), her claims about transgenderism have reflected and recreated dominant forms of silence through transphobia and transemnity. In her writing, she seems propelled by fear to colonize the bodies of people who are transgender and to use her academic voice and white, lesbian, feminist credentials as a battering ram. Because of the meanings Raymond makes of transgenderism and lesbianism (and because her politics are performed in many lesbian and gay communities), I learned about the homonormative nature of "mainstream" lesbian and gay spaces.[2] Raymond defines belonging through sex-normative embodiment and a pathologizing genetic determinism—all in the name of feminism and lesbianism. She limits lesbian desire and the sound of her voice lurks in my (possible) relationships, interpenetrating and interpellating my affections and belongings.

In my mid-thirties, I lived in one of Southern California's predominantly lesbian and gay neighborhoods. During this time, a friend of mine set me up with Alexie. The two of us met for the first time at a local coffee shop. We both had friends who would often go there to socialize, so it seemed like a "safe place" to get to know each other. Alexie and I had our first chat at a quiet table away from everyone we knew. Our conversation was friendly, but brief. We connected as friends, but not as lovers. As we left the coffee shop, mutual friends were sitting outside and called us over. When we approached their table, everyone said hello to us both and then exchanged furtive glances. The energy at the table was uncomfortable and it felt like we had walked in on a joke of some kind, like a prank awaiting us on a school playground. Because the group interaction was strangely uncomfortable, I left. Alexie remained at the table as I said good-bye.

During the next day or so, I ran into my coffee house friends, who seemed eager to speak with me when Alexie was absent. They laughingly talked about my dating Alexie and asked me if I knew that she was "really a man" who was clearly confused because she took hormones, lived as a woman, and had intimate physical and emotional relationships with both women and men. Harkening back to a time of freak shows, they defined Alexie as a liar and a freak—a spectacle to be ogled and ridiculed. In a flash, I fell into my pre-pubescent body. I lost my words and felt like the freakish object they were making her out to be. My intellectual self was both stunned and appalled at the transphobic violence emerging from a community that defined itself as "queer." They tried to engage me in cis-sex/gender bonding.[3] Just like those who engage in white racial bonding, my "friends" were making diligent attempts to bring me into their fold of sex and gender rigidity, and, simultaneously, to silence and erase Alexie's personhood and my own burgeoning trans-identification. The comfort I had felt in this coffee house space was pulled out from under me and I toppled into a new dimension of spatial hostility. The tumbling through time continued, transporting me away from junior high shock back into my present-day body, adult anger, and discomfort. I shifted from a passive silence characterized by shock and moved into a verbal voice others could read and understand.

My jaw grew tense and I engaged my body as I have learned to do in the heterosexist, racist, ableist, transphobic, and classist environments of public life. Stoic and rock-like I controlled the anger...I directed it at my "friends" as I verbally challenged their trans-hatred. I followed my verbal response with silence—working to remove their comfort in the physical and relational space they had created. Even in Alexie's hypervisible physical absence, I imagined her beside me and wondered how her relationships with this group and with me might shift as a result of the group's bigotry. My physical presence and Alexie's physical absence reminds me of C. Jacob Hale's (1998) claim that persons who are transgender, like other colonized people, "are coerced into silence or are dismissed as mad when we do speak" (p. 108). In my own (then) lesbian body, I felt frustrated and culpable. Even as I challenged the coffee klatch's transphobia and centering of mainstream homosexuality/homonormativity, I was confused and repulsed by their attempts to center my fatness, "lesbianism," whiteness, and class privilege. They flirted with me and attempted to seduce me with their sexes. They made jokes about Alexie and her "inability" to "commit" as straight or gay, woman or man—all code for their own rigid assumptions about bodies and identities. In the manner of a colonial power, they expressed disgust at her pansexuality and trans-identification. Through their laughter, repulsion, and flirtation, I felt like a weapon they were using to erase Alexie—they interpellated my body as the mediating force of silence and I felt caught in quicksand, being enveloped and smothered against my will. They didn't count on my identification with her or my desire for her. They were tricked by their perceptions of my body and mistook that perception for my identity. Bodies and identities clashing... shifting. I resisted their use of my body and disrupted this homo-genizing of my cells and skin. I worked to connect my monstrous flesh with hers in an expression of alliance.

The kind of silencing the coffee klatch engaged "is characteristic of any social formation anxious to promote its own interests and disinterested in complicating its own self of reality and self-realization by paying attention to other points of view" (Fernandez, 2006, p. 160). These were the same "friends" who worked for a local lesbian and gay pride organization that refused to include transgender persons in the organization's name and activism. They were happy to support cross-dressing queens, the Sisters of Perpetual Indulgence, or butch lesbians as long as the "biological covenant" wasn't broken. Their comfort with the gender continuum and sex binary was, as in many lesbian and gay communities, firmly grounded in a sense of "biological purity" that positions transsexuality as an aberration to the "natural" order. Priyanka Jindal (2008) speaks to intersectional limitations of some lesbian and gay communities: "... [M]y experience as a transgender person of color, and more so the experience of working-class and poor queer people of color, are not only marginalized and silenced but also trampled on in the name of gay 'rights'" (p. 41). I wonder if the same people would be mortified with appeals to racial purity, even as they easily slipped into a different kind of biological essentialism?[4] I refuse(d) and reject(ed) dominance in all its forms and the klatch met my enactment of silence with elision, laughter, and dismissive glances and gestures. They also isolated me as they attempted to hold me close.

In an emotional and intellectual rejection of their transphobia, I performed silence qwe'rely. As Cheryl Glenn (2004) states, "A rhetoric of silence has much to offer, especially as an imaginative space that can open possibilities between two people or within a group. Silence, in this sense, is an invitation into the future, a space that draws us forth" (p. 160). My silent rejection was not solely "in my mind." Silence was rhetorical and relational—a series of choices and performances that distanced me from one community and created the space for reflecting about what it meant to identify, to connect, to affiliate with another. It was also an invitation for my "friends" to choose alliance instead of erasure and epistemic violence. I wondered if the voice and silence I used might have created a bridge between Alexie and me. What might Alexie think about this writing and my construction of her body and identity?

Alexie and I remained in this community, organizing for lesbian and gay rights. By working with them at all, I felt Janice Raymond pulling at me, the distance and silence ever present. No matter how much I reject Raymond, her performance of lesbianism is always already written on my body, continually creating divisions that I must use silence and voice to resist. In asserting silence to the coffee klatch, I used my privilege within the community (although speaking back is often insufficient to hammer through a wall of silence or to form an alliance). In another performance of silence, I never spoke with Alexie about the struggle with the coffee klatch. I don't know how she made sense of them or of me. The ways that both of us addressed that particular lesbian and gay community seemed to inhibit us from talking, even when we spent time together. I don't know if silence is what allowed our continued friendship, but the fear living in the silence kept our bodies and intimacy distant.

Had this group moved through their silencing imposed on Alexie and taken up my silence, histories could have opened up the present relations between lesbian and gay and transgender communities; however, their quest was for mainstream acceptance of lesbian and gay lives—marriage, property ownership, health rights. They silence(d) "Others" to achieve their rights and imaginings. For them, gender had its boundaries as did same-sex love. Silence was their weapon of choice. It was also my chosen path of qwe're resistance. Alexie was my ally. I can only hope I was hers.

Silence, and the feelings that silence offers, provide portals that allow access to different spheres simultaneously. As I write this essay, my desk in the Midwest and the Southern California coffee shop merge. When my body shifts slightly in my chair, my perception also shifts—the coffee shop fading slightly—and other familiar locations fade in through the stillness. This next example presented itself as a tangible ghost moving through my body, caught in the feelings of connection and loss presented by my relationship with Alexie. Another moment of qwe're possibility emerged.

Qwe're/kuaer/quare silence and racism

In 1994, I learned how silence can function as a site of resistance and alliance building, all of which was facilitated by Minister Louis Farrakhan. For some, it may seem unusual to associate Minister Farrakhan and queerness. Yet, as I began writing this essay, the first experience that persistently tapped on my bones involved audiencing a speech delivered by Farrakhan at the university where I attended graduate school. Without knowing how or why, I knew this experience exemplified queerness as an affiliational possibility. As I've moved through the writing, I understand that this example illustrates for me how enacting silence can disrupt normative relations, even when appearing mundane or usual. By deliberately sitting in silence and listening to the absence of sound we can initiate connections that interrupt oppressive uses of power.

As a PhD student, I learned quickly how whiteness manifests problematically in/as silence—silence in the face of enacted racism, sexism, ableism, US nationalism, heterosexism, Christian supremacy, and classism. In the politicized environment in which I was growing, white, bourgeois liberals often demonstrated how *not speaking* and acting against racism reinforced white, middle-class, heterosexual privilege. In alliance *with* me, US and "third world" activists and academics of color (and a few critical white people) verbally challenged my complicit silences, such as my immersion in white narcissism, my failure to speak when white people expressed racism, or my desires to have other white people like me. In addition to learning the negativity of silence, I also learned from these allies the rhetorical, social and political *value* of silence as a strategy of resistance. I learned that in order to embody and resist dominance as a white woman—both personally and as a member of the general category—I needed to actively engage silence or *perform silence* to form intimate and meaningful alliances with those defined as racially "different." As much as silence can constrain, it can also enable and transform.

One significant lesson I learned about the power of silence to resist domination emerged during interaction with friends following our attending Farrakhan's speech. On campus, there was public conversation about his visit, both in terms of the importance of his critique of whiteness and the troubling nature of his rhetoric in relation to Jewish communities, people who are lesbian and gay, and women. At that point in my life, I was being pushed by the campus political climate (as a subset of the larger culture) and by my relationships to interrogate cultural dominance, particularly white supremacy, classism, and heternormativity. Being pushed was not a theoretical exercise for me, although I was saturated with critical cultural theory. Interrogating identity, particularly identity intersections, was relational—it was born out of interactions with people different from me and it assumed a central presence in all my relationships. My friends and colleagues often challenged my assumptions and embodiment and I often found myself the proverbial fish sitting outside the tank amazed (often horrified, guilty, sad, enraged) by the nature of the water. Attending Farrakhan's speech fit squarely into the relational terrain I was navigating and, as a bourgeois, white woman, I felt it was important to audience him directly instead of relying on media accounts of his rhetoric.

I don't remember specific elements of Farrakhan's speech, but I do remember the feeling of/in my body as I walked into the theater where he was speaking and moving out of the theater when the speech was complete. The space and bodies echo in my throat, heart, and solar plexus: A circular theater complex that seemed never to end; the men of the Nation of Islam standing strong and silent around each entrance to the theater and on stage with Farrakhan; the theater filled with people of color who outnumbered the white people in the room. I remember the feeling in my body as I listened to one of the most explicit critiques of white racism I had ever heard. I felt hypervisible...exposed...culpable...anxious...alone—conscious of my whiteness...whiteness made visible...whiteness critiqued...whiteness the public and explicit object of critique. I felt discomfort, anxiety, and a desire to become invisible. If I couldn't be invisible, I certainly wanted to be perceived as "a good white." Like most white people, I didn't want to be associated with the white supremacy that was being critiqued and I longed for a glimpse of forgiveness from those who were terrorized by whiteness. I struggled to speak to release myself from the eyes I felt watching me and from the guilt filling my chest.

Instead of meeting my white needs, my friends engaged a strategy commonly used in the face of white guilt—a strategy I've come to understand as an opportunity for alliance. As my friends and I left the theater when the speech ended, I couldn't figure out what to say and everything that I said seemed to echo conspicuously in the air. Most of my friends did not speak to me as we walked back to our offices. They were very polite to me, invited me to go out for coffee with them, but they did not actively initiate any dialogue. They walked beside me in silence. Because of the silence, I had no place to go. No words to hide behind. No language to use that would explain away the exposure. My friends allowed me to sit in the silence and be in the discomfort of my defensiveness, frustration, and guilt. I can recall the feeling of being obvious, as if my thoughts and emotions were plainly visible in a way I had not before experienced. Of course, I don't think I was any more obviously white than usual, but the context brought my whiteness to the surface of my own consciousness, so I was learning whiteness in a new way. The pretense of privilege had been peeled away with each word Farrakhan spoke and the subsequent silence in my interactions pushed me deeper into my own obviousness. I was oblivious and obvious, and wanted to run away from the silence, the pain in my body, and from the legacy of white supremacy and the racism that the speech made tangible to me personally. White guilt was oozing from my pores and dripped from the words I could muster. As Shannon Winnubst (2006) contends, "White guilt wishes to erase the sins of its past, not to do penance for them" (p. 172)—given the history of colonialism, white supremacy is infused with Christian supremacy and, thus, racism involves dialectical tensions of martyrdom/sainthood and guilt/innocence.

I didn't know what to do with myself or the ways language failed me, so I sat in the silence alone. And I worked to listen—to take in the silence extended to me. I did not walk away, nor did I "demand" attention and explanation. I wanted to ... I longed to. I remember walking side by side back to our offices—a physicality that mirrored how I was engaged through silence.

The silence of that experience—a silence full of words and sentiments—still lives within me and, although I fleetingly long for racial transcendence, white supremacy continually asserts itself and directs my life in ways that surprise and anger me. Humble reminders of the past collapsing in the present—and the illusion of progress. I find myself regularly returning to one particular passage from Mab Segrest's book, *Memoir of a Race Traitor* (1994). Early in the book, Segrest reflects on the distances that whiteness creates between white people and people of color, even as we work together to resist racism. She states:

> ... the Black people I encountered seemed to know as many versions of white people as Eskimos developed words for snow, and my place on the white spectrum seemed recognizable immediately in my inflection, body language and, especially, deeds ... I could feel Black strangers opening toward me or closing down, a constant calculus of distances. I learned also to cipher the distances in Black friends, when in the middle of a conversation I would feel the attention drift or shift, a sudden space between us. Sometimes their challenge would be

direct and swift, though seldom sharp; other times I would look back and recognize a subtle contradiction or re-routed conversation that left me searching through my words to find the point where I had thrown the switch. There was a constant possibility of small betrayals that could invoke the specter of much larger crimes. (pp. 19–20)

The walk back to our offices was long and I felt conspicuous in my inability to speak. What I didn't understand at the time was that the silence my friends enacted in their relation with me was a qwe're bridge between us—and a strategy many people of color regularly use with people who are white (that may be intended to distance themselves from white people and white supremacy). Silence as a distancing relationality, albeit likely mundane and an everyday act for my friends, created the possibility for me to know differently—whiteness generally, my whiteness, and the whiteness that my friends were asked to perform daily. As a result of our complex (nationalized, racialized, gender, and sexuality-marked) embodiments and political commitments, I learned more fully how hegemony impacts all identities and relations. Words would have covered this awareness. To challenge hegemony, I had to grapple with myself without the familiar cloak of excuses, diversions, or trite acknowledgments. In silence, the roar of domination was almost impossible to ignore. My ally-friends were being qwe're with me because they interrupted the quiet and insidious forms of racism (and other intersecting forms of dominance) in which I was invested. Because of their silence, I was provided a choice to *be* and *do* differently. Time and space shifted. History lived vibrantly in the silence. It pushed on my body and made the interracial corporeality and differential racialized consciousness a space of possibility—qwe're possibility. In that silent challenge to racism, my knowledge of all identities shifted, including sexuality, sex, and ability. It was as if the distinct histories of different oppressions fell against one another, making my cells fall together and different parts of my life collapse. In my consciousness, the "I" dissolved into "we." Did it have the same effect on my friends?[5]

My times during graduate school were filled with words. My friends and I often had intense verbal exchanges. Our use of sound was punctuated by silences. The grammar of silence exists not only in its complimentarity to written and oral articulations, but also in the distinctive ways of knowing that can only emerge through verbal absence. The rhetoric of silence is qwe're because it speaks beyond a logocentric model and also disrupts a logocentric flow. As my friends and

I walked back in silence from Minister Farrakhan's speech, our embodied presence *together in the silence*, was a loud moment of meaning making and, yet, a common performance of interracial division and connection. The histories of racism moved with and through our bodies as did our histories as feminists, lesbians, third world activists, anti-imperialists, bourgeois academics, gender conformers, and gender benders. The quareness, qwe'reness, and/or kuaerness of our experience was expressed in our relation and our broader commitments to disrupting raced, gendered, classed, sexed, and imperialist dominant cultural norms. By virtue of the histories inscribed upon us, we embodied coalitional possibilities and, at various moments, we qwe'red our community with performances of silence.

Continual going on

At the moment of my writing, the past lingers here with me. My friends of all kinds—allies, antagonists—cohabitate with me in this liminal space. I find myself thanking them for the pain they have helped me find and the kindnesses they have extended to me in the process. Alexie, the coffee klatch, Farrakhan, my graduate school colleagues, the scholars whose ideas guide me—all have helped me know silence as a qwe're performative and have reminded me of how silence is also a weapon. We can use silence to build community and to transform dominance. Silence can also—sometimes simultaneously—be used to divide, conquer, and oppress. It can also transform time, orient us to others, and highlight the role of bodies in generating knowledge and community.

Silence is queer when we relinquish linearity and narratives of progress (Halberstam, 2006). Once upon a time, I believed the Farrakhan story was a "before" picture—an experience that happened to the "ignorant Julia" that somehow magically transformed me into a racism-free zone. But there is no place to go with isms in the linear sense—no "cure" for bigotry. These Western narrative frames divide time and action into discrete categories—fixing/statically situating bodies, ideas, and practices. Herein I've argued that silence brings past, present, and future together—blurring the boundaries between what was, what is, and what might be. I did not look into my past to find isolated examples of silence. My body simultaneously brought the past and present together—and different moments from the past into overlapping sensibility. History repeats itself because the nature of silence repeatedly brings us back as it pushes us forward. The racisms I performed in the past reiterate in the present as do the rhetorical silences I assert to resist oppression.

The experiences I detail herein continue to give me an ever-present space of possibility and foreclosure—it reminds me that resisting white supremacy (or any dominant discourse) in a white body (or privileged body) never ends. It also prompts me to continually ask how privileged bodies might take up, cocreate, enter/engage/understand the qwe're moment of alliance possibility by refusing to think of ourselves as beyond any dominant discourse. Instead, we might ask ourselves questions such as "How do our experiences with domination help move us toward social justice?" or "How does deep and critical reflection about whiteness and race help one think deeply about ability status, gender conformity and sexuality, recognizing the points of connection and disconnection in these interlocking, yet distinct, histories?" Personally, I also ask myself.... How would Alexie respond to what I have written here? My friends from Massachusetts?

Richard Johannesen (1974) reminds me that "In our literate Western culture silence often is regarded as worthless (we must *verbalize* something) or is regarded as an act of unfriendliness. Silence generally is taken as an asocial if not antisocial...." (p. 27). In our assumptions that words are powerful, we negate the power of silence to orient us toward others and to connect with them. When we conceive of silence as presence, we can enter it with curiosity and move beyond our own truth worlds to find new meanings. Allying with others requires curiosity. It requires orienting ourselves simultaneously inward to understand our own beliefs and outward to receive the reality of others. It requires putting our own voices and knowledge aside to make space for new universes of meaning. While we can never fully know someone else's reality, we have the capacity to work toward understanding others deeply within the intentional spaces of silence. This effort to access others through silence is qwe're because affiliations and alliances require knowing both of self and of other. As my ally and friend Alison asked me, "What would it mean to take the oppression or criticism of others into our own bodies? What affiliational possibilities would this create?" How would this act of relational listening have transformed the relation between the coffee klatch, Alexie, and me?

Silence is accessible through the body. Moving into silence is a performance—a choice—to access new meanings and new realities. In our bodies, we can attend to the fuzzy edges of sound that exist *between* or *around* what is said as well as part of what is said (Achino-Loeb, 2006). Intentionally attending to our bodies, we can feel and disrupt the linear timetables that often define daily life. Therein exists the potential to feel/know/hear/perceive ourselves and each other more deeply and carefully. The trouble with bodies is that they feel and know pains and joys that the mind only imagines.

When I write, I sometimes use my mind to avoid my body so that I can run from the quietness that threatens to invoke the pains and traumas that echo within me. Pain, including trauma, can be generative (Cvetkovich, 2003), but we must move into the pain to access generative possibilities. Silence offers a space and place to feel the byproduct of dominant ideologies and to resist them. Ignoring the pain of oppression and domination erases our differences and the histories that contextualize our relations.

My body continually reminds me of the productive nature of pain. It steers my attention and shows me the ways time and space collapse through the memories silence helps me know. Pain has also developed my understanding about how oppression works on us. In the folds of silence, I have accessed that knowledge most deeply and found qwe're words to speak. Silence is a space of qwe're affiliational possibility—it makes room for contemplation and confrontation. It pushes us into our bodies and, hopefully, into the experience of others as we contemplate and learn from what is not said, and it can teach us how to better be *with* others.

I long to affiliate in embodied spaces where guilt and defensiveness do not define my affective life. We must learn to read the silences of our desired communities, recognize where we don't belong, who we long to be with, and read invitational moments. We must also learn to forge ahead without invitation and find our way in uncertainty and in the face of rejection. This is a qwe're space because it is not clearly defined as either with or against, but it is a space of temporal, affiliational, and structural shifts that are always already re-aligning with context and relationship. Community is always present, absent, and waiting.

I remain in anxiety about silence as I learn to embrace it more and more. As I finish this writing, my office fills with desire and I feel the voices of allies, colleagues, friends, strangers, and antagonists that reverberate in my core. No time or space can interrupt what they have taught me. Pain, joy, anger... they live in the silence with me—and, hopefully, qwe'rely.

Acknowledgments

My deepest thanks and respect to Karma Chàvez, Jackson Jantzen, Alison Kafer, Sheena Malhotra, Kimberlee Pèrez, Marc Rich, and Subrina

Robinson for their comments and encouragement as I completed this essay. You inspire and humble me.

Notes

1. I am using transgender as an umbrella term for persons who challenge the gender binary, which includes (but is not limited to) persons who iden-tify as transmasculine, transfeminine, transsexual, Two-Spirit, cross-dressers, gender queer, MTM (male-to-male), FTF (female-to-female), FTM (female-to-male), MTF (male-to-female), and/or intersex. It is also important to recognize that the category of transgender is often problematic (culturally, politically, socially, historically) for many (e.g. Driskill, 2004; Roen, 2001). Second, fol-lowing the example provided by Stryker, Currah, and Moore (2008), I place hyphenate trans- to highlight the "categorical crossings, leakages, and slips of all sorts, around and through the concept 'trans-' " (p. 11).
2. I also reject the investment mainstream lesbian and gay communities have in whiteness, bourgeois accumulation, homonormativity, and (Western) imperi-alism.
3. Cisgender refers to persons who are not transgender, but persons whose assigned sex (by doctors, parents, society, etc.), avowed sex, and gender identity are aligned.
4. See Somerville, S. (1997). Scientific racism and the invention of the homo-sexual body. In R. N. Lancaster & M. di Leonardo (Eds) *The Gender Sexuality Reader: Culture, History, Political Economy* (pp. 37–52). New York: Routledge.
5. Thank-you to Karma Chàvez for challenging the description of my friends silence as queer. She thoughtfully reminded me that people of color often use silence as a way to "comment upon their investment in racism" and, thus, what I might describe as a queer silence may not be defined as queer by those with whom I am in relation.

References

Achino-Loeb, Maria Luisa. (2006). Silence and the imperatives of identity. In Maria Luisa Achino-Loeb (Ed.) *Silence: The currency of power* (pp. 35–51). New York: Berghahn Books.

Barrie, John R. (2008). The deepest silence. *Parabola*, 33(1), 6–11.

Carrillo Rowe, Aimee. (2005). Be longing: Toward a feminist politics of relation. *NWSA Journal*, 17(2), 15–46.

Clair, Robin P. (1998). *Organizing silence: A world of possibilities*. New York: State University of New York Press.

Cvetkovich, Ann. (2003). *An archive of feelings: Trauma, sexuality, and lesbian public cultures*. Durham, NC: Duke University Press.

Driskill, Qwo-Li. (2004). Stolen from our bodies: First Nations Two-Spirits/queers and the journey to a sovereign erotic. *SAIL: Studies in American Indian Literature*, 16(2), 50–64.

Fernandez, James W. (2006). Silences of the field. In Maria Luisa Achino-Loeb (Ed.) *Silence: The currency of power* (pp. 158–173). New York: Berghahn Books.

Foucault, Michel (1990). *The history of sexuality volume I: An introduction*. New York: Vintage Books. Translated by Robert Hurley.

Glenn, Cheryl (2004). *Unspoken: A rhetoric of silence*. Carbondale, IL: Southern Illinois University Press.

Halberstam, Judith (2005). *In a queer time and place: Transgender bodies, subcultural lives*. New York: NYU Press.

Halberstam, Judith (2006). What's that smell? Queer temporalities and subcultural lives. In S. Whiteley & J. Ryenga (Eds) *Queering the popular pitch* (pp. 3–26). New York: Routledge.

Hale, C. Jacob. (1998). Tracing a ghostly memory in my throat: Reflections on ftm feminist voice and agency. In Tom Digby (Ed.) *Men doing feminism* (pp. 99–129). New York: Routledge.

hooks, bell (1997). *Wounds of passion: A writing life*. New York: Henry Holt.

Jindal, Priyanka (2008). Sites of resistance or sites of racism? In Mattilda Bernstein Sycamore (Ed.) *That's revolting! Queer strategies for resisting assimilation* (pp. 39–46). Brooklyn, NY: Soft Skull Press.

Johannesen, Richard L. (1974). The functions of silence: A plea for communication research. *Western Speech*, 38(1), 25–35.

Johnson, E. Patrick (2001). "Quare" Studies, or (almost) everything I know about Queer Studies I learned from my Grandmother. *Text and Performance Quarterly*, 21(1), 1–25.

Kafer, Alison (2003). Compulsory bodies: Reflections on heterosexuality and able-bodiedness. *Journal of Women's History*, 15(3), 77–89.

Lee, Wenshu (2003). *Kuaering* Queer Theory: My autocritography and a race-conscious, womanist, transnational turn. *Journal of Homosexuality*, 45(2–4), 147–170.

Lorde, Audre (1984). *Sister outsider: Essays and speeches by Audre Lorde*. Freedom, CA: The Crossing Press.

Moraga, Cherrie (1983). La Guera. In Cherrie Moraga & Gloria Anzaldua (Eds) *This bridge called my back: Writings by radical women of color* (pp. 37–34). New York: Kitchen Table.

Munoz, Jose E. (1999). *Disidentifications: Queers of color and the performance of politics*. Minneapolis, MN: University of Minnesota Press.

Puar, Jasbir K. (2007). *Terrorist assemblages: Homonationalism in queer times*. Durham, SC: Duke University Press.

Rich, Adrienne (1979). *On lies, secrets and silence*. New York: W.W. Norton.

Riddell, Carol (2006). Divided sisterhood: A critical review of Janice Raymond's *The Transsexual Empire*. In S. Stryker & S. Whittle (Eds) *The transgender studies reader* (pp. 144–158). New York: Routledge.

Roen, Katrina (2001). Transgender theory and embodiment: The risk of racial marginalization. *Journal of Gender Studies*, 10(3), 253–263.

Segrest, Mab (1994). *Memoirs of a race traitor*. Boston, MA: South End Press.

Stone, Sandy (1991). The *Empire* strikes back: A posttranssexual manifesto. In Julia Epstein & Kristina Straub, (Eds) *Body guards: The cultural politics of gender ambiguity* (pp. 280–304). New York: Routledge.

Stryker, Susan, Currah, Paisley, & Moore, Lisa Jean (2008). Introduction: Trans-, trans, or transgender? *Women's Studies Quarterly*, 36(3 & 4), 11–22.

Winnubst, Shannon (2006). *Queering Freedom*. Bloomington and Indianapolis: University of Indiana Press.

5

Silence Speaks Volumes: Counter-Hegemonic Silences, Deafness, and Alliance Work

Rachel Levitt

The telephone rings.

"Hello?" my dad answers. He looks excited at first, then struggles to hear. "Sorry, say that again." His eyes look darker, glossy. His chest sinks.

I look at my mom, my eyes asking who is it? Her shoulders tell me she doesn't know.

Dad looks over at both of us and signs "H-A-N-N-A-H ARRESTED."[1] He asks, "Is she the only one?" "What's happening?" He seems to struggle to hear the answers over what I assume is the crackle of the crowd's roars which I can hear from across the room. "Are you okay?" my dad asks Hannah's father.

Hannah wasn't the only one arrested that night. For months, the protests at Gallaudet University were met with increasing threats by the administration. That night, the police brought in a police van to cart away the numerous protesters. One of the protesters arrested used a motorized wheelchair. She locked the wheels and refused to help the police put her in the van.

I was raised in a home where American Sign Language was used out of convenience—when it was too noisy to hear my dad, when we were on opposite sides of the park and it was too far to yell, when it was some-one's birthday and we would be plotting what gift to get. I am hearing and both my parents are hearing, but I grew up signing to my dad and friends—a luxury that the brutal history of Deaf education and eugenics often denied Deaf subjects. It is easy to enjoy hearing privilege and not notice the myriad ways hearing norms oppress people. I struggle with how best to work against hearing normativity: when to be silent and when to argue with my peers. I struggle with when to interpret and "help," and when to refrain because my "helping" is a performance of hearing entitlement, a pathologizing posture, and a violation of interpreting ethics. Growing up in a household with parents who dedicated their lives to working with students with disabilities, I saw the important work that needs to be done to challenge the educational, social, and structural practices that center a normative, able-bodied subject against whom everyone is judged. It is with my activist parents, Deaf friends, and my own work in queer theory that I come to this conversation—seeking ways to better ally myself with Deaf Studies and Deaf social justice organization.

In this reflection, I weave narrative with theory to examine the everyday discursive logics and relational manifestations of oppression that police Deaf and Deaf-allied bodies. Kirsten Langellier and Eric Peterson (2004) note that our personal stories have implicit political implications. The stories I share here are personal encounters that highlight the banal processes by which hearing supremacy is evoked, sustained, and challenged. Myron Beasley (2007) echoes that "when we tell our stories against cultural backdrops that nourish them, we transcend self-indulgence and contribute to a rewriting of the governing cultural narrative" (p. 137). My hope is that through the following narratives I can help to draw attention to the discourses that support and sustain structures of oppression, and differently locate silence as a means of protest and a tool of alliance work.

The politics of alliance work are complex, and full of bumps and fissures that call for moments of speaking, but more often demand silences that refuse to participate in hearing entitlements. Both the politics of speaking and the politics of silence have been meaningfully theorized in feminist, postcolonial, critical cultural, and queer studies as well as productively implicated in the maintenance and production of power (Alcoff, 1994; Lorde, 1984; Moraga, 1981/1983; Spivak, 1988). In this reflection, I concentrate on the transgressive potential of silence while simultaneously noting the oppressiveness of silences invested in normativities. Silence builds, never providing an autonomous offering. It is a site of multiple meanings. The seemingly disparate types of silence I highlight intersect to support and invest one another with protests, opportunities for learning, and both transformative resistance and complicity.

As a child, I was engrossed by the things adults could do. They could make coins appear from behind my left ear, make table tennis balls disappear, and they could communicate without speaking. I used to look at my dad's hands when he was signing to figure out where the magic came from. I wanted to be just like my dad. What few signs I knew gave us a coded language through which we bonded. I'd sign "ONE-MORE" to get another cookie, or "GAME THROW GAME" to see if we could play a game of catch before it got dark.

The practice of sliding easily between speaking and signing didn't last. That special language that allowed me to communicate with my family and close friends would get me in trouble at school. It was important to my teachers that I use my voice with my Deaf friends. This meant letting the interpreter translate my contributions during small group work, which was, one of my teachers insisted, more "fair" to the other students. Signing was fine between classes, but not during class. My teacher outwardly expressed concern that the interpreter wouldn't cover everything I said and that it would hurt my grade. She claimed she didn't want the hearing students in our group to miss anything because of a delay in communication as we waited for the interpreter to finish voicing what I had signed, but there was another agenda there. School taught me that hearing students were the priority, that "fairness" was code for maintaining hearing privileges, and that if I, as a hearing student, presented my part of our group project in American Sign Language, I would get detention. My teacher separated me from my friend; she made us sit on opposite sides of the room facing each other. We were silent and appeared to have stopped signing in class, but our new geography made it easier to sign to each other with our hands in our laps where she couldn't see.

In the pages that follow, I explore silence as resistance to hearing norms, an act of solidarity, a pedagogical tool, and a counter-hegemonic strategy. Counter-hegemonic silence is a method of protest and a tool for allies working to support marginalized people and communities. For silence to be a counter-hegemonic strategy, it must contest an implicit hegemonic dynamic. In Douglas Kellner's (1978) powerful meditation on hegemony and ideology, he expands on Antonio Gramsci and Joseph Buttigieg's (1992) notion of hegemony as domination by consent. Kellner notes that ideologies function to legitimize the existing institutions and social structures of a given society. While Gramsci and Buttigieg and Kellner evoke hegemony as political and economic ideologies that underwrite capitalism, I argue that the category "hegemonic" can be extended to encompass the hearing-centric regimes that have promoted hearing supremacy. Audism and oralism, thought of as hegemonic ideologies, privilege the hearing body and oral communication (Humphries, 1975)—thereby producing knowledge about "deafness" as a pathology while simultaneously obscuring Deafness as a culture.[2]

While my use of "hegemony" is important to mark the social norms that pervade the discourse surrounding Deafness, it also has the potential to occlude the violent and coercive elements of audism. Audism has underwritten discourses advocating the sterilization of the Deaf, the structural and systematic foreclosure of access to language, the imposition of "corrective" cochlear implants on Deaf infants who have their bodily integrity violated without their consent, and the widespread denial of rights to people who are Deaf. To account for these profound bodily interventions, Harlan Lane (1992) connects the audist ideology that produces these types of material violence to the logics of colonialism. Chandra Mohanty (1984) explains colonization as "a relation of structural domination, and the suppression—often violent—of the heterogeneity of the subject(s) in question" (p. 333). Mohanty's conceptualization of colonization echoes Bhabha's notion of discursive colonialism. Discursive colonialism is a technology of power, "an apparatus of power" that both produces knowledge and subjects; and regulates what we know, how we come to be, and what we come to be (Bhabha, 1983, p. 23). Extending these accounts of imperial power, Lane (1992) suggests the category "colonial" can be used to shed light on the audist regimes that have systematically attempted to suppress Deaf culture. For Lane (1992), the colonial logics that construct the "native" as "defective" and in need of Western civilizing reciprocally construct the "deaf" as a population also in need of civilizing (p. 37). According to Lane "hearing paternalism likewise sees its task as 'civilizing' its charges: restoring deaf people to society" (p. 37). In this way, the Deaf subject is similar to the colonial subject in part because "hearing authorities," much like "colonial authorities," seek to regulate and control the Deaf subject by making them as "hearing" as possible (Lane, 1992, p. 37). Lane's work performs key epistemological labors by linking colonial dynamics with the logics of audism. In this discussion, I choose to mark silence as a "counter-hegemonic" rather than a "decolonial," strategy because anti-audist work doesn't necessarily work against colonialism, even though audism is implicated within the logics of colonialism. In other words, audism functions as a normativity that exacts violence on subjects and produces subjectivities invested in oralism. Audism and oralism are specific nodes of oppression, crafted by and produced in tandem with racism, heteronormativity, colonialism, and normative citizenship standards. Within this field of intersecting normativities, there is a two-pronged movement with which I am concerned: (1) the disaggregation of audism from other intersecting normativities that leaves audism uncontested; and reciprocally, (2) gestures to solidarity in which anti-audist work is not attentive to its own investments in other normativities. It is among these vexed politics that silence offers alternative orientations. By attending to some of the labor done by silence, I hope to more robustly account for the complexity of power dynamics at play in solidarity work, hearing norms, and consciousness raising.

Silence speaks volumes

Previous literature on silence and Deafness articulates a vision of silence that gestures toward silences holding counter-hegemonic pedagogical power. In "Silence Is Not Without Voice: Including Deaf Culture into Multicultural Curricula," H. Dirksen L. Bauman and Jennifer Drake (1997) argue that the classroom is a space in which hearing students can increase their understanding of multiculturalism and the complexities of oppression. They argue that texts, videos, plays, and other media provide an avenue for connecting hearing students to the important social, political, and historical contestations of power that Deaf communities have battled and continue to negotiate. Connecting Deaf struggles to other oppressive discourses like whiteness and heteronormativity highlights the similarities and important differences between and among these processes. At the core of their argument is what their title asserts—Deaf silence is not without voice.

My reading of the stories that follow takes Bauman and Drake's (1997) argument a step further. While they contend that silence does not equate to silenced (the negation of silence as lacking agency), I argue that silence speaks volumes (an affirmation of the power of silence). In the Deaf and Deaf-allied community, silence is a technique, a cloak, at times a space of invisibility and solidarity. For hearing people, silence can be an entry point into Deaf culture. It can be an important method of being in solidarity with Deaf culture and people who are Deaf. More profoundly, silence is a refusal to occupy the hegemonic space of speaking for and over those subjects that hearing norms render unintelligible. Silence is a demand for hearing accountability, one that rejects the expectations of audism and oralism which put the onus of adaptation and assimilation onto the Deaf community and Deaf body.

Silence as refusal

We were trying to figure out which game we wanted to play—volleyball or basketball. I was arguing for basketball because it was easier to sign to each other; in volleyball, we'd have no easy line-of-sight to communicate. Cia dismissed my concerns, "SIGN; DOESN'T-MATTER. HIT BALL; LOOK-AROUND, SAME-TIME CAN. DOESN'T-MATTER."

Suddenly there she was, the girl who sat next to me during algebra, standing in front of us on the edge of the basketball court, left hand clutching an index card showing the American Sign Language alphabet, right hand bouncing up and down flailing in harsh abrasive movements attempting to spell something unrecognizable. She was much too close for comfort.

Almost imperceptibly Cia rolled her shoulders making her posture even more perfect. Her eyes focused somewhere beyond the girl, eventually settling on me.

Eyebrows furrowed with my lower lip protruding, I waited to follow Cia's lead.

Cia's eyes indicated the Volleyball court. Then she signed, "COMMU-NICATION O-V-E-R-R-A-T-E-D," which she emphasized with an eye roll ending with a gentle stare that rested on algebra girl, who had finally finished spelling what may have been her name.

After waiting a second or two, the girl announced, "Aren't you going to say hi?! I learned your stuff, the least you could do is talk to me!" Looking first at Cia, then at me, a look of recognition came across her face and she exclaimed, "I've heard you talk in class. You're not even deaf."

I folded my arms, preparing to say something biting, but the expectations I had for myself were more than my 14-year-old brain could muster that soon after lunch. Before I said anything, our two other friends, Claudia and Réna, began walking toward the net.

I looked to Cia, who smiled and bowed with a subtle nod of the head, and the four of us left algebra girl with her moral indignation.

―――――――――

Here my focus is not the Deaf body or even the person attempting to coerce Deaf subjects to placate audist expectations to make hearing people comfortable. My attempts to use silence as a way to be in alliance with my Deaf friends in the face of hearing entitlement refused to afford audism a place at the table. The normalizing expectation of spoken English marked our silence and Cia, Claudia, and Réna's Deafness the problem, but "the 'problem' is not the person with disabilities; the problem is the way normalcy is constructed to create the 'problem' of the disabled person" (Davis, 1995, p. 24). The normalizing discourse of hearing privilege and entitlement not only constructs a matrix of intelligibility that artificially constructs the Deaf body as disabled through the elevation of hearing norms (Lane, 2008), but it also simultaneously demands placation to hearing subjects. Our silence served as a refusal to re-center the hearing subject. Maintaining the silence was both an act of refusal, and, for me, it was an act of solidarity. In this space, our silence and refusal to engage supports Bauman and Drake's (1997) negation of silence as lacking agency. However, it also suggests that there is an active and agentic power in deploying silence by Deaf and Deaf-allied subjects when confronted with adversarial hearing entitlements.

Silence as solidarity

We only had 20 minutes until the next debate started. I was rushing to explain in Sign what Marxist critiques of capitalism mean by false consciousness to one of my debaters. I was mad at myself because what would have taken me three sentences to say out loud was taking me five minutes to sign because I was out of practice. Janelle had a series of questions, which she voiced to me and the head coach:

"How do we know what is false? What if Marx was wrong about capitalism? How do we know it's not communism that's a false ideal?"

"Those are good questions," he said, facing her, so she could read his lips. "What do you all think?" he asked the other students.

Arthur was the first to respond. He quipped, "I think if she can talk, she should stop talking shit."

Frustrated, I think of the hours of practice debates and weekends of research I've spent coaching Arthur to help him articulate his heart-felt objections to the whiteness and elitism of competitive debate. At different junctures, I tried to help Arthur make the connection between the racism and classism he is dedicated to challenging and the audist policing Janelle suffers. My educational compassion for Arthur exists in concert with a fierce anger that wants to list all the arguments he's ever made about being inclusive and challenge his moral indignation. I looked to Janelle.

"W-H-A-T?" she asks, eyes searching, having not looked at Arthur when he spoke and missed the opportunity to read his lips.

Interpreting his comment, his aggression and anger leaked down my arms. Burning, my fingers convey his entitlement and policing. My palms throw meaning at her body. I interpret his words, "I THINK IF SHE CAN TALK, SHE SHOULD. I DON'T-WANT HER TALKING S-H-I-T," signing with facial expressions that convey the hatred and disdain of his tone.

Janelle furrows her brow.

I wait for her reaction. I want to follow her lead, but the debates were starting and everyone scattered to their various rooms.

At dinner, Janelle and I have a brief conversation in Sign about the last debate that knocked her out of contention. She asks me how our other teams placed. I point to Arthur to indicate he and his debate partner were on the cusp of making it to the quarter finals, but we were waiting to hear the official team match-ups.

Arthur stares at me, then says, "I told you to stop doing that around me."

"Excuse me?" I asked.

"I told you to stop doing that around me," Arthur repeats.

Traditionally, a politics of location argues that where we are—our social location—is the starting point for our politics. Aimee Carrillo Rowe (2005) reconceptualizes a politics of location as "a politics of relation" (p. 16). That is, a politics of relation envisions our political locations as relational. Who I am, the self I claim, is always in motion, negotiating the relationships and connections I have and pursue. Carrillo Rowe's (2005) work on reframing a politics of location to encourage a feminist conceptualization of relational politics "gestures toward deep reflection about the selves we are creating as a function of where we place our bodies, and with whom we build our affective ties" (Carrillo Rowe, 2005, p. 16). A politics of relation requires that we be allies, engaged in each other's struggles, willing to be self-reflexive as we wade through the deep and challenging conversations, as well as the silences.

My frustration with Arthur stems from a larger dearth of anti-audist alliance work among seemingly progressive hearing people, but it also signals my failure to attend to the ways whiteness and other normativities affected him. On one level, friends and colleagues that are dedicated to being anti-racist, anti-sexist, anti-classist, queer, decolonial allies often take for granted their hearing privileges and unwittingly help perpetuate discourses of hearing supremacy. In the field of Deaf Studies there is a robust offering that critically interrogates audism (Bauman, 2004; Gertz, 2003; 2008; Humphries, 1975; Lane, 1992) and its intersections with racism (Dunn, 2008), gender oppression (Kelly, 2008), heteronormativity (Bienvenu, 2008), and colonialism (Ladd, 2008; Lane, 1992). Yet, both the scholarship as well as the lived politics of hearing friends and colleagues seem to lack a dedication to challenging the epistemological and physical violence audism brings to bear.

However, on another level, this exchange with Arthur and Janelle was an opportunity to think through and connect the ways whiteness and anti-audist work are imbricated within larger structures and legacies of oppression. In other words, marking some failure on Arthur's part to recognize his own investments in audism also obscures my investments in whiteness. To H. Dirksen L. Bauman (2004), the parallels between hearing privilege and white privilege are profound. Using McIntosh's often-cited article on the taken-for-granted privileges of whiteness, Bauman argues that audism is similarly manifest and sustained through both the mundane and the systemic privileging of hearing ability. Eugenie Gertz (2008) echoes this comparison between racism and audism. However, these comparisons see audism and whiteness as separate, much like I did during the exchange with Arthur. It was easy for me to see the ways audism and racism are mutually constituted, but my initial reaction and reading of Arthur's protests lacked a sensitivity to the ways the pain of white supremacy was informing of his frustration with our signing. His was a tension-ridden politics of relation where his objections existed in tandem with an anti-racist and anti-classist appeal to access information and to be included in the conversation. Arthur's interventions signaled a troubled relationship between audist demands to center spoken communication and anti-racist and anti-classist demands for inclusion and accessibility in an elite, mostly white space. Silence can function as a form of solidarity that opposes the recentering of the hearing subject, a means of being in solidarity with anti-audist politics through maintaining a politics of relation with Deaf friends; however, our silence was also marked by a fraught politics of relation. In those moments when audism, whiteness, classism, and anti-audism come together to mutually inform a dynamic, silence can be used to shut down hearing entitlements, but it can also be complicit in maintaining racial and class normativities. In other words, silence as a mode of solidarity holds a contested relationship to power.

Silence as pedagogical practice

"She can lip read and she can talk, right?" my friend Stacy asked, sounding indignant.

"That's not the point," I say. I wipe my hands on the napkin in my lap, preparing to be as diplomatic and clear as possible with my friend who has never understood white privilege and seems to be heading in the same direction when it comes to audism. "We were at a conference. She requested interpreters so she could access the information at the keynote lecture and the audience questions at her own panel presentation. They made the executive decision that since she could lip-read, she didn't need interpreters."

"But the organization didn't want to spend the extra money on just one person."

"That's bullshit," I say louder than I had intended. I lean back to look around. Satisfied that our dining neighbors appear unaware of our conversation, I move in closer, moving my margarita to the side. "It's a feminist-oriented organization. Their mission isn't to make money, it's to foster social justice," I say more quietly.

Everything comes down to money with her. She's always defending racist policies and discriminatory practices because they are more economically viable.

"Conferences are places where you show off what you have to offer as a graduate student," I say. "To preclude her full participation means she is at a disadvantage when applying to graduate programs because she didn't get the same face time or the same information. It's about access, power, discrimination, and preserving hearing privilege."

I reach across the table. I dip my chip in the guacamole and finish my margarita in silence.

Silences carve out the space for profound reflections required for transformative learning. As learners, we seek answers—easily formulated, consumable nuggets of knowledge. Parker Palmer (1993) argues that instead of doing all the intellectual work, our teachers and allies help bridge us to consciousness not through brilliant, extended monologues, but instead through the silences they create that afford us the space to question and reflect on the nuances of power dynamics. The silences for which Palmer advocates implicate our thoughtful consideration of silent pauses as moments bursting with opportunity, freedom, and openness to learning.

Silence offers profound pedagogical spaces. For anti-audist alliance work, silences allow for spaces in which hearing privilege is critically grappled with and connected to power structures and discursive formations that produce and regulate both the Deaf and hearing body. Feminist, postcolonial, and critical theory are all invested in teasing out these investments and productions of power. In "Toward a Poetics of Vision, Space and The Body: Sign language and literary theory," Bauman (1997) argues that we need to connect marginalized literatures on Sign and Deafness with feminist, postcolonial, and multicultural theory. Silent pauses, moments of reflection, and guided considerations afford and invite the intersectional analysis Bauman requests. The silences we create and embody, rather than foreclosing the conversation, open the temporal and physical space to help us connect hegemonic discourses to our ideological commitments. And, most importantly, through such connections, they crystallize modes of oppression so that we can devise strategies of resistance, refusal, and protest.

Silence as counter-hegemonic

Silence is a method of resistance, alliance, and a strategy of counter-hegemonic protest. Silent protests refuse the dictates of audism and oralism, such as opting to not use or train one's voice to acquiesce to hearing expectations; however, silences can also be complicit in normativities, as my exchanges with Arthur attest. I employ strategic silences: moments when I refuse to voice the conversations I have had in Sign Language with my girlfriend at a party or the strategizing I do with students at a debate tournament. Hearing-centric paranoia assumes we are always talking about a "hearing them" instead of the "signing us."

Audism as a normalizing discourse privileges hearing bodies, spoken communication, and hearing culture over Deaf bodies, signed communication, and Deaf culture. There are important points of resonance between audism and racism (in its privileging of whiteness), homophobia (in its demonizing and pathologizing of Queer bodies), and colonialism (with its state-based exertion of power aimed at the suppression of difference through civilizing projects). The narratives I have foregrounded in this piece reveal that audism is more than an add-on to a laundry list of oppressions. It is a technology of power. The narratives I have shared illustrate the atomized modes through which these normativities are embedded within each other. They are interlocking and messy. The history of hearing people perpetuating a culture of hearing hegemony is long and exhaustive (Lane, 1992; Neisser, 1990), yet for

Gertz (2003), the coercive ethnocentrism of hearing culture does not negate the potential for there to be hearing allies (p. 2).

The relationships I hold between hearing and Deaf culture—between my parents and Hannah; my teachers and classmates; Arthur and Janelle; feminist organizations that withhold interpreting services and Deaf graduate students; between my entitled hearing peers and Deaf friends—are all relationships, coalitions, and alliances. Being in alliance takes many forms. It can mean being a space of refuge and understanding. It can be a space of disagreement and accountability. In the uprising at Gallaudet, students organized massive protests. The Deaf and Deaf-allied communities came together to support the students' work, before, during, and after their sit-ins, campouts, and rallies. Hearing people are often in a space to serve as bridges and to create sites of solidarity. Our hands, arms, mouths, and voices can act as conduits through which the statements of friends, lovers, siblings, parents, teachers, and students are communicated to others. But the work we do is complex, infused with power and normative ideological implications that play out on our bodies and minds and the lives of those with which we ally ourselves.

Centering silence

Interpreting codes of ethics require that hearing people arrest their own subjectivities and serve only as a conduit, a communicative tool when acting as a professional interpreter. As a professional interpreter, you do not have a choice when to speak out and when to remain silent. As an interpreter you are merely a vehicle. When you are a friend, a partner, or a coach, you choose when to speak, sign, or be silent. Anti-racist theories of alliance work foreground silence as a negative (hooks, 1989; Lorde, 1984; Moraga, 1981/1983). Not speaking up against racism, allowing white supremacy to go unchecked in organizations, conversations, and classrooms means you are culpable. Here, silence equals complicity. Aimee Carrillo Rowe (2000) has argued that white women's silence in the face of racism perpetuates white supremacy. For Linda Alcoff (1994), not speaking and refusing to engage as a scholar and teacher abdicates responsibility for understanding the nuanced arguments of critical scholarship. In this context, silence means to preserve the privilege of the powerful.

Both being silent and speaking out can uphold dominant regimes of power, but they can also be deployed in moments of alliance work. Refusing to stop signing around hearing people or to answer the entitled and disingenuous questions hearing people sometimes pose are acts of solidarity. My body and actions are implicated in systems of privilege and power. My arms, hands, voice, and eyes have the potential to be tools of resistance, deployed strategically in moments of contestation. In these moments, I act as a drawbridge. Gloria Anzaldúa (1990) explained in her powerful reflection on bridgework that those engaged in bridgework have agency. Conceptualized as a drawbridge, allies can sever their role as a bridge, withdraw the support system they created, and leave those previously bridged to be rejected. Silence is a method of bridgework, a tool of the drawbridge. Silence can protect me, and the communities I am in alliance with, from disingenuous hearing people. As a drawbridge, I close myself off to those who refuse to interrogate their hearing entitlement and their violent policing of signing bodies. Silence can be safety. As a drawbridge, I can also choose to speak out and challenge those that see access to communication as an economic issue rather than a right, then be silent and allow those I am challenging to contemplate the implications of my argument. Silence can be frustrating, at times enraging. But, silence and hearing people's support of silence can be a powerful demand for and means of acceptance of Deaf subjects. Silence can demand and support acceptance in the face of discourses of "fairness" or mere "tolerance." Much like the way white people can choose to "deal with or ignore" (Carrillo Rowe, 2000) racism, hearing people can choose to ignore audism or critically grapple with it.

If hearing people decide to deal with audism, our activism requires coalitional politics—alliances between people and communities that account for the ways audism is mutually constituted by other normativities and reciprocally, how anti-audist work can be complicit in those same normativities. When speaking means assimilation into an audist paradigm, silence asserts the value of Deaf culture. It resists the narratives that demand spoken language. Silence protests the demands for hearing inclusion. Silence rejects the double bind of assimilation or systematic exclusion. Inaudible does not mean unintelligible. Silence can be tactical, strategic, and transgressive, but it is not a pure politics of resistance. Silence is a sticky and tense site of political action. It is never without the potential to be complicit in norms. However, silence clearly does not preclude communication, and as this reflection attests, it can be a form of resistance, solidarity, reflection, and, at its best, a counter-hegemonic protest. Indeed, silence speaks volumes.

Acknowledgments

I wish to extend my thanks to Brandi Lawless, Dr H.L. "Bud" Goodall, Andrew Marcum, and Calinda Shely for their thoughtful feedback on earlier versions of this manuscript. I am also deeply appreciative of Dr Sheena Malhotra and Dr Aimee Carrillo Rowe for their profoundly helpful engagements throughout the development of this article.

Notes

1. When representing American Sign Language in text, capital letters are used to gloss signs. When letters appear separated by hyphens, these words are finger spelled.
2. Eugenie N. Gertz (2003) delineates between (little "d") deaf and (big "D") Deaf. She explains that Deaf "denotes individuals who, in addition to having a significant inability to hear, function by choice as members of the Deaf community, subscribing to the unique cultural norms, values, and traditions of that group" (Gertz, 2003, p. 1), whereas deaf "denotes anyone who has a significant audilogical loss regardless of their cultural or group identity" (Gertz, 2003, p. 1). Similarly, I use "Deaf" to signify the cultural group and "deaf" to mark the category of people constructed as having hearing loss as a pathology.

References

Alcoff, Linda (1994). The problem of speaking for others. In Susan Ostrov Weisser and Jennifer Fleischner (Eds), *Feminist nightmares: Women at odds: Feminism and the problem of sisterhood* (pp. 285–309). New York: NYU.

Anzaldúa, Gloria (1990). Bridge, drawbridge, sandbar or island: Lesbians-of-color hacienda alianzas. In Lisa Albrecht and Rose M. Brewer (Eds), *Bridges of power: Women's multicultural alliances* (pp. 216–231). Philadelphia, PA: New Society Publishers.

Bauman, H. Dirsken L. (1997). Toward a poetics of vision, space and the body: Sign language and literary theory. In Lennard Davis (Ed.), *Disablity studies reader* (pp. 355–366). New York: Routledge.

Bauman, H. Dirsken L. (2004). Audism: Exploring the metaphysics of oppression. *Journal of Deaf Studies and Deaf Education*, 9, 239–246.

Bauman, H. Dirsken L., & Drake, Jennifer (1997). Silence is not without voice: Including deaf culture into multicultural curricula. In Lennard Davis (Ed.), *Disablity studies reader* (pp. 307–314). New York: Routledge.

Beasley, Myron (2007). Migrancy and homodesire. In Karen E. Lovaas & Mercilee M. Jenkins (Eds) *Sexualities and communication in everyday life* (pp. 134–144). Thousand Oaks, CA: Sage.

Bhabha, Homi (1983). The other question—the stereotype and colonial discourse. *Screen*, 24(6), 18–36.

Bienvenu, M. J. (2008). Queer as deaf: Intersections. In H. Dirsken L. Bauman (Ed.), *Open your eyes: Deaf studies talking* (pp. 264–275). Minneapolis, MN: University of Minnesota.

Carrillo Rowe, Aimee (2000). Locating feminism's subject: The paradox of white femininity and the struggle to forge feminist alliances. *Communication Theory*, 10(1), 64–80.

Carrillo Rowe, Aimee (2005). Be longing: Toward a feminist politics of relation. *NWSA Journal*, 17(2), 15–46.

Davis, Lennard J. (1995). *Enforcing normalcy: Disability, deafness, and the body.* London: Verso.

Dunn, Lindsay (2008). The burden of racism and audism. In H. Dirsken L. Bauman (Ed.), *Open your eyes: Deaf studies talking* (pp. 235–250). Minneapolis, MN: University of Minnesota.

Gertz, Eugenie N. (2003). Dysconscious audism and critical deaf studies: Deaf Crit's analysis of unconscious internalization of hegemony within the deaf community (Unpublished Doctoral dissertation). Los Angeles: University of California.

Gertz, Eugenie. (2008). Dysconscious audism: A theoretical proposition. In H. Dirsken L. Bauman (Ed.), *Open your eyes: Deaf studies talking* (pp. 219–234). Minneapolis: University of Minnesota.

Gramsci, Antonio and Buttigieg, Joseph A. (1992). *Prison notebooks.* New York: Columbia University.

hooks, bell (1989). *Talking back: Thinking feminist, thinking black.* New York: South End.

Humphries, Tom (1975). *Audism: The making of a word.* Unpublished essay.

Kellner, Douglas (1978). Ideology, Marxism, and Advanced Capitalism. *Socialist Review*, 42, 37–66.

Kelly, Arlene B. (2008). Where is deaf HERstory? H. Dirsken L. Bauman (Ed.), *Open your eyes: Deaf studies talking* (pp. 251–263). Minneapolis, MN: University of Minnesota.

Ladd, Paddy (2008). Colonialism and resistance: A brief history of deafhood. In H. Dirsken L. Bauman (Ed.), *Open your eyes: Deaf studies talking* (pp. 42–59). Minneapolis, MN: University of Minnesota.

Lane, Harlan (1992). *The mask of benevolence: Disabling the deaf community.* New York: Knopf.

Lane, Harlan (2008). Do Deaf people have a disability? In H. Dirsken L. Bauman (Ed.), *Open your eyes: Deaf studies talking* (pp. 277–292). Minneapolis, MN: University of Minnesota.

Langellier, Kirsten M., & Peterson, Eric E. (2004) *Storytelling in daily life: Performing narrative.* Philadelphia, PA: Temple University.

Lorde, Audre (1984). *Sister outsider: Essays and speeches.* Freedom, CA: The Crossing.

Mohanty, Chandra T. (1984). Under western eyes: Feminist scholarship and colonial discourses. *Boundary 2*, 12(3), 333–358.

Moraga, Cherrie (1981/1983). La guera. In Cherrie Moraga & Gloria Anzaldúa (Eds), *This Bridge called my back: Writings by radical women of color* (pp. 27–34). New York: Kitchen Table: Women of Color Press.

Neisser, Arden (1990). *The other side of silence: Sign language and the deaf community in America.* Washington, DC: Gallaudet University.

Palmer, Parker (1993). *To know as we are known: Education as a spiritual journey.* New York: Harperone.

Spivak, Gayatri (1988). Can the subaltern speak? In Cary Nelson & Lawrence Grossberg (Eds), *Marxism and the interpretation of culture* (pp. 271–313). Urbana, IL: University of Illinois.

Part II

Learning to Listen: Academia, Silence, Resistance

6

Imposed Silence and the Story of the Warramunga Woman: Alternative Interpretations and Possibilities

Robin Clair

> It is customary, upon the death of the husband, that the Warramunga of Australia impose silence upon the widow for a period of approximately two years. "Occasionally the women prefer to remain under the ban for a long time, and among the Warramunga there was one old woman who, from choice, had not spoken a word for twenty-five years."
>
> (Spencer and Gillen, 1912, p. 396)

The above story has crossed continents and centuries. It has been lifted from its time and place, to be used, and at times abused, by scholars, for purposes of theoretical and ideological commentary. This snippet of a story has been interpreted according to various perspectives, but always with the intention of addressing the meaning and practices of silence.

Silence has drawn the attention of many scholars, especially those who wished to reclaim silence from the backdrop of communication (Courtenay, 1916; Picard, 1948/1952). Early on, these scholars began to realize the complicated relationship between speech and silence, as well as the aesthetic nature of silence (Picard, 1948/1952). Bernard Dauenhauer (1980) suggests that Max Picard's work provided a treatise that represented what phenomenologists such as Martin Heidegger and Maurice Merleau-Ponty were asserting with respect to the essence of silence—that silence is expressive. Adam Jaworski (1993) did not refute the phenomenological or aesthetic element of silence, but he did challenge this portrayal as limited, lacking the political and pragmatic meanings embedded within silence.

For feminists, silence, as a topic of concern, can and has been approached from various perspectives, including both the aesthetic and the political (Clair, 1998). As early as 1973, radical feminist, Mary Daly spoke of the "Great Silence" of women that erased all clues to the possible existence of matriarchal societies and the accomplishments of women. By 1980, Dale Spender, drawing on the work of Julia Stanley (a.k.a. Julia Penelope, a liberated pseudonym) and Cherise Kramer (a.k.a. Cherise Kramerae, a liberated pseudonym), narrowed the focus on silence to understanding the power of language to name women. Debarah Tannen and Muriel Saville-Troike (1985) added to this body of knowledge by exploring the power of silence from a linguistic perspective, specifically addressing the bits of silence between consonants and vowels that allow language to be shaped and take form. But they also proposed an "institutionally-determined silence" (p. 14) that explored the rules regarding silence as found in churches and libraries. Robin Clair (1998) extended these perspectives suggesting a linguistic, aesthetic, and ideological take on silence. In general, the feminist perspectives of the past positioned silence as the means and method of marginalization. However, Clair (1998) provided an exception by arguing that silence could be thought of as either oppression or resistance, indeed, silence exists both as oppression and resistance in many cases. Silence, then, is a dynamic and dialectical form of expression, a simultaneous and self-contained opposite (Clair, 1998). This perspective suggests that silence is not only marginalizing but also can behave as a form of resistance. But even this more sophisticated feminist take on silence may have relied on an accidental and incomplete interpretation of a case of *imposed silence*.

The focus of this chapter is on that famous story of *imposed silence*, a story of one Warramunga woman that has been repeated by sociologists, philosophers, anthropologists, and communication scholars to make a point. Often that point was that women are positioned in a lower place than men in "archaic" societies (Durkheim, 1915/1976), that patriarchy has unduly "silenced" women literally and figuratively (Daly, 1973), and that silence can be both a form of oppression and a form of resistance (Clair, 1998). There is some truth in each of the previous interpretations; but by turning to the first published version of the story of the Warramunga woman, additional and alternative possibilities might unfold with respect to the interpretation of silence.

Silence is oppressive;

Silence is resistance;

Silence is simultaneously oppression and resistance;

Most recently, Kris Acheson (2008) mentioned the story of the Warramunga woman in an essay on silence as gesture, relying on Emile Durkheim's story. Clair (1998) relied on Mary Daly's telling of the story. Daly (1973) cited Durkheim as her source. And Durkheim (1915/1976) credits Sir Baldwin Spencer and Francis J. Gillen. It is Spencer and Gillen (1912) who actually traveled across Australia to study the native societies of the early twentieth century. It is they who first published the story of the Warramunga woman; however, publishing a story does not necessarily make it the Truth and we will never know "the story" as it was lived at the time. Nevertheless, the partial readings from the various versions speak of how the story is captured and expressed, borrowed and reinterpreted, and this speaks more of those who would interpret the Warramunga woman's actions and silence than of her. The story has been repeated for one hundred years and the various interpretations are deserving of closer examination, not simply as a means to condemn the silencing of women and celebrate their resistance, but also to explore, by means of the first published version, alternative possibilities concerning silence.

Interpreting the story of the Warramunga woman's silence

Each and every scholar brings their own personal and cultural background and heritage, respectively, to his or her work. For Durkheim, the father of sociology and founder of the *Anée Sociologiques,* understanding societies meant engaging them from an anthropological perspective. His school of ethnography held great promise, but faced severe obstacles in establishing itself. He had trained multiple students in the practice of ethnography only to have World War I interrupt his students' studies. Worse yet, the war claimed the life of several of his students, including his only son. The only survivor, Marcel Mauss, Durkheim's nephew, remained to carry on this sociological tradition (Clair, McConnell, Bell, Hackbarth, and Mathes, 2008). Durkheim relied heavily on the work of Mauss as well as other field anthropologists, including Spencer and Gillen, to develop his own theories of religion (1915/1976) and labor in society (1893/1984). But these were difficult times for both Durkheim and Mauss: the war had taken its toll, leading Durkheim to study suicide and Mauss to write on the "greeting by tears" (see Garces and Jones, 2009, p. 6). Each took an interest in rituals and ceremonies of death, grieving, and burial practices.

Mauss (1921) explored the obligatory expression of sentiments while Durkheim focused on the rituals of native peoples. It is important to note that Durkheim did not necessarily respect his subjects. For example, he assumed "that he who saw one native American has seen them all," whereas "By contrast, among civilized peoples two individuals can be distinguished from one another at a glance" (1893/1984, p. 89). With respect to the Warramunga, Durkheim's biases could be felt as well. For instance, Spencer and Gillen describe the men of the Warramunga society standing in a straight line, legs apart, and the women crawling through their legs during a particular part of the burial ritual. Durkheim changes the description to have the men standing in "Indian file" (1915/1976, p. 397). Nor would it be fair to say that Spencer and Gillen (1912) are without prejudice, as they inform the reader that the Warramunga are the equivalent of children, and with respect to rituals of self-mutilation, Spencer and Gillen (1912) suggest that "the Australian native cannot be supposed to feel pain as acutely as the average white man does" (p. 505). Aside from these personal prejudices, all three men are intent on understanding the ritual of silence in the Warramunga burial ceremonies.

It is part of the burial ritual in the Warramunga tribe to have the widow remain silent following the death of her husband, usually for a period of one to two years. Durkheim reports that "Spencer and Gillen knew one old woman who had not spoken for over twenty-four years" (1915/1976, p. 394). Future scholars who relied on Durkheim's interpretation tended toward a one-sided interpretation of the imposed silence. For example, Durkheim's wording led Daly (1973) and Clair (1998) to interpret the imposed silence as patriarchal, and the extended silence as a form of resistance. Clair interpreted the extended silence as a refusal to speak once one was allowed to do so: the woman demonstrated resistance, the right to decide when she would speak. Clair further wrote, "it is a wonder that one woman's story has moved from the Warramunga tribe—across time and space—to become a collective narrative—a symbol of silence as both oppression and resistance" (p. 163). But Clair added that the silence should be treated as "open to interpretation" (p. 147). For example, who is to say that this woman did not love her husband so much that she chose to remain silent? The possibility exists, but the interpretation is always tentative without more of the story. Or ironically, without speaking to the woman in order to understand her silence. Actually, numerous alternative interpretations are possible. And it is those additional possible interpretations that I turn to here.

I take the stance that past interpretations have been limited by the incomplete portrayal on which scholars have relied—myself included. And while we can never have a complete and unmediated view, a view which stems from the first telling rather than secondhand derivatives may be of some value by opening possibilities for further or alternative interpretations. And for that we must turn to Spencer and Gillen's (1912) work. First, the ritual begins with loud lamenting, wailing, crying, howling by mostly the women of the society, which led Durkheim to assume that the women are the mediators of death, and yet the men also have periods of silence alternating with loud mourning and many of the participants express their feelings with great intensity. Those feelings include frustration, anger, fear, loss, abandonment, and even a rejection of any responsibility on the part of the collective for the death—they sing these lamentations. That is, the wailing includes pronouncements as well as cursing, and it is mandatory and must continue for anywhere from ten days to several months. These wailings are accompanied by periods of cruel self-mortification, self-mutilation, the cutting of chunks of flesh, slicing the scalp, or beating each other with sticks. Chris Garces and Alexander Jones (2009) have suggested that the cutting and clubbing which the participants engage in willingly may indeed allow them to meet their obligations to cry over the deceased for months; for this interpretation the authors rely on Marcell Mauss's (1921) "L'expression obligatoire des sentiments" and suggest that Mauss would say the Warramunga do this to show respectful levels of grief for the deceased. These loud periods are juxtaposed to periods of silence, for both the men and women, except for the widow who carries on the mourning cries. Moments of silence in this case may be considered relief from one's obligations to express concern. In silence one can hear one's self breathe again. That is, as Mauss and other phenomenologists might argue, one can *exhale,* feeling the whole body, the whole human being (Garces and Jones, 2009).

Silence is relief, it is a breath, a chance to hear oneself inhale and exhale, a relief that the widow has not yet experienced for any substantial length of time. Her period of imposed silence allows for, and it would seem encourages, the continued wailing of grief by the widow. The moments of silence may be sanctuary.

Silence is sanctuary;

Many cultures engage in acts of purification surrounding rituals of transformation. Births, coming of age, marriage, and death ceremonies—all mark important moments, often symbolized by stripping oneself in preparation for a new role, redressing oneself in new apparel. The Warramunga may be stripping spoken words from their daily interactions during this momentous time of transition from life to death as a way of purifying their interactions, a way of giving extreme attention to their wails, songs, and cries of bereavement. Silence may be the equivalent of fasting from food, purifying the body. One gives up the day-to-day way of being in the world and undertakes the intense obligation to mark transition.

> **Silence is purification through absence;**
> **Silence marks transition;**

The women of the Warramunga society who lose a husband and are committed to silence are not permitted to work during the period of silent mourning. One might be tempted then to re-interpret the woman's choice to be silent for a long period of time. As a matter of fact, Spencer and Gillen (1912) report that many women extend their mourning period, just none had ever extended it as long as 25 years before, according to their information. Could these women be taking a break from work, from hunting and gathering, weaving, and other daily tasks? Is it possible that silence is rest, is restorative; in part, perhaps it is, but before considering this interpretation as conclusive, it is important to know more of the ritual and to keep in mind that if the woman is not working she must be dependent on the kindness of others to supply her with meat and yams.

> **Silence is restorative;**

Spencer and Gillen (1912) tell us that it is not uncommon to have several widows in a state of mourning—imposed silence—at the same time, and these women, as suggested above, are not permitted to work. If the widow is caught working, for example, hunting for yams, her older brother-in-law has the right to spear her. Spencer and Gillen explain this practice as related to the marriage rituals. The widow, at the end of her mourning period, when she chooses to end her silence (and begin working again), will marry her younger brother-in-law. If caught working, she might be speared because she is not demonstrating respect for the dead brother, or as Spencer and Gillen also suggest, she may be speared out of resentment by the older brother-in-law who is not in line to marry her. The older brother-in-law may release his frustration by spearing the widow. One can now see, remaining silent allows the widow to remain unmarried. And she may do this as long as she chooses, even for 25 years, if she so desires. It is possible then that silence is protective and even liberating, freeing.

Silence is liberating;
Silence is freeing;

Again, Durkheim (1915/1976) translated Spencer and Gillen's (1912) work, concluding that the women could not speak during the mourning period; however, to be silent and not to communicate are not one in the same. Spencer and Gillen explained that during the silent mourning period, women freely communicated by way of a finger language. The anthropologists were very impressed by the finger language which they assert was not like sign language as they knew it; sign language is based on words and the spelling of words, at least at that time, whereas the finger language had its own system of signs. The authors report of the imposed silence:

> The women did not seem to mind...they chatted away gaily with their fingers. Without making any sound, except that of laughing, they easily communicated with one another by means of their remarkable system of gesture language. (1912, p. 390)

The authors provide illustrations in their book of the finger language, demonstrating the ways in which animals are symbolized as well as how sounds are communicated silently. The authors were enamored with this creativity, which was, perhaps, spawned by silence.

Silence is gay;
Silence is light;
Silence is creative;

When the woman chooses to end her silence, she removes the white clay-painted covering from her body, which she has been wearing to signify her mourning. She is free to leave a streak of clay across her forehead, to symbolize that she is recovering from her grief, but is not completely ready for marriage. Or she may remove all the clay, bring food to the appropriate male and bite his hand before giving him food to announce her eligibility. Silence is partial; as in the above, the women found ways to communicate and the imposed silence could be redefined as less than total, less than overwhelming. Silence has often been portrayed as a complete and utter lack of sound, of communication, but perhaps silence is like the night sky with the light of the stars and the moon.

Silence is partial;

Even still, the above portrayal of the rather lengthy burial ceremony has not provided a full and complete picture. For example, following numerous ceremonies of crying, singing, and mutilating oneself, the body is removed from the village, taken about a mile away, and placed on a platform and not returned for one year. At the one-year mark the ceremonies change. Complicated rituals are carried out, including the breaking of the bones, all of which are buried in an anthill except for the arm bone. This bone is returned and carried by the widow in a wooden bark box to the appropriate male kin and then the widow returns to silence once again with the exception of wailing at night. And it is also during this daytime ceremony that the women crawl between the legs of the men—the act that stimulated Durkheim to note the "great sexual assignment" (p. 397), but while there are moments of distinct differences between males and females there are many shared rituals as well. Respect, no matter what aspect of the ritual is taking place, seems to be the motivating factor: respect for the dead so that evil is not done and so the dead can see and hear from renewed cries that the collective is treating the deceased with respect (Spencer and Gillen, 1912). The men undertake silence as well on behalf of a dead relative and they are freed from their imposed silence by a younger male. These practices may still appear patriarchal, but one should know that the Warramunga believe in reincarnation and the spirit will enter the woman's womb one day carrying the deceased back to life. But perhaps even more important to our feminist understanding of silence among the Warramunga depends on knowing that reincarnation, for the Warramunga, is an alternating spiritual phenomenon. That is to say, for the Warramunga, women come back as men and men come back as women. Each will take the role of the other, eternally alternating one's sex, one's gender, one's role in the community into eternity. Thus, in this case, there is the proposition that silence is shared.

Silence is shared.

Conclusion

Past research has told us that silence is expressive (Clair, 1998; Courtenay, 1916; Picard, 1948/1952), a gesture (Acheson, 2008), a sacred way of being, especially for Native Americans (Awiakta, 1993; Carbough, 1999; Clair, 1998), and relative across cultures (Roberts, Magutti, and Takano, 2011; Tannen and Saville-Troike, 1985). Silence is oppressive (Daly, 1993) and it is resistance (Clair, 1998); for that matter, it is both oppression and resistance (Clair, 1994, 1998). Silence is political and ideological (Jaworski, 1993; also see Clair, 1997, 1998). Silence has many meanings. And we scholars lay intriguing, albeit partial, interpretations upon silence. Indeed, previous interpretations of the lengthy silence, self-imposed after the usual time of mourning by one Warramunga woman, has been partial at best, and likely continues to be partial even with this more detailed exploration. Perhaps, we can only and always content ourselves with partial understandings. But one thing we know; silence is filled with meaning, perhaps debatable and partial, but meaningful, nonetheless.

Silence is meaningful.

References

Acheson, Kris. (2008). Silence as gesture: Rethinking the nature of communicative silences. *Communication Theory*, 18: 535–555.

Awiakta, Marilou (1993). *Selu: Seeking the Corn-Mother's wisdom.* Golden, CO: Fulcrum Publishing.

Carbough, Donal. (1999). "Just listen": "Listening" and landscape among the Blackfeet. *Western Journal of Communication*, 63: 250–270.

Clair, Robin P. (1994). Resistance and oppression as a self-contained opposite: An organizational analysis of one man's story of sexual harassment. *Western Journal of communication, 58,* 235–262.

Clair, Robin P. (1997). Organizing silence: Silence as voice and voice as silence in the narrative exploration of the treaty of New Echota. *Western Journal of Communication, 61,* 315–337.

Clair, Robin P. (1998). *Organizing silence: A world of possibilities.* Albany, NY: SUNY.

Clair, Robin P., McConnell, Megan, Bell, Stephanie, Hackbarth, Kyle and Mathes, Stephanie (2008). *Why work: The perceptions of a "real job" and the rhetoric of work through the ages.* West Lafayette, IN: Purdue University Press.

Courtenay, Charles (1916). *The empire of silence.* New York: Sturgis and Walton.

Daly, Mary (1973). *Beyond God the Father: Toward a philosophy of women's liberation.* Boston, MA: Beacon Press.

Dauenhauer, Bernard P. (1980). *Silence: The phenomenon and its ontological significance.* Bloomington, IN: Indian University Press.

Durkheim, Emile (1976). *The elementary forms of the religious life* (J.W. Swain, Trans.). London: Allen and Unwin. (Original work published in 1915).

Durkheim, Emile (1984). *The division of labor* (W.D. Halls, Trans.). New York: The Free Press. (Original work published in 1893 and original English translation published in 1933).

Garces, Chris and Jones, Alexander (2009). Mauss redux: From warfare's human toll to "L'homme total." *Anthropological Quarterly, 82(1)*, 279–310.

Jaworski, Adam (1993). *The power of silence: Social and pragmatic perspectives.* Newbury Park, CA: Sage.

Mauss, Marcel (1921). L'expression obligatoire des sentiments. *Journal de Psychologie, 18*, 425–434.

Picard, Max (1952). *The world of silence* (S. Godman, Trans.). South Bend, IN: Regnery/Gateway. (Original work published in 1948).

Roberts, Felicia, Margetti, Piera and Takano, Shoji (2011). Judgments concerning the valence of inter-turn silence across speakers of American English, Italian, and Japanese. *Discourse Processes, 48*, 331–354.

Spencer, Baldwin and Gillen, F. J. (1912). *Across Australia, Vol. 2*. London: Macmillan.

Spender, Dale (1980). *Man made language* (2nd ed.). London: Routledge & Kegan Paul.

Tannen, Deborah and Saville-Troike, Muriel. (1985). *Perspectives on silence.* Norwood, NJ: Ablex.

7
Silence and Voice in a More-than-Human World

Jeff Bile

To talk with the animals is the stuff of Western mythology. But really listening to nonhuman nature? The very suggestion is quickly and efficiently dismissed as sentimental, romantic, naïve, befuddled, deluded, or crazy. Our culture anticipates an inarticulate nature. We therefore tend to "participate in a grid of knowledge" that constructs human communication as filling "a void left by nature" (Manes, 1995, p. 43). The purpose of this chapter is to set aside taken-for-granted common sense to creatively contemplate the uncommon wisdom of what is not-to-be-taken-seriously. I adopt the nonsensical stances of the "less-than-human" to consider the possibilities of a more-than-human world. In the process, we may uncover the possibility that the dominant social paradigm is constructed, ontologically frozen, and illusory. Isn't that crazy? I first consider the communicative construction of our culture of alienation.

Communication and the construction of nature

In contemporary Euro-American culture, other species, ecosystems, and the earth itself are typically considered incapable of communicating. A silenced natural world is background against which the voices of *Homo sapiens* (especially more powerful humans) are foreground. Christopher Manes (1995) contends that "nature *is* silent in our culture" because "the status of being a speaking subject is jealously guarded as an exclusively human activity" (p. 43). Human discourse prioritizes language and thereby creates the illusion of extra-human silence. In the process of making it easier to attend to some things, human language makes it harder to listen to others—like the voice of nature. We have compressed "the entire buzzing, howling, gurgling biosphere into the narrow vocabulary" of our own language (p. 43). We tend to have little patience for expressions of nature which fail to comply. Therefore, our discourse "marginalizes nature, mutes it, pushes it into a hazy backdrop" (p. 44) and creates "an immense realm of silences, a world of 'not saids' called nature" (p. 45).

Human communication also silences the voice of nonhuman nature by objectifying it. Objectifying nature is essential if it is to be exploited without recrimination and remorse. Therefore, we routinely construct human-articulate/nonhuman-inarticulate distinctions. As Derrick Jensen (2000) puts it, the modern world must destroy "the larynx of the biosphere," to transform the living world into a lifeless thing (p. 16). Our rhetoric takes the voice of the nonhuman subjects by rendering them as objects. One way that discourse accomplishes this muting is through the imposition of function. Trees turn into *lumber* and animals are rendered *meat*. Unfortunately, "by transforming what exists into what is useful to *us*, life is silenced" (Rogers, 1998, p. 250).

Finally, human cacophony masks the voice of nonhuman nature. Even a marginalized and objectified natural world expresses itself. Sadly, human activities drown out what residual voice we might otherwise hear. As David Abram (1996) puts it, our attention is "hypnotized" by a host of human contrivances "that only reflect us back to ourselves" and make it "too easy for us to forget our carnal inherence in a more-than-human matrix" (p. 22). The voice of nature is snowed under by "the incessant drone of motors that shut out the voices"; "by electric lights that eclipse not only the stars but the night itself; by air 'conditioners' that hide the seasons; by offices, automobiles, and shopping malls that finally obviate any need to step outside the purely human world at all" (p. 28). Human communication plays an especially important role in masking the more-than-human world. The noise of cultural communication ultimately overwhelms the voice of nature. We may have "heard the world" when we were young but, "like static on the radio," socialization begins to interfere with our perceptions (Jensen, 2000, p. 2). Manes (1995) observes that speaking our language "veils the processes of nature with its own cultural obsessions" (p. 43). Selective exposure and attention mean that humans do not perceive what we might...if we were just quiet and listened.

Listening to nature

Unfortunately, there are "political, social, ecological, and economic implications of living in a silenced world" (Jensen, 2000, p. 2). The ecological implication is that our culture has become deaf to urgent feedback from an expressive planet. In a culture that conceptually links "the natural" and "the feminine," the social implications also include the repression of women (and whatever is associated with women). "Women are identified literally and symbolically with the natural world. Mutually associated and mutually devalued, both are subjugated" simultaneously (Johnson, 1993, p. 15). Therefore, gender oppression and ecological domination "are inextricably fused in theory and practice" (p. 15). In this section, we consider two rationales for quieting human communication: deconstructing the "silence" of the natural world and reconstructing its "voice."

Deconstructing nature's "silence"

If nature was voiceless, it would not follow that humans should turn a deaf ear to it. There may be value in simply listening to even an inarticulate nature. For millennia, peoples around the world learned from animals, plants, even sticks and stones. They read the signs to predict weather, gather sustenance, and locate water. Clearly, we can learn much by listening to nature, whether or not it is specifically speaking to us. Only in our own silence can we really hear more than the sound of our own voice. The suggestion is that we simply listen. "Only by listening deeply with a quiet mind" can we ever really hear nature (Cornell, 1987, p. 10). Scholars working in many fields have acknowledged the advantages of a listening model for ecological studies. The example of geneticist Barbara McClintock is instructive. She employed a research method of "feeling for the organism by being intuitive" and was ostracized for her approach—until she won the Nobel Prize (Loer, 1997, p. 288).

Listening to nature is an idea whose time has, once again, come. Ecosystem feedback can be apprehended as communication from the natural world which, currently, we are not really hearing over the sounds of our own voices. Consider what we might learn from other species if we simply take time "to listen to what they might already be saying" (Jensen, 2000, p. ix). Attending to the unnatural quietude of the natural world is crucial "for it is within this vast eerie silence" that exploitation of nature has produced ecological crisis (Manes, 1995, p. 44). "We need to learn how to listen" to nature because "our survival depends on it" (Rogers, 1998, p. 255). Addressing our eco-crisis will require alert attention to the nuances of a more-than-human world. As Donna Haraway puts it, perhaps our hopes "turn on re-visioning the world as coding trickster with whom we must learn to converse" (in Warren, 2000, p. 35).

It is time for us to sharpen our perceptions, to pay better attention, to listen for the murmurings of a more-than-human world, and to imagine the possibility that a seemingly silent planet might yet reveal something that we need to hear.

Reconstructing nature's "voice"

In this culture, nature seems voiceless. In contrast, for animistic cultures, Manes (1995) contends, nonhuman subjects are "perceived as being articulate and at times intelligible subjects, able to communicate and interact with humans" (p. 43). While such a view is usually relegated to the realm of fantasy in our culture, it is a "sophisticated and long-lived" experiencing of nature that is implicit in many others. In fact, Jeannette Armstrong maintains, "attitudes about interspecies communication are the *primary* difference between western and indigenous philosophies" (in Jensen, 2000, p. 24). Animism undergirds many contemporary tribal societies, just as it did our own millennia ago. Indeed, "overwhelming evidence" supports the importance of animism in human history (Manes, 1995, p. 45). "For the largest part of our species existence," Abram (1996) notes, "all could speak, articulating in gesture and whistle and sigh a shifting web of meanings that we felt on our skin or inhaled through our nostrils or focused on with our listening ears" (p. ix).

What if our contemporary culture embraced an animistic world? What if we didn't deny nature's voice? What would happen if we were silent and really tried to hear what the earth, and all her children, had to say? Could we? Inspirational precedents do exist. Indeed, the urge to communicate with a more-than-human world survives in spite of our largely anthropocentric, even logocentric, culture. Suspicions that the animal world communicates are not limited to myth and fiction. Even scientific study is beginning to confirm animistic assumptions. Tim Friend (2004) reports that "there have been an enormous number of recent discoveries about animal communication" (p. 3). "Many species have been shown to possess a basic language capability through the attempts to teach artificial languages to species such as dolphins, parrots, and nonhuman primates" (p. 249). Why, one might ask, would these animals "possess a fundamental capacity for grammar and syntax if they did not make use of them somehow in their own species-specific ways to communicate?" (p. 249). Human uniqueness is challenged by "whales with globe-spanning languages" and "gorillas who acquire extensive sign language vocabularies" (Seager, 2003, p. 952). Scientists have even "caught wild primates in the act of speaking—communicating specific messages through a pattern of vocalization" (*The Week*, 2008, p. 23).

The evidence is even more compelling when not viewed through anthropocentric lenses. Friend (2004) contends that much previous theorizing about animal communication reflected a "glottocentric bias" in that it presumed "that language should necessarily have to take the form of human speech and involve vocal learning" (p. 240). However, we should give more attention to "the vocal, visual, and chemical signals that constitute the ancient natural language of animals" (p. 85). "Sure, some of us have amazing powers of speech, while others use clicks and sonar, or wave their hands, or flash brilliant feathers, or bark, or chirp, or whinny" (p. 250). Why not listen?

A growing understanding of anthropocentric prejudice is consequential. If we do develop an appreciation for interspecies communication, the rewards could be substantial. Scott Friskics (2001) argues that "despite our habitual inattentiveness, nature's creatures may yet grace us with their presence in dialogue" (p. 391). Believing is seeing, and hearing, what was there all along. When we behave as if our fellow earthlings have something to say to us, "we find ourselves ever more ready to take up with those whom we encounter" (p. 406). "Over time our dialogical encounters with our fellow creatures—encounters which at first glance might appear as isolated and episodic occurrences—begin to gain a certain enduring quality" (p. 406).

Such dialogues may be personally enriching, but they are also consequential. "Ideologies of domination and manipulation, in effect, silence nature" (Rogers, 1998, p. 245). However, Manes (1995) argues, "dialogical encounters with our fellow creatures furnish the experiential ground of ethical action with respect to them" (p. 391). "To regard nature as alive and articulate has consequences" since "moral consideration seems to fall only within a circle of speakers in communication with one another" (p. 43). The Euro-American ethos of environmental exploitation is founded on the unnatural silence of nature. We must therefore "expose and overcome the unwarranted claims that humans are unique subjects and speakers" (p. 49).

Conclusion and new beginnings

This chapter is organized around two paradoxes. First, much like the editors of this volume, my voice is not so much a univocal imitation of other voices as it is an appreciation of a unique multivocal orchestration of them. I heard this chorus in an authentic and very personal way. That truth introduces the second paradox. I am refusing to remain silent about the need for human silence as a vehicle for ending the apparent silence of a more-than-human world.

I have chosen to set aside taken-for-granted common sense to creatively contemplate uncommon wisdom. I adopted the stances of the "less-than-human" to consider the possibilities of a more-than-human world. Here is what I learned. Humans have "occluded the natural world, leaving it voiceless" (Manes, 1995, p. 49). "Our obliviousness to nonhuman nature is today held in place by ways of speaking" that deny it voice (Abram, 1996, p. 28). But "a real world awaits us, one that is ready to speak to us if only we would remember to listen" (Jensen, 2000, p. 7). We must, as Manes (1995) puts it, reconstruct voice and "reestablish communication with nature" (p. 52). The mission is to restore humans to the "humbler status of *homo sapiens*: one species among millions of other beautiful, terrible, fascinating—and signifying—forms" (p. 52). "For half a millennium, 'Man' has been the center of the conversation in the West.... The time has come for our culture to politely change the subject" (p. 52). All that requires is our silence.

References

Abram, David (1996). *The spell of the sensuous: Perception and language in a more-than-human world*. New York: Pantheon Books.

Cornell, Joseph (1987). *Listening to nature*. Nevada City, CA: Dawn Publications.

Friend, Tim (2004). *Animal talk: Breaking the codes of animal language*. New York: Simon and Schuster.

Friskics, Scott (2001, Winter). Dialogic relations with nature. *Environmental Ethics, 23*, 391–410.

Jensen, Derrick (2000). *A language older than words*. New York: Context Books.

Johnson, Elizabeth A. (1993). *Woman, earth, and creator spirit*. New York: Paulists Press.

Loer, Joseph R. (1997). Ecofeminism in Kenya: A Chemical Engineer's Perspective. In Karen Warren and Nisvan Erkal (Eds), *Ecofeminism: Women, culture, nature*. Bloomington, IN: Indiana University Press, pp. 279–299.

Manes, Christopher (1995). Nature and silence. In Max Oelschlaeger (Ed.), *Postmodern environmental ethics*. Albany, NY: State University of New York Press, pp. 43–56.

Rogers, Richard A. (1998). Overcoming the objectification of nature in constitutive theories: Toward a transhuman, materialist theory of communication. *Western Journal of Communication, 62*, 244–272.

Seager, Joni (2003). Rachel Carson died of breast cancer: The coming of age of feminist environmentalism. *Signs: Journal of Women in Culture & Society, 28*, 945–972.

The Week (2008). Proof that monkeys can talk. 8 (355): p. 23.

Warren, Karen J. (2000). *Ecofeminist philosophy: A Western perspective on what it is and why it matters*. Lanham, MD: Rowman & Littlefield.

8

Inila: An Account of Opening to Sacred Knowing

Sarah Amira De la Garza

July 1992. Everything was shades of Payne's gray and dark Irish green as I drove west on Highway 20. I was headed toward the little town of Lusk, Wyoming, looking for a hotel room. For the previous two years, I'd driven this road on numerous long solo journeys, traveling to and from South Dakota to my home in Arizona. Just a couple of hours before this particular drive, I'd been on the Pine Ridge reservation of the Oglala Lakota, in the towns where I'd come to be familiar with the families and summer gatherings. I spent time buying gas and washing clothes in the town of Pine Ridge, preparing to "leave the field," as the ethnographic literature calls it. Technically, this meant I was supposedly finished with my fieldwork; it was time to begin my analysis and writing. However, this entire project had not been technically, or practically, anything quite like it was supposed to be. In this project, I'd never consciously voiced what my next steps would be. The road home was to teach me to hear the lessons in the silences.

I headed through Nebraska, for Wyoming, not quite sure how I was ever going to write about what I'd been observing and recording—what, in many ways, I'd also been living. My interest in the sun dance community and its extended networks of spiritual and native cultural practice and friendship had evolved from a personal exploration of my own Native American, or Indian, ancestry. I'd spent time living in Mexico, and it had left me with a deep yearning for insight into the history that could have contributed to my grandfather's deep connection to the land and my grandmother's supernatural sensibilities, her simplicity, and effortless detachment from material excess. These were my

101

"Indian" grandparents. I longed for what they'd never spoken, while inside myself I was aware that asking too many questions was violating a code I did not understand.

Over the years, I nurtured these unformed questions, seeking occasions that would provide answers or hints. Based on geography, and informal oral tradition, my native ancestry was Comanche, Apache, and Rarámuri (or Tarahumara). Due to the fact that our ancestry is Mexican and therefore not part of the US Bureau of Indian Affairs system of tracking blood quantum to determine "legitimate" Indianness; we have no official tribal claims like US American Indians. In Mexico, once you cease speaking your native language and move into a Europeanized lifestyle, you cease to be Indian. Like many other Chicano/as and Mexicans, I came to learn that my ancestry was also a blend of Spanish/ Castilian, Sephardic, and Basque. The seventeenth-century caste system of Mexico, combined with the culture of the Spanish Inquisition, had made the ambiguous "mestizo" classification—with its silencing of stigmatized ancestry—a safer ethnic hiding place. So, like many who live with such silences, I knew little about these origins or traditions growing up. Unlike many, however, I wanted to explore them, wanted to understand what was hidden in the silences of our official discourse as Mexican Texan Roman Catholics.

This thirst formed the backdrop for the questions I asked of Native Americans and those expressing Indianness. What I claimed to be studying was how people with no Native American ancestry became deeply involved and identified with the spiritual practices, traditions, and identity of the Lakota. It was the projection of my inner thirst for the shadowed identities that history had silenced within my own life.

Excuse me?
did you say you are Indian?
what tribe?
where did you grow up?
are you tribally enrolled?
oh, you're Mexican
you know, we've got to be careful.
Whites are claiming to be Indians to get our jobs,
our scholarships, to make money off our spirituality.

I was less concerned with the notion of fraud than I was fascinated by "the non-Indian desire to become Indian.... As each individual's life was by nature complex, it baffled me to want to add to that complexity. Why would someone want to add to the confusion of personal identity by attempting to take on an identity judged to be inauthentic, or as many asked, 'why would someone want to be who they're not?'" ("Painting the White Face Red," González, 1997, p. 486[1]). My questions were naïve in their simplistic avoidance of sociopolitical factors that informed the very silences regarding my own ethnic history and roots, but that naïveté held an unconscious awareness of the psychic violence blaming one set of ancestors to privilege another can cause.

---

hey you . . .
yeah, you!
"you walk like an Apache," I hear
his words as I carry my bucket of water
—I walk like an Apache—
just who encoded this body of mine
to declare my ancestry without a word?
perhaps in other places, other times
I walk like a zombie, like a good girl
like someone burning in a pyre for
walking like a Jew. But when around
the People, and living on the land
I walk like an Apache whose body
hides the mind of a confused human being.

Almost three years later, I found myself driving out of Chadron, Nebraska, having spent a good part of the summer in South Dakota. That afternoon, everything had a hue of gold to it, as I drove along the two-lane road in Nebraska, the image of massive thunderhead clouds forming on the horizon striking me. Incredibly beautiful, one cloud in particular, coming from the southwest, reflected the golden sunlight in a palette of brilliant violets and deep orange-tinted pinks. It was magnificent and spellbinding, and the substance of the clouds seemed to grow before me. So this is what the call of the sirens must have felt like. All around me was quiet and still, even as I drove speedily along the road, seemingly summoned into this place of storms. There were no cars besides my red Ford Ranger anywhere to be seen, and I was having a hard time keeping my eyes on the road. It suddenly felt obscene to focus on my driving when nature was calling me to attention. Still, I resisted. I pulled my truck to the side of the road, but told myself it was to take a photo. I grabbed my camera and stepped out onto the gravel, standing on the side of the road, transfixed, gazing up at the clouds that were calling me. It was as if my mind had been washed clean, my emotions blown away by a still wind.

I don't know how long I stood there; it could have been seconds, or many moments. The golden luminous clouds filled the horizon and towered into a turquoise blue sky. As I stood there, I tried to take a picture like a mindless tourist, only to discover that my camera had no more space on the film for a photo.

These things are not meant to be recorded...

The words of the Lakota elders and teachers rang through my mind. Over the years of fieldwork on this project, I'd had to abandon traditional field notes and interviews out of respect for the authenticity of the ritual events I was attending. I'd had to learn to trust that what and how I *remembered* it would be the determining factor of what my work reported. I couldn't turn to recorded interviews or long transcripts of notes to see what I'd forgotten. I had to learn to revere the human vessel and oral tradition as a method—rather than elevating critical or historical concepts I'd learned to a place of more authenticity than lived experience. Looking at my disposable Kodak camera—with no room for the image—I felt myself wake up, with the uncomfortable feeling of embarrassment before Creation, realizing that perhaps this two-legged human I called myself was being called to a new form of attention.

> They say you steal the soul
> or the spirit...when you take a photo
> Is it possible the spirit that is lost
> is in the silent connection possible
> when human beings dare to be present
> together, unimpeded by technologies
> of knowing or unknowing.
> In the surrender of my knowing

I come to know without being told
…something is stirring in the great Oneness
you must receive it in the Old Ways
if you wish to share it…you must.

———————

The cloud was rolling toward me. I could feel it drawing me. Was this madness? My eyes felt glued to the way the cloud was moving, rolling over on itself, moving while staying still—staying in place while it came ever closer as its immensity grew. I wanted to stay, resisting my Texas upbringing and ranch wisdom to flee from the environmental signs, warnings of tornado. I'd grown up around this. The golden yellows, pinks, and turquoise hues were classic precursors to a funnel cloud approaching. Yet I was glued there, my emotions and sensibilities suspended in a moment of pure, silent Power.

———————

You too are a churning cloud within
oh you frail two-legged scurrying ones
why do you run from the power?
Stay with me.
That place you hunger for, that you
keep filling with words in lines,
must twist and whirl, uplift
all the weak little shelters you've
called home, called knowing
called explanation.

———————

Without words or discernible reflection, something had shifted, as I returned to my body standing on the desolate country road about to be visited by a tornado. "You've got to get out of here!" ran through my veins. I jumped in my truck and, driving away, I tried to remember if I'd learned to stay in my car if the storm came, or if that was an earthquake, or both.

Thirty minutes later, I was on the road to Lusk. The sky had turned a dark stormy gray, the brilliant golden hues only a memory. It was the sort of darkness that feels as if night has taken over day. The light is dark. The radio broadcast I was listening to announced that a twister had been seen to touch down in the area near Chadron. Yes, I know,

I thought without words. Something larger than my knowing self was governing the day, as had been the case throughout this entire study. But I'd been shielded from this awareness, struggling with the latent and stubborn seeds of academic method.

> *How am I going to report what*
> *I have not been allowed to record?*
> *Who will believe my absence of axioms &*
> *axial coding, theory with no logico-deductive*
> *framework or a litany of citations? You*
> *call yourself a scholar?!?*

The darkness intensified as the rolling green fields became the color of a deep green sea and the clouds so gray they were black. I knew I needed to stop and avoid driving until the next day. I was not in the way of the twister anymore, but the stormy downpours that accompany a tornado were patiently giving me time to get out of their way. Comforted by my decision not to drive much longer, I decided to stop at the first motel I saw, and relaxed.

I began to reflect back on many events in the fieldwork of the previous years. I began to hear my thoughts as if they were speaking to me:

> "...so distanced from themselves...
> ...that when they see...
> ...for the very first time...
> ...their own face...
> ...when they sense for the very first time...
> ...their own soul...
> ...they think it is something Indian..."

("Incognito," González, 1997, p.70)

I repeated the words as if I were learning a song. It was a chant of wisdom that explained much about the bittersweet ignorance in the void of US American ethnic identity—a void motivating the rush to sweat lodges and sun dances. Every explanation I'd tried to articulate about the focus of my study had rung harshly with a tinge of judgment or anger, of ethnic or ideological superiority or feigned authority. These

words, in their lyrical form, were telling me how to "report" my observations in a different way. They were also voicing the silenced inner
needs of my ancestral self.

Throughout the two and a half years I'd been conducting my research,
I'd traveled with a Dictaphone voice recorder, purchased for interviews.
Other than a few formal lectures delivered by some of the elders at public gatherings, I had not recorded anything else. Maybe it had been
intended for another purpose. I reached for it and began to speak the
words that were coming to me. I quit listening to my radio for the
remainder of the 24-hour drive to Arizona, playing music that helped
me stay in the spirit of the events I'd shared. Later, back in my fluo-
rescently lit and air-conditioned faculty office, I would transcribe the
words. They became the ethnographic collection of poetry, "Painting
the White Face Red," a title that came directly from the words of
one poem.

Wa cante wiya. Woman.
Woman with a heart. For others.
That's you. My teacher's words to me
the last time I saw him walking on this earth . . .
That's your name. I'll help you with your
writing. Just put out a cup of coffee. I'll be there.

The elder who, in 1991, guided me through the fasting and ritual for
my *hanbleceya,* or "vision quest," on the flat topped hill outside his land
on Rosebud reservation, passed on from this life while I was working on
this project. In my cock-eyed academically blinded fashion, even in the
heart of the insights personally gained from the *hanbleceya,* I didn't hear
his promise. Today, there's a cup of coffee sitting by me as "I" write this.
That day, driving in stormy Wyoming, I was just beginning to hear—
to learn—that what I was called to offer through my research was not
about what "I" have to say, or what I have managed to get others to say,
but what I can get out of the way to understand.

In this vein, my academic preparation, ideological tendencies, and
personal preferences are my artist's toolbox. They should not determine
what or how insight and understanding arrive, but they are ready to be
used when *awareness* indicates to me the need for the particular brush,
ink, paper, pen, or even computer. This change in the habitus and force

of expressive authority is a difficult adaptation to make within a society and profession that continues to live in the shadow of the middle ages, fearing metaphysical wisdom and received knowledge due to the experienced brutality of zealotry and inquisitorial politics. It is a profession that far too easily becomes the accomplice to generationally maintained silences of those of us who carry the DNA of histories too complex to simplify through essentialist or politically correct ethics.

I shared the poetry with academics who knew nothing or little about the type of contexts where I'd spent my time during the study. This was the era of Kevin Costner's "Dances with Wolves" and the publication of Lynn Andrews' "Medicine Woman" series of books. Ethnic fraud was a topic debated on college campuses as "white Indians" cropped up when job announcements seeking ethnic diversity were posted. Individuals with no previously demonstrated history as ethnically anything but white were reporting Native American or American Indian ancestry, distorting the demographics needed to support departments' proposals for hiring of Native Americans. There was great concern that these "ethnic hires" were gaining employment, but bringing no added cultural diversity or insight to the departments where they were hired.

Meanwhile, I shared the poetry with members of the sun dance community who I'd spent so much time with. One young Lakota woman in South Dakota asked for a copy of the poems to give to her grandmother. Upon sharing a few of the poems in a keynote address at a conference for women of color, a Lakota woman honored me by giving me the earrings she was wearing as an expression of gratitude for capturing what she said others failed to see in her people. Two drummers from the sun dance expressed appreciation that one of the poems was clearly about them. I realized that there was something very intimate in the poetry, but in such a fashion that it gave something to the people about whom the poems were written. They recognized themselves and found confirmation of their experiences. The poems were not idyllic or complimentary. They were often quite blunt and revealing. They held the complexity of intercultural and interracial relationships as I had carried them within myself as a Chicana. I wanted to share them widely but struggled when it came to the question of publishing them.

I listened to the ways the poetry I'd written was seized through academic interpretation. I watched their meaning publically warp as I tried to analyze or describe them in static written text to satisfy the needs of a particular publication or meeting, or to respond to individuals' attempts to claim the poems as evidence of their pet academic theory or ideological standpoint. It was problematic. Gradually, my concern grew until I knew I couldn't publish the collection then. Publishing them in an academic venue, particularly during the trends of the times, seemed a betrayal of the people. I was encouraged to write an annotated manuscript, but the idea of explaining the meaning of the poems seemed to defeat the purpose.

Both Indian and non-Indian participants in the community I'd been with over the years were not anonymous subjects in an academic project. I was the observer and guest in their homes and sacred events. Even though the poems held a wealth of opportunity for intercultural discussions, placing the whole collection on the level of academic discourse created a discourse that dominated the quietly powerful insights in the poetry. Further, it appeared that rather than being significant because of their topic and the cultural issues they raised, it was simply the fact that my ethnography *was* in poetic form that was of more interest to many scholars. My participants would be invisible...their garments more interesting than their lives. No, this was not going to happen. Was it possible that what I had worked on for so long was actually going to remain silent in the academic world within which it was assumed any work of value I do must appear?

> *Inila—*
> *the Lakota word for...silence.*
> *There is a time for you to speak*
> *as we move around the Circle*
> *you must believe that if something*
> *is meant to be known it will find its*
> *way into the world through the Circle.*
> *If it's your turn, the Circle will make*
> *a space for you. This world where*
> *words move in lines...it's an odd one*
> *so busy making sure you get a place*
> *makes the words stand out...we can't hear you*
> *lots of words, but not what you meant*
> *to share...what you could say by listening...by waiting.*

Our research is shared in printed words and conference presentations, then cited and recited over time in a dance that serves to keep us employed. "Painting the White Face Red" taught me that the relationships and knowledge/wisdom garnered from deep immersion and sharing of others' life experiences are not just about our careers or preferred expression of politics. In fact, they are far more political than many an intentional public statement on behalf of others might be. The academy has challenged my deeply held awareness in a greater reality and Source, which always leads me to question what I am actually doing in authentic relationships with others. This is in opposition to seeking research relationships specifically or primarily to further my career. It also opposes speaking the politically charged rhetoric of the disempowered in settings where the words carry more ego than spirit. To choose not to speak where I am expected to speak, or to be silent when I feel myself puffed up by my own voice is a political act, on behalf of those who are essentialized and hidden by the clatter of too much talk. I would venture to say that even the commonly privileged fail to be known and heard because they are far too vocal and taken for granted.

By claiming our research as alive within the embodied selves who have experienced the lived contexts about which we write, we dare to acknowledge our work is never complete. Our work is our lives, our presence as the carriers of the voices that have shaped our inner understanding in unspoken ways. We may write something, but our texts are never completed. They continue to develop through the dialogue and conversation we have as members of the community that shares the knowledge we have published or performed. We enter a setting carrying all of this within us, and as such, each breath transformed into words in any setting carries it as well. I have often said that my doctoral dissertation used five percent of the coded interview data for the written document. The rest of the information was alive in me, as the ethnographer.

By entering and living within the sense making contexts we study, we come to experience the blurring of boundaries. The more successfully we can cease to be a "walking, talking study," and become mindful participants, capable of sitting with silence rather than a mind full of predetermined questions, the more likely we are to come to embody our insights. Anthropologist Ted Conover reflected upon his experience living with and experiencing the life of undocumented Mexican workers in the USA in his book, *Coyotes* (1987), that he was "bound to stay (at the borders he had studied) for a long time." Upon reflection, I don't think it is that we stay *"there,"* but rather, that the experiences stayed *with us.* More accurately, they stayed *within* us. As the ethnographer who was present, I now embody the knowledge of what I experienced, and this knowledge enters with me into every setting and context where I am present.

When I completed the transcription of the poetry collection, "Painting the White Face Red," I had not even begun to understand the nature of the journey I had invited by playing with the sacred. I had profound experiences, but my maturity at the time was low, and my ethical arguments stereotypically wild as those of a zealous advocate or activist. While I chose not to "speak" with the publication of the poetry, I ranted and raved at any opportunity in a fashion that decried my immaturity and lack of wisdom. Speaking at length about the wisdom of not speaking is obviously contradictory at an ontological level. At the time of writing and performing the collection of poetry that expressed and analyzed my ethnographic experience, I saw the ways the knowledge and insight I had garnered was regarded chiefly as possession, or material that could be taken or used. In some ways, I think that remains true, if we consider how information can be manipulated to suit the needs or intent of authors and speakers of many a perspective. However, this conceptualization is very limited, and by focusing on protecting the "property," the silent insights in the verses were not recognized amidst the defensive din of a trendy academic idea.

Where are the words to tell about
the day you didn't show up to dance,
I stood in the arbor, sage in my hand,
knowing you were pierced by life somehow.
I walked through the veil that day
left my researcher mission with the books.
This was real life, not a piece of literature
the sun dance leader calling us forth to sacrifice
four small bits of flesh—did they help as you danced
on the edge of death that day, so the people might live?

The poem is not simply a piece of creative writing; it is ethnographic poetry. It documents real situations and a specifically intended theme based on actual focused events. In the unstated awareness of the issues and concepts this poem encodes, it becomes a sacred text, able to be read through the body that was there. While I acknowledge that there is no word spoken or written that is immune to subjective interpretation, that is precisely the point: *because* of the ever present dynamic of personal interpretation of the shared word, a level of consciousness of the texture and potential of what we will share is called for. When we begin to carry the history of the worlds we represent through our work, the longer we live, the more significant those words become. And if we want that knowledge to be remembered, then we must choose words that evoke the desire to recall and re-tell the stories. Our role as scholar-teachers becomes more important.

Although I have often remarked that as ethnographers and persons engaged in naturalistic inquiry we carry the data in our selves, for many years I did not do this with the awareness that I had become the vessel for something sacred. I was defending methodology against the dominant evaluative voice of deterministic and quantitative epistemologies. In that defensive posturing, I was blind to the deeper implications of this methodological reality. I did not have the capacity to sit in the silent spaces created by intentional withholding, and rather, filled those spaces with polemic fluff and rebuttals that left me feeling nauseous after seminars and conferences.

While working on the ethnographic project, "Painting the White Face Red," I experienced great frustration as I presumed that there was a dead end in the academic road I felt had been my vocation. I had become an ethnographer because of my passion for understanding others, my calling to be an advocate, and my love of shared experience *in vivo*. Out of this frustration, I sat down one day and imagined what ethnography would be like if my Native American ancestors had conceived the practice. In "The Four Seasons of Ethnography" (2000), I compared ethnography to a ritual of natural cycles, and this piece has become the cornerstone of my own academic work and pedagogy. I did not publish the full collection of "Painting the White Face Red," but out of the wrestling with my decision to honor the silence, emerged my life work. I did not lose my vocation.

My teachers and those who have gone before me have endowed my scholarship in its ideal form upon me; those teachers include the many participants in their everyday lives whom I have had the privilege of observing. When I share what I have learned, it is their silence that carries the most weight. I have learned that my voice must be tempered by this awareness. What I produce is a manifestation of my practice, and that practice requires what the institution of the academy might at times consider untenable: my own silence...and the gradual awareness that deep within what I know and *don't* articulate are often deeper messages that will come in their own time and in their own way. Today, I celebrate the awareness of the deeper messages about the silenced creation of Chicana mestizaje I carried inside myself that this poetry helped reveal. I've learned there is a silencing that kills truth...and there is a silence that awaits the sharing of truth so that those who have been harmed are not carelessly harmed by an academic or political hearing of their own stories.

———————————

...Inila...
...silence...
There is no absence in this space
no void in the emptiness you perceive
this body has lived with others and
carries the seeds of a voice yet
unheard...but it moves wherever I move.
They danced so the people might live
and we watched with sage clutched in
our hands, supporting and believing in
something we could not understand.
Their bodies were pierced and now they
are scarred. Beautiful scarred bodies like
those of us who witness with our bodies
carrying the voice of our people, silent as
we claim the privilege to speak in our own way.

Note

1. María Cristina González is the previous name of the chapter's author, Sarah Amira De la Garza.

References

Conover, Ted (Ed.) (1987). *Coyotes.* 1st edn. New York: Vintage.

González, Maria Cristina (1997). Painting the White Face Red. In Judith Martin, Thomas Nakayama, and Lisa Flores (Eds), *Readings in Cultural Contexts.* Mountain View, CA: Mayfield, pp. 485–494.

González, Maria Cristina (2000). The Four Seasons of Ethnography. *International Journal of Intercultural Relations,* 24: 623–650.

González, Maria Cristina (1997). Incognito. In L. Perry and P. Geist (Eds), *Courage of Conviction: Women's Words, Women's Wisdom.* Mountain View, CA: Mayfield, p. 70.

9
Attuned to Silence: A Pedagogy of Presence

Alexandra Fidyk

Silence and pedagogy

What has directed my work (teaching, research, and writing) for as long as I can remember is a pedagogy of presence.[1] Such a pedagogy is rooted in an ontological way of being, not an epistemological doing. As such, it values silence. It is sustained, in part, by an on-going contemplation about what silence, experienced as active, generative, creative, and meditative, might mean to one's daily practices in life, to one's teaching and writing.

Pedagogy, from the Greek *paidagogia*, once referred to the work of leading children to school, but today it takes on a much wider signification, including both the formal practices and professions of teaching and the complex network of activities that surround general care for the young (Smith, 1999). Today pedagogy exists as a fluid dynamic whereby a tensionality emerges from "indwelling in a zone between two curriculum worlds"—the worlds of "planned" and "lived" curriculum experiences (Aoki, 1986/1991/2005). Stated otherwise, pedagogy exists in the overlap between an ontological position (a way of being) and epistemological practices (ways of knowing and doing). As Ted Aoki aptly explains, "the quality of life lived within the tensionality depends much on the *quality* of the *pedagogic being*" that the teacher *is* (p. 161, emphasis added). Every teacher is confronted by this tension. What she chooses to do with this tension tells much about who she is and how she sees and so lives with the world. Too often the teacher seeks to control, remove or sublimate tension as if it is not a valuable aspect of learning, as if life was without its own resistance and force.

In my curriculum and pedagogy course, the initial reading for undergraduate students is Aoki's "Teaching as Indwelling Between Two

Worlds" (1986/1991/2005), whereby the guiding question becomes "who are you as a pedagogic being?" The calling into presence of two curriculum forms, even though often singularly understood, allows one to understand more fully the pedagogical life of teachers. Aoki speaks of the quest we undertake for a change from the "is" to the "not yet." He explains:

> [... I]ndwelling dialectically is a living in tensionality, a mode of being that knows not only that living school life means living simultaneously with limitations and with openness, but also that this openness harbours within it risks and possibilities as we quest for a change from the is to the not yet. This tensionality calls us as pedagogues to make time for meaningful striving and struggling, time for letting things be, time for question, time for singing, time for crying, time for anger, time for praying and hoping. Within this tensionality, guided by a sense of the pedagogic good, we are called on as teachers to be alert to the possibilities of our pedagogic touch, pedagogic tact, pedagogic attunement— those subtle features about being teachers that we know, but are not yet in our lexicon.... We must recognize the flight from the meaningful and turn back again to an understanding of our own being as teachers. (p. 164)

One of the "subtle features" about being a teacher is one's relationship to silence and one's ways of respecting it within the curriculum, the classroom, and the "not yet."

Questions of relevance to pedagogy include but are not limited to: what is generative silence? How might silence open up creative possibilities? And how might silence, itself, be a pedagogic act? What follows is a philopoetic address of these questions. By philopoetic I mean a love of metaphoric knowing, a maieutic art, that beckons ways in, lifting to the body latent things. Poetry or dialectic will "use [a] system to draw what needs saying further along" (Lilburn, 2002, p. 2). Here it seems that with writing, the text itself is doing the thinking, the bringing to consciousness, rather than the "author" who contributes her pressing to know and willingness to follow where the writing wants to go. Many philosophers and poets of this tradition say that, "what is wanted is a kind of negative attention, an alert emptiness" (p. 2). So this text is not an unraveling of a single thought, an argument, nor a guide on how to proceed. There is no position or technique—where language comes to claim and bring closure—just the drift of attunement: "all the writing has an open ear, proceeds by this ear: a certain form of speech can be an attempt to hear"

(p. 2). This way harbors a kind of politics that grows from alacritous attention, and echoes the meditative focus and capricious movements of silence.

Silence as active experience

Central to understanding a pedagogy of presence is the space of silence. Silence in classrooms typically has existed as forced silence. Traditionally, students have been subdued, expected to be quiet when they are attending to assigned tasks. This form of silence has been imposed from the outside-in as a form of discipline, order, and obedience. Silence too exists as a form of classroom participation or even resistance, both of which cannot be read as a simple matter of power or lack of power, voice or lack of voice. Cheryl Glenn (2004) explains:

> [S]ilence is too often read as simple passivity in situations where it has actually taken on an expressive power: when it denotes alertness and sensitivity, when it signifies attentiveness or stoicism, and particularly when it allows new voices to be heard.... Silence can deploy power; it can defer to power. It all depends. (p. 18)

"It all depends" acknowledges and respects the complexity of the factors relevant to silence, such as distinguishing between types of silences, especially those that can be unfamiliar, uncertain, and paradoxical. When silence is considered generative, creative, meditative, and paradoxical, however, it can be a nourishing space in the classroom or in any daily practice. Such cultivated silence calls for a discipline from the inside-out. Its teaching manner cares for the well-being of youth and ourselves with the genuine inclusion and valuing of silence. Michel Sciacca suggests that this kind of silence "has a weight... that we don't find in any word: it is heavy with everything that we have lived, are living now and everything that we shall experience" (cited in Fiumara, 1990, p. 105).

Conceived as primordial, this silence is an active experience; it is neither muteness nor mere absence of audible sound. Silence is more like an "inner virtual condition" into which we can submerge and from which further understanding can emerge (Fiumara, 1990, p. 104). It is an "autonomous phenomenon" (Picard, 1948/2002, p. 15), "a force," a constitutive principle distinct from but associated with other forces, such as spirit and word, in the constitution of the human world (Dauenhauer, 1980, p. vii). That is, silence is the *necessary* ground for building knowledge and relationships among self and others, animate and inanimate. Silence brings one into "living contact with the mysterious depths of ourselves, the creative spirit, the mysteries of love" (Lane, 2006, p. 96). And it is "the only thing that confronts us with our own life. It recapitulates it for us there, in that instant, entirely present" (Sciacca cited in Fiumara, 1990, p. 105). When this silence appears within a teaching situation, it enfolds those present in a kind of field that is experienced through its feeling tone, a quieting, an opening in the way that something is heard and embodied. It casts a spell that often prevents insignificant speech as a way to sustain itself and its effects.

Mapping generative silence

Creativity, deep attendance, meditative stopping, forgetting, insight, and de-reflection are concepts that are used to characterize generative silence. As silence cannot be directly known, analogies, images, metaphors, and poetry assist to map its terrain. Their presence threads this text not by way of argument but as an approach that speaks to their relationship with teaching and writing. A braid of silence, transformation (movement toward authenticity), and paradox, herein guides the reader to where these concepts overlap, skip, circle back, and even blur at the edges. Meaning thus becomes layered and interwoven through the text where what is apparently absent may be intensely present.

Similarly, one is reminded that "meaningfulness always contains an absence as well as a presence," and sometimes in the absence of things one becomes conscious of a presence that one may have long overlooked (Smith, 1999, p. 71). In this way "silence is as much as declaration" (p. 71); silence is not an absence, not a lack. Generative silence is ripe, full, fertile; it is always already becoming. While one may create a space for its "radical presence" (O'Reilley, 1998), so that at any moment silence may break forth, nothing, however, in the previous moment guarantees its arrival. I recall this happening when a student came to my office, excited to share a teaching encounter. He told me about it, but the words failed to capture the "feel" of what he experienced. Frustration seeped in as the telling fell short and his voice dropped off. He paused and grew quiet. Eventually, he looked up as he could feel me listening deeply. We continued to sit for a few minutes, neither of us speaking until he said, "it was like this." I smiled and nodded, both of us reluctant to say anything more. Mary Rose O'Reilley's work reminds us, "Presence to another can be this informal" (p. 24). It implies deep and intentional listening. In order to "practice radical presence—to come home to your heart and listen deeply to others who look for you there"—someone must have first listened to you (p. 16).

When one is able to attend to images, feelings, and words anew, this is a creative act. As Toni Packer (2007) teaches, "There is nothing more miraculous than thorough attention, no matter what the activity may be" (p. 77). Through such attention, one may discover that silence itself is a creative act and can arouse creativity for when the mind or voice grows quiet; a door opens to the unknown, to a place where things can emerge. "In its creative function," writes philosopher Gemma Fiumara, "silence basically represents a way of being *with* the interlocutor; it indicates...a proposed interaction, an invitation to the development of a time-space in which to meet, or clash, in order to share in the challenge of growth" (p. 101).

As this understanding of silence and creativity suggests, there is a spiritual basis to attendance, a humility in waiting upon the emergence of a pattern from the world—from students' questions, queries, and challenges. The willingness to assimilate what has been seen or heard draws other life into increasingly inclusive definitions of the self. Such fresh attention to the familiar is one creative purpose of silence. Bateson continues: "looking, listening, and learning offer the modern equivalent of moving through life as a pilgrimage" (1994, p. 11). Here there is an invitation to attend, to be present sometimes with companionship, sometimes with patience, sometimes with solitude. It means to embody a caring, receptive attitude. The willingness to do what needs to be done—'the pedagogic good'—is rooted in attention to what is. Here the best care for students is founded in felt observation or contemplation and may be unexpected, even contradictory, depending on the context. To be attuned to learning, one needs to develop an authentic and deliberate kind of attention: attention that turns and turns again. Such attention does not imply that something must be done; rather, it emphasizes a profound respect of attending deeply beyond the sensate.

Deep attending characteristically precedes profound silence and has a subsequent response of undoing some knots or what some perceive as problems. For some it is easier to run, repress or ignore such challenges rather than being with what on the surface appears troublesome, time-consuming, or useless. Learning to dwell in these difficult situations or zones of tension creates a sense of faith in a particular kind of presence, one that is not readily named or described. When dwelling in these places, there may come a moment

> when the wholeness of the phenomenon bursts upon you. When that moment occurs, an intense joy accompanies it, a moment in which you are caught up in the wonder of the thing itself. And there is also this pause, this pregnant point, when you and the phenomenon itself—at this moment of interwoven, participatory consciousness—are suspended in time in a state of dynamic tension.
>
> (Buhner, 2004, p. 187)

It is after glimpsing such wholeness that one may experience a shift in consciousness. This transformation happens in the badgering and bothering (and correcting and grading); it happens as well in the ground of silence. It happens in good teaching and counseling where members know that their individual inward attention is part of what may emerge on any given day when one is willing to be vulnerable, take risks, and be present to what unfolds. Upon such repeated experiences, trust, courage, and confidence often arise or deepen.

When one acquires the skill of deep attendance, one in a sense forgets oneself and yet becomes something more than previously imagined. By forgetting oneself, I am not suggesting a form of escapism, abandonment, or repression of self, memories, or narratives; indeed, memories and narratives are necessary to develop a sense of one's multiple selves and one's enduring self. The proposed forgetting typically occurs after one has developed a strong ego and so teaches from an authentic being, which has integrity. Not everyone can readily sit with what the mind and body (or another) may toss up as one grows quiet. A strong ego is developed in part by one's capacity to be comfortable in silence, in the ability to slow down, take leave, and dwell in quietude—elements of a pedagogic practice that radically alter the way learning unfolds. Such forgetting implies dwelling in the here and now, not grasping onto memories of the past or expectantly anticipating the future. Musician John Cage (1967) explains that he learned to take his likes and dislikes out of the creative process so that he could more fully meet what unfolded without projecting his own ego desires. "I have always tried to move away from music as an object," he describes, "moving toward music as a process, which is without beginning, middle, or end. So instead of being like a table or chair, the music becomes the weather" (Nisker, 1986, p. 4). His work found its rhythm through the integration of art, life, and meditation.

Silence as meditative

Rarely is one able to focus solely on a task wherein nothing else happens. The trick then, among on-rushing events and emotions, is the ability to drop into presence—even just a one-breath meditation: straightening the back, clearing the mind for a moment—which can be like a refreshing breeze on a stifling day. Although the term meditation has mystical and religious connotations for many people, it is, as I mean it, a simple and plain phenomenon. And while it may occur collectively, it is a solitary act. It is deliberate slowing, stillness, and silence. The quietened mind has many paths, many of them tedious and ordinary, and some unexpected. But each path is one chosen from innumerable refuges from the hurry of external events. A person meditating, however, may be simply experiencing a wider ground of consciousness and thus avoids excluding or excessively elevating any thought or feeling (see Fidyk, 2011).

An act of presence, such as meditative stopping or pedagogical leave taking, is vital to creativity and renewed visions central to learning. "Meditative stopping," writes David Smith (1999), "makes possible a new kind of stillness in which can be heard or recognized...all of those voices, intuitions, dreams and aspirations...which have been suppressed under the dispensations of the dominant order" (p. 86). Meditation, which has to do with gaining a fuller measure of one's situation, is achieved through "a stopping of all those daily rituals and habits which inevitably act to sustain status quo conventionalities" (p. 85).

To become forgetful, to break from the structures and conventions of one's ego, practice, and worldview is to release into recognition the deep interdependency of any subjectivity, with a fuller acknowledgment of the way in which "I always already am that of which I speak, even when I speak of the world and others as objects" (p. 85). "To forget oneself," as Buddhist scholar David Loy (1990) describes, "is to wake up and find oneself in or, more precisely, as a situation—not confined by it but one with it" (p. 497). In this way, partaking in practices of silence can lead to a sense of self that is always in relation with others, woven as a dynamic web of interconnectedness.

Such forgetting and insight also contributes to pedagogical authority. Authority that flows from the wisdom of respecting others, from deeply understanding what it is to live authentically, not authority which is concerned with delegating or sharing power, as if it were a commodity. Rather, it "leads us to understand authority in terms of the wisdom that comes from having lived well as a very human being" (Aoki cited in

Pinar, 2005, p. 67). Its accompanying inner knowing and doing directs pedagogical leave-taking, knowing when to and the importance of stepping back, encouraging the student to make her own way. Aoki says, the pedagogue

> must take leave... he (sic) must withdraw, such that in the very event of withdrawal, there may inhere a pedagogic creativity, a coming into being that is vibrant with pedagogic possibilities. Hence, pedagogic withdrawal may, within a seeming negating of self, confer in the silence of the pedagogue's absence an opening wherein the student can truly learn what it is to stand, what it is to be in one's becoming. (p. 67)

Such withdrawal is antithetical to much teacher training today. To take leave at a "pregnant point" so that the student may step into her own becoming opens the moment for a "meaningful striving or struggling" and "intense joy." This pedagogic knowledge is not accumulative, not a process of expanding outward or the desire for something whereby every void is filled. It is a process instead of "de-reflection." While reflection is championed in teacher education, it takes place within one's mind as a self-contained activity. While significant, without a reflexive or inter-subjective quality, one's reflecting is limited by the way that one sees and so thinks of the world, just as a mirror reflects back what stands before it. De-reflection, on the other hand, where one suspends individualism and openly engages with others, can usher in a discovery or recovery of a world already imbued with creative value.

Writing and speaking silence

For many, people teach and write because they know; they have something to say. It may sound like an absurdity to teach and write because one wants to know and so inquires, listens, and waits for something to take hold. Like waiting during teaching for an image to take root or flight, Smith (1999) suggests that "before anything can be written, something must be seen, and because insight is the necessary condition for good writing, preparation for writing inevitably lies in the realm of existential preparedness" (p. 70). Seeing and 'insight' indicate a readiness for otherness—a kind of welcoming the not-yet-known. This kind of seeing dwells on the edge of conversation between student and teacher, where each glimpses what the other says yet does not understand. Here both seek to make meaning. They participate in a dance, negotiating concepts, terms, and paradigms, to put forth his and her thinking and yet are receptive to the other's as well. Similarly, "being prepared to write," Smith continues, "involves an attunement or attentiveness to reality most closely allied not to epistemology (knowing how to write) but to Wisdom (knowing what should be said)" (p. 70). Again, it is a relationship to *ontos* and *ethos*, not procedure or technique, that is central to writing. Just as different types of silence are but splinters of Silence—that which was there first—"Writing is a holy act, an articulation of limited understanding oriented to a pre-existent Whole. Anything else is a cultural fetish driven by and towards secondary aims" (p. 70).

As in teaching, the acts of writing and speaking of silence are paradoxical. This paradox becomes apparent as one confronts the limits of language. Cage (1967) and Susan Sontag (1969), respectively, say it thus: "No silence exists that is not pregnant with sound" (p. 135); and, "[s]ilence remains inescapably a form of speech" (p. 11). For Gabriel Marcel, one ought to think of the word as "coming forth from the fullness of silence" and the fullness of silence conferring on the word as if it were its real purpose (cited in Picard, 1948/2002, p. 10).

However stated, silence and sound—like research and writing or teaching and learning—are always interrelated. Parker Palmer (1998), in the classic *The Courage to Teach*, presents six paradoxes that he sees as essential in teaching and learning spaces. The sixth paradox is, "The space should welcome both silence and speech" (p. 77). In meaningful exchanges, silence may actually mediate communication, so much so that even an appropriate word may disrupt a previously unexplored communicative level. Sometimes when we do communicate in the midst of silence, we are tempted to shatter it with an innocuous articulation. This temptation derives from a need to escape an overabundant communication. In such situations, expressions are not used to say something but to attenuate what is being said. For instance, often after reading aloud a particularly affective piece of literature in class, silence befell us. The language (content, voice, context, etc.) touched upon the deep, and no questions or comments broke forth. It was as if our timespace reality shifted and "we" were no longer in the separate roles of individuals as students and teacher, rather we were knitted into a listening, feeling whole. It took practice to learn to let this silence be and not shatter its weight by an unnecessary question or comment. I had to learn 'pedagogic withdrawal,' to let silence breathe so 'pedagogic possibilities' could emerge where students learn to shift the balance, to swerve, disrupt, multiply, even renounce the privilege of a single voice. We were held together in those moments, first by the intent of the words, and, then, by silence itself. However, I had to become comfortable with "letting" this happen, being present to silence—attending it without any expectation or ego direction (Fidyk, 2008). Although teachers are often considered the "guardians of language," students learn more in those moments, "when [they] find [them]selves standing at the threshold of deep insight or reverence—and fall silent in awe—" than they do from language-directed courses (Warland, 2008, p. 15). In creating communal silences in classes, there rises a recognition that generative pedagogical silences are built on teachers' personal silences—their ability to listen to themselves and wait in the seeming emptiness of sound. As Stuart Sim (2007) urges in his manifesto for silence: "Silence matters, and there should be more of it" (p. 170).

Given the nature of human beings' intricately layered selves, awareness arises on many different planes. One reaches subtler states through activity that draws attention inward rather than outward. The means of conveying such states may best be presented by metaphor, poetry, art, and performance—not exposition. To write of silence requires other methods of representing knowledge, skills, and attitudes both in class and beyond. Metaphor is one, for it keeps words close to the intense moment of experience; it is not just the best words in the best order, but rather "experience in the most dynamic syntax" (Peterkiewicz, 1970, p. 43). Turning inward offers another side of dwelling, where one may be astonished to find one's own poetic desire by feeling no need for a voice. Hence, the act of turning inward, attending a course by moving slowly, reading material deeply rather than broadly, and using metaphor, poetry, and art provide guidance for teaching—and any address of silence.

Poetry, poetics, and "the tunnel of silence"

Writing and living poetically and the tradition of deliberate attention to consciousness are as old as language for humankind. Meditation looks inward, poetry breaks forth. One is for oneself; the other is for the world. One enters the moment; the other shares it. However, in practice, it is never clear which is doing which. Gary Snyder (1995) reflects on this ambiguity between the apparent inwardness of meditation and the apparent outwardness of poetry: "Poetry steers between nonverbal states of mind and the intricacies of our gift of language (a wild system born with us). When I practice *zazen*, poetry never occurs to me, I just do *zazen*. Yet one cannot deny the connection" (p. 113). This connection echoes the insight: "meaningfulness always contains an absence as well as a presence," and similarly, "good" pedagogy means "living simultaneously with limitations and with openness."

To poet Adrienne Rich (2001), the matrix of a poet's work consists not only of "what is there to be absorbed and worked on, but also of what is missing, *desaparecido*, rendered unspeakable, thus unthinkable" (p. 150). It is through these gaps or "invisible holes in reality" that poetry makes its way (p. 150). Max Picard (1948/2002) likens these gaps to "empty spaces," "places of authentic silence," "nature in repose" (p. 146). For Rich, the human "impulse to create begins—often terribly and fearfully—in the tunnel of silence" (p. 150). She writes passionately:

> Every real poem is the breaking of an existing silence, and the first question we might ask any poem is, *What kind of voice is breaking silence, and what kind of silence is being broken?* ... [S]ilence is not always or necessarily oppressive, it is not always or necessarily a denial or extinguishing of some reality. It can be fertilizing, it can bathe the imagination, it can, as in great open spaces, ... be the nimbus of a way of life, a condition of vision. (p. 150)

As it happens, the first evidence one has that a work is a poem is the greater blank space around its page. That space is silence. Silence draws near the aesthetic experience which requires conscious and unconscious participation in a work. For a poem's task is to seduce. Its readers or listeners must find in the poem "something irresistible, something to which they want to surrender" (Hirshfield, 1997, pp. 184–185). In any good poem, even one as brief as *haiku*, there is a moment of transformation. Something happens over its course to the writer and to the reader:

> Up the barley rows,
> Stitching, stitching them together,
> A butterfly goes.
>
> (Sora, translated by Harold Henderson, 1958)

For such a change to come about in our teaching, one must access a poetic or metaphoric consciousness, a "going out of energy, an ability to notice what is there to be noticed in the play, the poem, the quartet" (Greene, 1995, p. 125). Knowing "about," as we are typically taught, is wholly different from composing "a fictive world creatively and entering it perceptually, affectively, and cognitively" (p. 125). To become part of this engagement requires a balance between assisting the young (and oneself) to be present "to attend to shapes, patterns, sounds, rhythms, figures of speech, contours, and lines" and to step back from control of grammar and thought by allowing them freedom to compose meaningful works (Greene, 1995, p. 125). The same stepping back, poetics, and attendance are needed in approaches to research. Many conduct studies without breathable gaps, denying any possibility to compose afresh or to be surprised. Worse, many fail to realize that there are different paradigms in which to address questions and so critique them from within the dominant discourse, failing to see that there are other ways to be, do, know. Lisa Mazzei (2007) attempts to redress such concerns in her call for a new sensibility in approaches to research. As in pedagogy, one needs to develop

> a methodology that helps us listen to the voice of silence and also develop a theoretical understanding of silences as *meaning full*....Such purposeful attentiveness to the inhabited silences in discourse-based research will serve to provide a more textured and nuanced understanding than can be obtained when simply focusing on the words that are spoken. (p. xii)

In research and pedagogic activities, one needs to allow the '*meaning full*' to be discovered and to unfold without restricting its potentialities.

Like poetry, silence unfolds with no external stimulus aimed at any particular organ. It happens. One hears with an inner ear and one sees with an inner eye. As such one's body—the "heart of silence"— becomes the instrument through which the rhythm plays (Prendergast and Bradford, 2007, p. 3). Silence registers viscerally and one absorbs it as carnal knowledge. Poetry arises from this dance of energy and cadence. Verses and voices arise—"It *is* the voices, intuited first without words"—with a "polyphonic tumble" so that one is only the vessel, a body for its arrival—a function of it, so to speak, rather than vice versa (Lee, 1998, p. 181). Indeed, this writing at times takes direction from this felt flux of energy. Teaching and research, too, can arise from this living flux by listening into the cadence where silence beckons 'a coming into being that is vibrant with pedagogic possibilities.'

Silence as pedagogy of presence

Deliberate attention to silence illustrates that it cannot be written or taught in a tight, preset structure. It is an 'autonomous phenomenon' that resists any attempt to make it work in particular ways as in "uses of" or "methods to." Readers here find the slide, saunter, and halt that are intrinsic to silence as meditation so that images, poetry, and ideas have room to breathe, stretch out, pause, feel around. Words lose linearity and form into a whole, an image—"a pattern that is not seen but felt" (Sardello, 2008, p. 112). Moving in this free-form way mirrors the movement of tracking something that matters and marks the dance of a life lived in and with attunement. That trek itself constitutes a way of being, an ethic of attendance, a pedagogy of presence. In turn, silence enlivens the gesture so that one feels the creative energy reverberating into the depths of one's being (Sardello, 2008). Living (teaching, researching, writing) as meditation—a form which silence beckons—involves the mind, but also the heart, the body, the spirit. Sardello explains, "As we enter the mystery of Silence, its presence resonates throughout the fibers of our flesh, while extending beyond the flesh to the soul inwardly and to the cosmos outwardly" (p. 8).

When one is no longer externally directed (valuing power, control, and predictable outcomes) and attunes to a deeper, inner resonance, the ego grows quiet and there arises an energy greater than itself. Here "living in tensionality" is not a case of either—or rather both—and, marked "with limitations and with openness." Recalling Aoki's dialectic reminds those in education to reach under the "lofty and prosaic talk ... of conceptual abstractions," and to turn back to an "understanding of our own *being* as teachers." Such understanding is grounded in "purposeful attentiveness," "Wisdom," creativity, poetics, and "the presence of what we live among." It is here where silence might emerge as active, generative, creative, meditative, and paradoxical. It is here that Silence might inspire "what it is to be in one's becoming."

Note

1. The ideas and voices present here are the heart of my research in *Silence and Eros: Beckoning the Background Forward* (Fidyk, forthcoming).

References

Aoki, Ted (1986/1991/2005). Teaching as indwelling between two curriculum worlds. In William Pinar & Rita Irwin (Eds), *Curriculum in a new key: The collected works of Ted T. Aoki* (pp. 159–165). Mahwah, NJ: Lawrence Erlbaum Associates Inc.

Aoki, Ted (2005). The sound of pedagogy in the silence of the morning calm. In W. Pinar & R. Irwin (Eds), *Curriculum in a new key: The collected works of Ted T. Aoki* (pp. 389–401). Mahwah, NJ: Lawrence Erlbaum Associates Inc.

Bateson, Mary C. (1994). *Peripheral visions: Learning along the way*. New York: HarperCollins.

Buhner, Stephan H. (2004). *The secret teachings of plants: The intelligence of the heart in the direct perception of nature*. Rochester, VM: Bear & Co.

Cage, John (1967). *Silence*. Middletown, CT: Wesleyan University Press.

Dauenhauer, Bernard (1980). *Silence: The phenomenon and its ontological significance*. Bloomington, IN: Indiana University Press.

Fidyk, Alexandra (forthcoming). *Silence and eros: Beckoning the background forward*. Rotterdam: Sense Publishing.

Fidyk, Alexandra (2008). The writing of poetry. In Betsy Warland (Ed.), *Silences in teaching and learning* (p. 130). Gatineau, QC: Gauvin Press.

Fidyk, Alexandra (2011). Suffering within: Seven moments of ignorance. In Eric Malewski & Nathalia Jaramillo (Eds), *Epistemologies of ignorance and studies of limits in education* (pp. 129–165). Charlotte, NC: Information Age Publishing.

Fiumara, Gemma C. (1990). *The other side of language: A Philosophy of listening*. London: Hobbs.

Glenn, Cheryl (2004). *Unspoken: A rhetoric of silence*. Carbondale, IL: Southern Illinois University Press.

Greene, Maxine (1995). *Releasing the imagination: Essays on education, the arts, and social change*. San Francisco, CA: Jossey-Bass.

Henderson, Harold. (1958). *An introduction to haiku: An anthology of poems and poets from Bashō to Shiki*. Toronto, ON: Anchor Books.

Hirshfield, Jane (1997). *Nine gates: Entering the mind of poetry*. New York: HarperCollins.

Lane, Jane (2006). *The spirit of silence: Making space for creativity*. White River Junction, VT: Chelsea Green Publishing.

Lee, Dennis (1998). *Body music*. Toronto: House of Anansi Press.

Lilburn, Tim (Ed.). (2002). *Thinking and singing: Poetry and the practice of philosophy*. Toronto: Cormorant.

Loy, David (1990). *A Buddhist response*. A paper presented to the Invitational Conference on Derrida and Negative Theology, at the Calgary Institute for the Humanities, University of Calgary, AB.

Mazzei, Lisa A. (2007). *Inhabited silence in qualitative research: Putting poststructual theory to work*. New York: Peter Lang.

Nisker, Wes (1986). John Cage and the music of sound. *Inquirying Mind 3*(2), 4–5.

O'Reilley, Mary Rose (1998). *Radical presence: Teaching as contemplative practice*. Portsmouth, NH: Boynton/Cook Publishers.

Packer, Toni (2007). *The silent question: Meditating in the stillness of not-knowing*. Boston, MA: Shambhala.

Palmer, Parker (1998). *The courage to teach: Exploring the inner landscape of a teacher's life*. San Francisco, CA: Jossey-Bass.

Prendergast, John, J., & Bradford G. Kenneth, (2007). Toward an Embodied Nonduality: Introductory Remarks. In John J. Prendergast & G. Kenneth Bradford (Eds), *Listening from the heart of silence* (pp. 1–34). St. Paul, MN: Paragon House.

Picard, Max (1948/2002). *The world of silence*. Wichita, KS: Eighth Day Press.

Pinar, William. (2005). "A lingering note": An introduction to the collected works of Ted T. Aoki. In W. Pinar & R. Irwin (Eds), *Curriculum in a new key:*

The collected works of Ted T. Aoki (pp. 1–85). Mahwah, MJ: Lawrence Erlbaum Associates Inc.

Peterkiewicz, Jerzy (1970). *The other side of silence: The Poet at the limits of language.* London: Oxford University Press.

Rich, Adrienne (2001). *Arts of the possible: Essays and conversations.* New York: W. W. Norton.

Sardello, Robert (2008). *Silence: The Mystery of wholeness.* Berkeley, CA: North Atlantic Books.

Sims, Stuart (2007). *Manifesto for silence: Confronting the politics and culture of noise.* Edinburgh: Edinburgh University Press.

Smith, David (1999). *Pedagon: Interdisciplinary essays in the human sciences, pedagogy and culture.* New York: Peter Lang.

Snyder, Gary (1995). *A place in space: Ethics, aesthetics and watersheds.* New York: Counterpoint.

Sontag, Susan (1969). *Styles of radical will.* New York: Farrar, Straus & Giroux.

Warland, Betsy (2008). Editor's note. In Betsy Warland (Ed.), *Silences in teaching and learning* (pp. 15–16). Gatineau, QC: Gauvin Press.

10
Hear I Meet the Silence:
The Wise Pedagogue

Cheryl Lossie

> There is a way between voice and presence
> where information flows.
> In disciplined silence it opens.
> With wandering talk it closes.
>
> (Rumi, translated by Barks, with Moyne,
Arberry, and Nicholson, 1995, p. 32)

I woke up on the morning of my last classes for the semester knowing I had to do something differently. At the beginning of the week, I had gone into the classroom feeling overwhelmed—and it showed. I was trying frantically to cram in everything I thought the students had to know before we parted ways at the end of the week. I was babbling, really. I simply could not find one point of focus. Reflecting on that moment of pedagogical floundering, I knew something needed to change. And so, as I inhaled deeply and greeted the morning, I began to reflect on where I'd become so lost and to imagine what I could do differently—much differently.

I could see that I had prepared my lessons days before, so there really was no need for this chaos and fretting. Even so, I was torn between shoveling in the last of the information and doing something else. And while I was craving it, I did not even know what that something else might be. I could not stand the stress running through my mind and body any longer. I realized I had to slow my pace—to simply accept that this last class was all I had. I resisted the impulse to dash. I gave myself room to breathe. To clear out the clutter, the noise, in my mind. I took twenty minutes for t'ai chi. Stilling. Grounding. Breathing. Stretching. Moving mindfully, slowly letting my body ride the gentle ebb and flow of my breath. In my determination to find that different way, that something else, I took thirty more minutes for meditation. Calming. Slowing. Sinking deeper into the stillness. The place where the noise begins to quiet.

As I drove to the university, I easily found the words I wanted to share. My body settled into the way I wanted to be. It all just popped into my head, as they say, as if "out of nowhere." I laughed out loud in gratitude for this Voice finding me, just in the nick of time to which, amazingly, that still small Voice inside replied: "I'm always here. It's just that today you gave me some space to speak, and you were still enough to hear."

Giving space to speak and being still enough to hear. I believe the first time I met Silence was in a community-building circle. We actually started with three minutes of silence, or so it was called. Although no words were spoken, my world was anything but silent. I could hear an incessant chatter in my head: "I'm scared. Why am I scared? What's going to happen? What did I get myself into? What will they think of me? What will I think of them? I wonder if the person sitting next to me can hear my heart pounding, my nervous gulping?" Breathing—I did a lot of that in those circles. Deep breathing. It helped calm the noise in the silence. Somehow it kept me grounded—in my chair. And so we waited for someone to dare to speak out of the silence. That was one of the guidelines: to speak only when you're moved to speak. And, conversely, to not speak when you're not moved to. Eventually someone would bring voice into the circle, sharing a story, a fear, or a frustration. And we would begin our work with the dance between voice and silence.

In this essay I examine the space of silence as one of tremendous possibility for teaching. I look for the source of my craving—that "something different"—by following a trail of memories and questions, starting with the work of M. Scott Peck, who argues for the importance of listening to explore the notion that in "hearing" we might meet the silence. I then look to a series of word patterns and a favorite definition of feminism which eventually helps me see how embracing silence can inform my teaching.

Reflecting on silence brings me back to memories of community-building circles and M. Scott Peck's (1994, 1987) work. He said that community building has four stages: pseudocommunity, chaos, emptying, and community. Pseudocommunity is easily recognized. It's water-fountain conversation, polite, surface. Once you get a real look at it, though, you realize it's the stage where we show our masks—the ones we hide behind. The second stage he called chaos. That's when we just get sick and tired of playing pretend and start challenging each other—arguing, cajoling, criticizing, and trying to fix, heal, and convert. Chaos is not a pretty scene. And, for the purpose of this discussion, chaos can be seen and felt in words *and* in silences—words imposed and silences imposed—words not carefully chosen and silences not carefully chosen. Loud words. Unkind words. Judging words. Scared words. Words. Words. Words. Often not leaving room for others to speak. No spaces. No room for some voices to chime in. No room for even a whisper. For me, chaos is frightening and generally noisy. Even when not noisy in the circle, noisy in my head. It often makes me want to run. But another of the guidelines is to hang in there. And so I do, by staying firmly planted in my chair and breathing, when I remember to, breathing. Peck said that chaos creates an opportunity for movement—movement in the decision to move backward to a more organized form of pseudocommunity, or, for the courageous, to move forward into the next stage—emptying. Emptying is so hard to define. It's amorphous. It has no edges. It clearly falls into that category of "you just had to be there." During this stage we—each person sitting in the circle—begin to put down our notions, our expectations, our judgments—all those things that keep us from being in community with this particular group of people. In essence, we toss our masks into the center of this growing safe container. There is a clear energy shift during this stage—a movement from the raucous, often rapid-fire voice of chaos, to a slower pace. Spaces actually start occurring between words, between speakers, between my thoughts. It becomes easier to breathe. I feel less afraid. And here I meet the Silence. (Note to self and reader: I felt the impulse to write "hear" I meet the silence, immediately caught the "error," but then decided to listen—and so I will follow that prompting.) And *hear I meet the Silence*. I hear quiet in my head. I hear quiet in the circle. I hear my breath, and it's almost as if I can hear the breath of the circle. It's slow. I hear my heart. I hear the heart of those sitting with me and hear I meet Presence. Silence leads me to Presence. Presence—fully being with you, opening the door to Listening—real Listening. And from this point forward, when someone speaks, including me, I can clearly hear the Voice. Because we have now moved to what Peck called the fourth stage—community—even more amorphous than emptying, because it seems that this stage just suddenly, and with no effort and no noise, morphs into the stage of unity. This place where we can feel, and see, and hear all of our unique distinct differences in the wholeness of this circle. This place where we can clearly meet and hear each other's voices—where we listen. Unity amidst diversity and diversity amidst unity.

So what? So what does community building have to do with finding my Voice on the last day of a semester? When I'm looking for answers, I often look to related words and their meanings.

I love words. I love to trip around in the paths they lead me through. Sometimes very spiraling, labyrinthical, yet always leading, always inviting me to hear not only their individual voices, but also the harmonious choir they sing together. Being so, I found myself visiting with each one, leaning in to listen—to hear.

```
voice
silence    sound
           still       vibrate
                       quiet      speak
                                  hear       mouth
                                             ear

                                  words
                       attend     listen

           presence
space      absence
                       yin
                       yang       passive
                                  active     oppose
                                             fuse
```

And, again, I ask, so what? What do these seemingly opposite words have to say about the tension I was feeling on the last day of classes? Thinking of dueling dualities always leads to my next favorite path: feminism. Feminism has so many facets and dimensions. I like to spend time with its teachings when I have questions. One is a statement by Mary Pellauer (1985) that has always appealed to me: "Feminism insists upon a commitment to listening with open ears to women's experiences [and I would add—all experiences] in order to reformulate our actions and thoughts" (p. 34). "A commitment"... "A commitment to listening"... "listening with open ears"... "listening with open ears to women's" [to all experiences]. And why? "... in order to reformulate our actions and thoughts." I love that.

And so it seems to me that:

Space + Stillness = the place where Voice and Silence meet and join
Therein lies the paradox
Voice and Silence being separate unique entities and blended
at the same time

Space/Making Room + Stillness opens the door to Silence
Silence leads us to Presence
the place where I Attend
to You
and Me
Presence
the place where I am not away from you or me
the place where I am really Listening
to Voice
Space + Stillness = the place where speaking and hearing meet
where Silence and Voice fuse, even to the point of exchanging places
and if I sit Still long enough
and Breathe
keep Breathing
the place where Unity and Diversity blend

Many in the West are familiar with the concept of yin and yang in Eastern thought. "Yin is the feminine principle of the two opposing cosmic forces into which creative energy divides and whose fusion in physical matter brings the phenomenal world into being, and is characterized by passivity," among other qualities; whereas "yang, the masculine principle, is characterized by activity," among other quali-ties...and "each containing a 'seed' of the other" (Simpson, Weiner, and Oxford University Press, 1989). Might Silence and Voice be seen as two opposing forces—the yin and yang? The passivity and activity? The stillness and the motion? And might each truly contain a seed of the other? And might the opposition between the two create resistance, hostility, obstacles? Fighting for control, dominance.

This type of tension was indeed what I felt on my last week of the semester, and indeed what I have experienced in the community build-ing circles. In both cases, the voices: noisy, chaotic, overwhelming, frantic, stressed, not focused, fearful, crowding in, crowding out. And also, in both cases, the shift. I don't know what causes the shift though. Maybe it's simply that when one remembers to breathe (or is it gasping for air?), Grace is able to slip through the crack, riding in on the breath. And in doing so, she stretches, and we feel that space. And in that space, we recognize the need to create more room. And so we keep breathing and stretching—slowly, mindfully, moving into Presence. Or maybe it's just that we weary of the pressure, resistance, hostility, and obstacles. We weary of holding our breath. And so we sit down and breathe—or we stand still and slowly stretch. And at that point, without the clutter, the obstacles, the resistance, we hear the Voice that slipped through the space, carried on the gentle wave of the breath, say, "I am always here. It's just that you finally gave me some space to speak, and you were still enough to hear." Hear I meet the Silence—the Wise Pedagogue.

And so I think what happens is that life infuses our world with two opposing cosmic forces: silence and voice. Ultimately, their goal is to fuse and "bring the phenomenal world into being." Not knowing that, or maybe forgetting, they grapple for control, driven by what the ecofeminist calls the hierarchical dualisms that undergird dominance (Adams, 1993; Plumwood, 1986). Some dualities related to this conversation are: sound–stillness, vibration–motionless, speaking–hearing, mouth–ear, voiced–muted, yang–yin, oppose–fuse, absence–presence. Ecofeminism (Adams, 1993) asks us to revisit the way we look at, and live with, these dualities. And instead of seeing them as either/or, better/worse, higher/lower scenarios, to embrace them as both/and, equal/mutual, to transform the consciousness of these hierarchies of domination into a consciousness that sees them as mutually interdependent, integrating the dualities.

I look at it this way: for a while silence and voice come together as opposing forces—dualities fighting for domination—and surely we have been living through times where voice has been on top. But somewhere along the line, when one of them is either gasping for breath or plain old sick and tired and so sits down or stands still, breathes and stretches, Grace slips in and creates some space, and then more space, and more space. And that space becomes the container, the inspiration, for the alchemical fusion of the two forces. In that fusion, the silence begins to Vibrate and raises Voice and the voice becomes Still and receives the Silence. And even if only for a brief moment, allows us to see the cosmos as my dictionary defines it: "the world as an embodiment of order and harmony (as distinguished from *chaos*)" (Barnhart, 1967, p.274). In other words, unity amidst diversity and diversity amidst unity—opposing forces fused and blended into mutual interdependency.

So what, I kept asking? So what? How do all of the pieces fit together? Where might my trail of questions be leading me? Throughout these reflections, I've asked myself how the Pedagogue of Silence can not only inform that frantic moment of the past on my last day of classes, but also enlighten all of my future teaching. At a National Communication Association Convention, Rod Troester (2010), a Professor at Penn State University Erie asked a question about his research topic that I thought was relevant to all of our teaching: "Why should I care about this as a teacher and as a scholar?" That led me to a search for those in the wider community who are heralds for the Wise Teacher Silence. Who else is writing about silence and presence, and how might we juxtapose their sentiments to influence our classrooms? It was the work of Carol R. Rodgers and Miriam B. Raider-Roth (2006) in their article, "Presence in Teaching" that brought the final piece. Finding their research on the tail end of writing this essay shed light on the struggle with which I was grappling. They explain that their work "seeks to address the current educational climate that sees teaching as a check list of behaviors, dispositions, measures, and standards, and to articulate the essential but elusive aspect of teaching we call presence" (p. 265). It was, in particular, two contrasting statements in their article that brought it together for me. The first speaks of the shadow side: "The forces that militate against presence are daunting. These include: a national and state level push to 'cover' set amounts of material within predetermined time frames at each grade level, causing teachers to 'cover' material regardless of whether students learn it..." (p. 283); while the second statement speaks to the light side, an explanation of why it is worth facing the forces that push against presence:

> The experience of presence is one most will recognize, particularly from their experiences as learners. Many of us have come across a teacher who, with the metaphorical touch of a finger, could give us exactly what we needed, neither more nor less, exactly when we needed it. A teacher who was present to, who could apprehend, make sense of and respond skillfully to, our needs, strengths and experiences as learners. From the learner's point of view the moment is one of recognition, of feeling seen and understood, not just emotionally but cognitively, physically and even spiritually. (p. 267)

Their words helped me to understand my quandary. On that last day of classes I was feeling a struggle between shoveling in the last bit of information and something else—something that I couldn't see yet, but that I knew was there. And by daring to be with and breathe through the struggle and listen for the guidance in the Silence, I was eventually able to hear that something else was Presence. By going back into my memory to the first time I met Silence in a community-building circle, recalling my experience with the dance between Voice and Silence, I remembered my first introduction to Presence and the power of Listening. And, by reflecting on those moments in the circle, I was reminded that the chaos serves to push me to empty of all that is standing in the way of me hearing—hearing my own inner voice and the voices of those around me, and that the circle creates the space to hold those tensions while I slow down long enough to hear the Voice in the Silence. Those memories then led me to Pellauer's reminder that "feminism insists upon a commitment to listening with open ears…in order to reformulate our actions and thoughts" (p. 34), which prompted me to keep asking what exactly was I needing to reformulate? That's when the ecofeminist voices popped in to remind me of the dueling hierarchical dualities—voice and silence, yang and yin—and on that last day of classes the seeming dualities—covering content and presence. I clearly saw that in my thoughts the compulsion to cover content had been dominating so much that the practice of presence had been snuffed out—silenced. I finally heard that what I am called to reformulate in my thoughts and actions is to fuse and blend what I had perceived as opposing forces into mutual interdependency. It is the braiding of the Content of our subject matter and Presence—not the resistance or the struggle between the two—but the braiding, the honoring of their interdependence, the integrating of the dualities that allows for the learning process. As Rodgers and Raider-Roth (2006) said: "[The experience of presence] is a feeling of being safe, where one is drawn to risk because of the discoveries it might reveal; it is the excitement of discovering one's self in the context of the larger world" (p. 267). Why is that so important? Because, they say, "…presence offers us a moral imperative, a psychological stance and an intellectual trajectory that can root the world of teaching and learning in its essential purpose, the creation of a just and democratic society" (p. 284).

And so what exactly did the Wise Pedagogue of Silence reveal to me on that last day? I simply plainly heard that I wanted to be present with my students. To look each and every one of them in their eyes and soak up their individual, unique, diverse magnificence. I wanted to acknowledge how these young women and men had touched my life for the last 16 weeks. I wanted to embrace our human moment together, giving that connection the same value I had given to the course information all semester. And so that is what I did. Rather than burst into the room in a mad dash to cover an inordinate amount of information while barely noticing the students in the room, I breathed. I was mindful of my every step, word, gesture. I let go of the voluminous details that I compulsively thought I had to cover, and instead I reviewed the basic information they needed to go into the final. I encouraged them to take what they had learned throughout the semester to help them to not only raise Voice in their worlds, but also to Listen to those in their worlds. And throughout our entire last hour together, I stayed ever Present with my breath, which allowed me to stay vigilantly present with each one of them, making certain to look each one of them in their eyes, impressing the memory of their faces, which contained the stories of their lives, in my mind and heart. For more than ever, I knew that spending time with Silence had led me to Presence. And that Silence, the Wise Teacher, reminded me that if I do not value the human connection in the classroom as much as I value the content material, I will always be stressed out. For that stress, that chaos, is just a sign that I have tuned out and silenced the voice that is my Wise Pedagogue—the Voice that reminds me that it is in honoring our human connections during the learning journey, blended with the content material, that the information begins to matter. And dare I never forget that embracing presence as part of the learning experience is ultimately to, as Rodgers and Raider-Roth (2006) said, "...root the world of teaching and learning in...the creation of a just and democratic society."

That is my call. So now you might ask yourself: Why should you care about this as a teacher and a scholar? What does listening with open ears call you to reformulate in your actions and thoughts—in your classrooms and in your life? How can Voice, Silence, Presence, and Listening inform your personal pedagogy? And as we continually work for a just and democratic society, can we collectively remember to be still and listen for the humble yet empowering voice of the Wise Pedagogue of Silence? On that day, I have no doubt we will hear it say, "I have always been here. You just gave me space to speak, and you were still enough to hear." Hear we meet the Silence.

References

Adams, Carol J. (Ed.). (1993). *Ecofeminism and the sacred*. New York: Continuum.

Barks, Coleman (Trans.) with John Moyne, A. J. Arberry & Reynold Nicholson (1995). *The essential Rumi*. Edison, NY: HarperCollins.

Barnhart, C.L. (Ed.) (1967). *The American college dictionary*. New York: Random House.

Peck, M. Scott (1987). *The different drum: Community-making and peace*. New York: Simon & Schuster.

Peck, M. Scott (1994). *A world waiting to be born: Rediscovering civility*. New York: Bantam Books.

Pellauer, Mary D. (1985) Moral callousness and moral sensitivity. In Barbara H. Andolsen, Christine E. Gudorf, & Mary D. Pellauer (Eds), *Women's consciousness, women's conscience: A reader in feminist ethics*. Minneapolis, MN: Winston Press, pp. 33–50.

Plumwood, Val (1986). Critical review. Ecofeminism: An overview and discussion of positions and arguments. *Australasian Journal of Philosophy*, 64: 120–138.

Rodgers, Carol R. & Raider-Roth, Miriam B. (2006). Presence in teaching. *Teachers & Teaching: Theory & Practice*, 12 (3): 265–287.

Simpson, John A., Weiner, Edmund S.C., & Oxford University Press. (1989). *The Oxford English dictionary* (2nd edn). Oxford/New York: Clarendon Press/Oxford University Press.

Troester, Rod (2010). *The civility solution to the bully problem in organizations: Creating a positive communication climate.* Paper presented at the National Communication Association Convention, San Francisco, CA, November 2010.

11
The US Day of Silence: Sexualities, Silences, and the Will to Unsay in the Age of Empire

Gust A. Yep and Susan B. Shimanoff

> Silence, in all its diverse forms, contributes to the creation of our social realities, from the mundane micro-level practices of our everyday expressions to the structuring of our macro-level institutions and back again.
>
> (Robin Patric Clair, 1998, p. 24)

> The notion of silence has long been a trope in liberation and social justice movements in the United States, including feminist, lesbian/gay/bisexual/transgender, and civil rights and antiracist struggles and movements of people of color.
>
> (Patti Duncan, 2004, p. 7)

As one of the largest student-led activist actions in the United States, the Day of Silence (US DOS) was established in 1996 to call attention to the quotidian and ubiquitous acts of violence committed against lesbian, gay, bisexual, transgender, and queer (LGBTQ) individuals in this country. As two educators who are deeply committed to social justice and inhabit distinct social locations, we decided to participate in the US DOS in an effort to reflect on the complexities surrounding the politics of silence. Using a combination of personal narrative, conventional academic writing, and dialogue, we examine and reflect on the multiple meanings of silence and their potential for social change.[1] To accomplish this, our essay is divided into five sections.[2] The first, "Exploring the complexities of silence," examines the meanings of silence in LGBTQ communities and proposes a "queer methodology" (Halberstam, 1998, p. 10) for this examination. The second, "Historicizing silence: A brief history of the US day of silence" provides an historical context

139

for this yearly event. In "Reflecting aloud," our third section, we draw on our own biographies and histories to make sense of the day. In the fourth section, "Conversing about silences and voice," we engage in dialogue to discuss the complex relationship between silence and voice, presence and absence, agency and resistance, oppression and liberation. In the final section, "Continuing our exploration," we pose a number of questions to continue with the investigation of the complexities of silence, particularly in our current era of globalization and empire.

Exploring the complexities of silence

Silence is an extremely complex communication phenomenon (Achino-Loeb, 2006; Clair, 1998; Glenn, 2004; Jaworski, 1993; Kurzon, 1995). To understand its complexities, Robin Clair (1998) identifies four approaches used by researchers: literal, epistemological, ontological, and ideological. Literal perspectives view silence as the space between utterances and how it functions in interaction (e.g. silent treatment, shared understanding). This approach is the most prevalent in communication research. Epistemological perspectives view silence as knowledge or experience that cannot be readily expressed or articulated. They may focus on artistic expressions to describe experiences that everyday language cannot adequately capture. Ontological perspectives focus on the "silence of being" and the "silence of life" (Clair, 1998, p. 6), which are presumed to instill feelings of awe, inspiration, and amazement. They highlight the existential dimensions of silence. Finally, ideological perspectives view silence as powerful manifestations of oppression as well as possible means of resistance and emancipation. They recognize the power of silence by exploring its micro- and macro-level practices.

In her discussion of the relationship between language and silence, Clair (1998) writes, "A dynamic relationship exists that allows communication to both express and at times silence individuals, issues, and interests. There also exists the possibility for silence to sequester as well as express experience" (p. 38). In other words, communication can be silencing and silence communicates. When communication is silencing, power relations are distorted, social inequities are disguised, and acts of resistance are taken away. For example, the pervasiveness of heteronormativity in the USA and numerous other cultures produces and perpetuates a powerful form of silencing of sexual and gender minorities including LGBTQ individuals (Yep, 2003). But this silencing is rarely complete as individuals and groups find creative ways to expose unequal power relations and unjust social arrangements. Silenced groups, in this instance, might creatively and skillfully use silence to communicate resistance. In fact, as an expressive and embodied human activity, silence communicates a wide range of experiences, social relations, and cultural conditions—ranging from negative to positive, individual to collective, disempowerment to empowerment.

In the USA, LGBTQ groups have had a complex history of, and with, silence. From "the love that dares not speak its name," the shame and stigma of the closet, the "silence=death" slogan during the early era of the HIV/AIDS epidemic to the "don't ask, don't tell" policy that existed for many years in the US military, LGBTQ individuals have experienced silence as oppressing, repressing, undermining, erasing, and annihilating. Given this history, it is not surprising that the rhetoric of the US LGBTQ movement has celebrated voice and speech. According to this rhetoric, the closet, for example, has been viewed as a "life-shaping" social pattern that involves fashioning a public life to hide—and silence—one's non-heteronormative sexuality, which must be abandoned and replaced by public acts of disclosure (Seidman, 2002, p. 8). Although "coming out" is connected to dynamics of privilege associated with whiteness, race, social class, gender, and nation (Yep, 2009), it has been largely elevated as the vehicle to achieve visibility, equality, and social legitimacy. In this sense, silence has been equated with sexual oppression and speech with sexual liberation.

In addition, the rhetoric of US sexual liberation, with its language of identity, desire, community, subjectivity, agency, and freedom, has had a global reach (Adam, Duyvendak, and Krouwel, 1999). Observing the rapid globalization of these ideas, Dennis Altman (2001) writes, "increasingly the institutions and ideologies which link sex and politics are themselves being globalized, as concerns around gender, sexuality, and the body play a central role in the construction of international political, social, and economic regimes" (p. 9). US neoliberal ideologies and politics of a free-market economy, privatization, profit, and the vigorous push for market expansion have resulted in the massive commodification of sexual identities for consumption in the global marketplace (Yep and Elia, 2012). This US move in the global stage is what Anna Agathangelou and her colleagues (2008, p. 138) call a "moment of intensified empire-building." In the process, a hegemonic construction of social equality and sexual freedom might become inextricably connected to the language of voice and speech.

However, the view of silence as antithetical to the liberation of LGBTQ people, fails to recognize the multitude of forms and meanings that silence may take. Patti Duncan elaborates,

There are qualitative distinctions between being silent and being *silenced*. Similarly, as I have suggested, it is a quite different process to be silent than it is to be unheard. One may speak and simply not be listened to, understood, or taken seriously .... Hence, we might ask, How effective are "speaking out," "finding a voice," "breaking silence," and "coming out" as liberatory rhetoric and political acts when such notions rely on the very discursive practices through which social and political domination occurs?

(2004, pp. 13–14, original emphasis)

This more nuanced perspective on silence suggests that it is not necessarily or exclusively oppressive or liberatory; it can be both depending on the discursive, material, historical, and geopolitical contexts in which it is deployed (Achino-Loeb, 2006). The US DOS is an important example of this deployment.

To explore the intricacies of silence in the US DOS that we participated in, we make use of personal narratives and dialogue, informed by our own biographies and histories, for this undertaking. This combination of approaches might be aptly characterized, in Judith Halberstam's (1998, p. 10) terms, as a "queer methodology," that is, "a political positioning that infuses research processes with ethical considerations" (Browne and Nash, 2010, p. 12).

Such a methodology is, according to Susy Zepeda, useful in research "particularly when there is a critical engagement of ... tensions via images, narratives, and representations that work against homogenizing histories, sexualities, violences, and instead center on honoring and building from differences and complexities" (2009, p. 622). This methodology is sufficiently sensitive and supple to respond to the nuances of silence as we navigate the worlds of thought and our own "archive of feelings," which Ann Cvetkovich (2003) defines as "an exploration of cultural [events such as the US DOS] as repositories of feelings and emotions, which are encoded not only in the content of the [events] themselves but in the practices that surround their production and reception" (p. 7). Before we engage in this exploration, we provide a brief history of the event.

Historicizing silence: A brief history of the US day of silence

The origins of the US DOS began in 1996 with the actions of a single woman inviting others to join her. Growing out of a history paper on nonviolent protests and her membership of the Lesbian, Gay, and

Bisexual Union at the University of Virginia, Maria Pulzetti started the first US DOS in 1996, because she "knew that if we held panel discussions and events like that, the only people who would come would be the people who already were fairly aware. I also wanted the event to involve straight allies" (quoted in Greene, n.d.). In the following year, her partner Jessie Gilliam joined her to make it a national event, growing from one university to 200 (Day of Silence, 2008c) by using the only resource they had beyond themselves—the internet—to send out e-mails to every LGBTQ college list they could find. Gilliam noted "unlike events such as rallies, people who did the Day of Silence were everywhere" and as a result of the support she observed, she "felt a lot more able to talk and be open in classes, knowing that I had allies surrounding me" (quoted in Greene, n.d.). *The Cavalier Daily*, the student newspaper of the University of Virginia, quoted Pulzetti's description of what motivated her:

> By far the most striking evidence of homophobia in my college community was the silence imposed on LGBT issues. Few students and fewer faculty members were out; the administration did not provide any resources to LGBT students; the Greek-dominated social scene did not acknowledge the existence of options other than heterosexuality. I had never before felt so invisible.
>
> (quoted in Gullapalli, 2000)

In 2001, the GLSEN (Gay, Lesbian and Straight Educational Network) became the national sponsor of the event (Day of Silence, 2008b). Participation has grown from about 150 students at one university to hundreds of thousands (Day of Silence, 2008c; GLSEN, 2008a).

Some critics have complained that silence is insufficient to bring about real change (Lee, 2004), but the US DOS is not completely "silent." Participants are encouraged to tell others about the day before it occurs and to distribute cards that explain the "silence." For the 12th US DOS in 2008, GLSEN recommended the following wording for the cards:

> I am participating in the Day of Silence (DOS), a national youth movement bringing attention to the silence faced by lesbian, gay, bisexual and transgender people and their allies. My deliberate silence echoes that silence, which is caused by anti-LGBT name-calling, bullying and harassment. This year's DOS is held in memory of Lawrence King, a 15 year-old student who was killed in school because of his sexual orientation and gender expression. I believe

that ending the silence is the first step toward building awareness and making a commitment to address these injustices. Think about the voices you are not hearing today.

(Day of Silence, 2008a)

The organizers see the event as a positive educational experience (Day of Silence, 2008d). In support of that objective, GLSEN (2008b) provides optional curricular materials for the US DOS and encourages "Breaking the Silence" events. These events take many forms (e.g. rallies, parties, speak-outs, dances, performances) with a common objective "to bring communities together to celebrate, augment, and share the impact of the Day of Silence" (GLSEN, n.d.). Clearly, the deliberative silence of the event is just a beginning in ongoing dialogues and actions.

On Friday, 25 April 2008, students from more than 7500 middle- and high-schools and 1000 universities (GLSEN, 2008a) participated in the 12th US DOS. Our personal reflections in this chapter are from our participation on this day.

Reflecting aloud

Susan's day of silence

In preparation for the US DOS, I had conversations I ordinarily would have had that day on an earlier day, I moved an appointment, and I sent out an e-mail telling colleagues about my participation. When I awoke on 25 April, I began the day by being mindful of my goal of spending the day in silence. But within fifteen minutes, I heard myself greet Alex, the family dog. I stopped before I completed the greeting, heartsick. How could I forget already?! If I couldn't be silent for even fifteen minutes, how was I going to make it through the day? I wanted to quit, but I knew members of LGBTQ communities often didn't have the option of quitting. Okay, I had made a mistake. I re-dedicated myself to follow through with the spirit of the day. I proceeded to get ready for work, resolved to speak no more.

Within an hour of my resolution, I had already spoken aloud to Alex two more times and even to myself. Now I felt demoralized. Didn't I care? How could I make so many mistakes in such a short period of time? Was I even thinking? Then another kind of self-reflection interrupted my debilitating guilt. This voice said something like: "Okay, you blew it. But remember that you have more than fifty years of being identified as a white, middle class, heterosexual woman. And you have a PhD. You have a lot of practice in the privilege of speaking your mind. You are not very schooled in monitoring your speech. How privileged is it to be sniffling over such trivial discourse?" I thought about how my participation in this political silence was attuning me to my privilege of speech and I was humbled.

As I walked to my car, carrying more food than I should reasonably eat in one day and more reading than I could possibly complete in the day's silence, so I wouldn't have to talk, I thought about how my anxiety led to over preparation. As strangers approached me, I looked down hoping they wouldn't speak to me. I didn't want to be rude or break my commitment, yet again. Suddenly, I rushed back into the house. I realized I needed something to give to people, when I didn't speak to them. I speedily prepared labels that read, "Day of Silence" and included the URL for more information. Although frustrated with the amount of time and energy all this was consuming, I was also embarrassed by my irritation over these expenditures, minuscule in comparison to that experienced by LGBTQ communities, and I was humbled.

I picked up the morning's newspaper and saw the headline: "Effort Heats Up to Ban Same-Sex Marriage." And I felt angry. How can people peddle hatred as righteousness?! I wondered what it feels like for LGBTQ communities to repeatedly pick up a newspaper, watch television, read a book, and overhear or participate in conversations, where they learn someone hates them without even knowing them, and I was humbled.

I made it to my office, already prepared for my silence, and I was largely left alone. I found it hard not to answer the phone. As I overheard conversations all around me, I felt left out—what were other people learning that I was not? What fun were they having? What plans were they making without me? I wondered how often members of LGBTQ communities feel left out, and I was humbled.

When I arrived home, not talking with my family made me feel like an outsider. But they knew my silence was temporary and they valued its intention. I knew that for many members of LGBTQ communities their silence was neither temporary nor valued. Following dinner, as I watched my son play a game, my husband walked in and told us Alex, our family dog of thirteen years had died; that she was in the backyard in the grass. This seemed inconceivable. She had been fine at dinner, happily eating a full meal and then going outside as she had done so many nights before. We rushed out to see her. For the first time, I purposefully broke my silence. We talked and cried together for hours. I told my son that the first time I broke my silence was to greet Alex. "Good, I'm glad you did that," he said.

For a while, I felt like I should not finish writing my reflection, as it seemed so trivial in light of Alex's death. But then I thought about the many tragic consequences of homophobia, one of which is not sharing daily occurrences and significant events with loved ones. I knew my privilege made it easier for me to engage in such speech, and I was deeply humbled. The words of the morning, which I had once thought of as mistakes, were now gifts of immeasurable value and in the context of the US DOS, additional reminders of the importance of speaking out against oppressive silencing.

Gust's day of marking silence

When I picked up my copy of the *Bay Area Reporter*, a weekly paper for the San Francisco LGBTQ communities, and read a front page article titled, "Pink is in for Day of Silence" (Hemmelgarn, 2008, p. 1), I was reminded of Susan's e-mail stating her intention to observe this day of silence. It was the evening before Friday, 25 April 2008—the official US DOS day. I felt unprepared and frustrated with myself. How could I have forgotten this day? In a moment of honesty, I found myself thinking, "I must have repressed it!" The thought had a degree of resonance and veracity that struck me.

Why would I repress an event that calls attention to LGBTQ bullying and harassment in this country? As a teenager, I was bullied and harassed by some of my high school classmates. It probably had less to do with my sexual identity than my utter lack of interest in performing teenage male hypermasculinity. Instead of displaying interest—either real or feigned—in competitive sports participation, I was genuinely drawn to the math, literature, psychology, journalism, and fine arts clubs and student government activities. I preferred reading and solving math problems to playing soccer. In other words, I was a nerd and nerds get disciplined by bullying and harassment. But as a nerd, I also had power: Classmates often needed my help with schoolwork and they were often conscious about not making me angry. Perhaps my forgetting was related to residual feelings about being bullied and harassed in high school.

As I reviewed my calendar that evening, trying to decide whether to participate in the US DOS, a flood of feelings gave me the answer I was seeking. I was, and still am, very ambivalent about purposefully subjecting myself to silence when I am, in many ways, silenced in this culture. Although my profession gives me a platform to speak and be heard, my identities as a queer-identified person of color often render me invisible or unimportant in a number of settings. Why would I want to be silent on this day when I often already feel silenced in the social world? In spite of this imposed silence, in other situations, I find silence to be a safe haven for me—calm, still, reflective, comforting, and full of possibilities. How can I meaningfully participate in this event without compromising my feelings of discomfort and uneasiness? As I was doing my routine bedtime reading, I decided to participate in the event.

I intended to be more mindful about silence the following day to allow silence to "speak to me." Besides keeping my appointments and meetings for the day, I would try to be silent and pay attention to what feelings, thoughts, and sensations emerged. I committed to live in my head as well as in my heart and body, challenging my sense of self as someone who primarily responds to the world with thoughts. I promised myself that whatever came up, I would stay with it, instead of distracting myself with something else. I decided to speak in my appointments and meetings and to tell everyone about the event. I imagined saying to people this rehearsed line, "I want to tell you that today is the US DOS. It calls attention to anti-LGBTQ violence everywhere and I am using my voice to let you know about this yearly event."

I woke up listening to the news and quickly shut off my radio. I reminded myself to turn inward. I gave Dino, my sweet Pomeranian companion, his "good morning" hug without saying a word. He gave me a kiss and let me pet him before his breakfast. I wanted to turn the radio back on but resisted. As I was having breakfast, I wanted to read the morning paper but decided to just focus on my eating. I normally read when I am eating. My chewing seemed loud, obnoxious, and ritualistic. I was feeling anxious and uncomfortable. "Stay with it," I told myself. The thought that surfaced, "You ignore your inner world by focusing on external things," was not particularly reassuring at that moment. Slowly, I started to taste my morning oatmeal like I have never done before: its texture, flavors, smell, and warmth. Even my English Breakfast tea felt more soothing. I worked at home before heading out and began to feel a sense of peace and tranquility.

Once I left the house, countless external factors competed for my attention: the traffic and impolite drivers ("don't people signal any more?"), garbage on the street ("why aren't people using a garbage can?"), an elderly Asian woman walking her dog ("what kind of dog is that?"), another Asian woman carrying her groceries and talking to a little boy ("is that her son?"). When I got to the restaurant for lunch, I told the server about the day before ordering. She looked perplexed but politely replied, "OK." I wanted to say more but stopped myself because she was very busy. The silence I experienced earlier felt very different than the silencing I just did to myself. Then I went to my first meeting, which lasted three hours. Besides telling people about the US DOS, the meeting felt like any other—easy and comfortable. One of my colleagues knew about the day but was not observing it. The rest of my meetings were very similar; people were receptive and I felt surrounded by allies. At the end of my day on campus, I felt fortunate to be a member of my university community. As I drove home, I returned to my silence and took in the magnificent views of the city. "I am glad to be living in beautiful and politically progressive San Francisco," I thought with a smile.

Dino greeted me excitedly when I got home. Continuing with my silence, I spent the rest of the evening contemplating, reflecting, and feeling immense gratitude with Dino next to me.

Conversing about silences and voice

In this section, we engage in an e-mail conversation about silence. Our dialogue was driven by two questions: (a) what does silence mean to us? and (b) what are the politics of silence?

> *Gust:* As someone who was trained in the communication discipline, I have focused a lot of my personal and professional attention to understanding voice as produced by speech. Although I haven't formally researched silence as a communication phenomenon, I have always known its power and complexities. This dialogue represents an opportunity for me to explore—however clumsy—the intricate world of silence and voice.
>
> First of all, silence, to me, is not the "constructed other" of speech and voice. That is, silence is not the opposite of articulation and certainly not the repository of all the negative attributes we want to disown (e.g. passivity, oppression, powerlessness) when we create relational dichotomies to celebrate speech in Western cultures. Speech, in this sense, is not the master category or activity that is being upheld by its shadowy and subjugated other—silence. Although the two are interrelated, silence is not speech's opposite, but rather is a different form of discourse. As such, it has its own characteristics—expressions and manifestations, modes of intelligibility, and grammar. Let's explore them.
>
> *Susan:* I value your challenge to interrogate common conceptualizations of silence as negative, as passivity, oppression, powerlessness, and I would add "ignorance" to the list. Yet I must also acknowledge that I have been both a "victim" and a "perpetrator" of such

perceptions. At times when I have used silence as a vehicle for discovery, I have been chastised for being hard to get to know or for withholding my insights. Similarly, I am embarrassed by the many times I read my students' silence as a lack of preparation or critical thinking. I have to work to remind myself that some individuals, including me, want more time to think before speaking, and do not consider it necessary to speak just to reiterate what others have said. While I embrace the desire to change how silences are viewed and used, I do not find the negative cultural associations given to me easy to transcend.

Gust: I agree with you. Ignorance is another common negative association with silence. It is also worth noting that all of these negative qualities can also be associated with speech (e.g. passive voice, oppressive language, powerless speech, ignorant articulation). However, the negative associations with silence remain powerfully inscribed in US culture. To the degree that we attach these negative meanings to silence more than to speech suggests the subjugation of silence in our cultural landscape. This is exactly the binary that I wish to move away from because in this system, silence will always be the inferior "constructed other" of voice and speech. Let's explore the complexities of silence. Silence has many forms and expressions, and the term should be more accurately used in the plural. Silence is both a verb (i.e. doing) and a noun (i.e. being). To silence is an action that might be imposed by self (e.g. self-censorship), people in our social world (e.g. groups that subjugate a person's identity and subjectivity), the culture at large (e.g. a sociocultural system that makes certain individuals and groups invisible and unintelligible), or a combination of the above. Silence is also a quality (e.g. peacefulness), state (e.g. moment of silence), place (e.g. a site in the practice of self-contemplation), and expression (e.g. to register social protest) associated with individual inner and outer worlds, social activities, and cultural events.

These multiple forms of silence occur at both individual and social levels. That is, silences are not merely personal expressions (e.g. a LGBTQ person remaining silent about his/her sexuality in a violent heteronormative world) but cultural and systemic ones as well (e.g. the lack of language for transgender individuals who do not identify with the gender binary system in Western cultures). We need to pay attention to how the individual and the structural interact to produce, maintain, and/or change silences in our culture.

Susan: I identify with your reference to self-censorship. I am painfully aware of occasions when I purposefully silenced what I wanted to say. Yet, in the reflective moment of this dialogue, I wonder if it is ever really censorship by the self alone. It seems unlikely to me that the crying, babbling infant is born desiring to censor the self and knowing how to do so. We are given explicit lessons about taboo topics and who has the right to speak, and more implicit lessons about whose words and actions are valued. For example, as a female I have received messages such as "only boys can do that," "hide your intelligence," "the full-ride debate scholarships are for males only," "girls would rather party than work on debate," "it is selfish for a woman to get a PhD, think of your husband and children," "hide your interest in gender research." It is harder for me to value my own voice when the discourse of others seeks to silence me.

Gust: Yes, self-censorship must be viewed in a larger social and cultural context. We live in a culture that upholds and perpetuates white heteropatriarchal dominance. Those of us who deviate from the nucleus of power of this system—namely, white, male, financially secure, heterosexual, able-bodied, Christian, and US American—are disciplined. I am glad that you were able to transform those painful experiences.

Your observations serve as a powerful reminder that silence must be understood in relationship to culture, history, and power. Silence means different things in different cultures. For example, Asian cultures view silence much more positively than Western societies. Similarly, some Native American cultures, such as the Blackfeet, perceive silence as deep connection among group members (Carbaugh, 2002). Given the intricate connection between culture and silence, it is critical to attend to the cultural particularities of silence and avoid the impulse to universalize current Western conceptions.

Susan: Karlyn Kohrs Campbell (1989) has noted that "for much of their history women have been prohibited from speaking, a prohibition reinforced by such powerful cultural authorities as Homer, Aristotle, and Scripture" (p. 1). Women were denied access to the podium and even to instruction in public speaking. They were considered too ignorant to be trusted with public persuasion and immoral if they tried to do so. When I studied public address in the late 1960s and early 1970s, my instructors provided no examples of women speaking, even though many women had struggled against public prejudices to gain a voice. The absences of such speeches in class appeared to be largely unnoticed by others, but for me the silence was personally invalidating. When social identities are missing from classrooms and other cultural institutions, the silence leads to judgments about who and what is valued.

Gust: Yes, that's why history is so important in understanding silence. Women were not only silenced but those who went against powerful cultural norms—and spoke up—were essentially buried in the official, hegemonic version of history. To top it all off, the silencing and erasure of women were naturalized as most students in your class did not notice their absence.

Your observations continue to point to the importance of examining silence by understanding the cultural and historical context. But your past experiences of pain and suffering also arouse feelings of anger and rage in me. Although we have been trained in the academy to bracket and contain—indeed discipline and suppress—our emotional reactions and affective life in our writing, I wonder what this new perspective on silence might look like if we incorporate our thoughts, emotions and minds as well as our bodies and hearts in this undertaking. For example, how do we feel about silence? What kind of affective experiences does silence trigger?

Susan: I experienced a roller coaster of different emotional states on the US DOS. I felt shocked to learn 2008 was the twelfth annual observance and I was learning about it just three days before; excited to be taking part in an event with such worthy goals and to join thousands in collective action; disappointed and embarrassed to behave clumsily when using a communication practice with which I had little experience; empathy and awe to glimpse temporarily and only in miniscule portions the daily oppression of members of LGBTQ communities; anger to reflect on violence directed toward LGBTQ communities; guilty to fail to meet the expectations of others; isolated to avoid encounters where I would have to explain myself or where I might violate my own commitments; intrigued to discover the lessons found in silence; and humbled to explore my own privileges and taken-for-granted assumptions.

Gust: So you have multiple feelings associated with silence. I have experienced a range of feelings about silence ranging from extremely positive (intense joy) to extremely negative (complete erasure). Do our feelings associated with silence mirror the negative meanings we attach to it to uphold the superiority of speech and voice end of the dichotomy we discussed earlier? Based on my earlier reflections about feeling silenced, this seems to be at least partially true.

Silence is intricately connected to power. As such, we cannot conceive of silence outside of power. Silence can be manifested and expressed under conditions of oppression (e.g. "to be silenced"), resistance (e.g. to refrain from engagement), and agency (e.g. to exercise the will to "unsay"). To "unsay" is an act of refusal, to push back at hegemonic forces, to fight against domination. It is a very active and powerful process. For example, the will to "unsay" has been deployed by numerous communities to fight against US ideological and economic expansion associated with empire building (Prokosch and Raymond, 2002).

I see silence as deeply political. Silence can, and has been, used to marginalize, oppress, and erase individual expression, identity, and subjectivity (e.g. silencing LGBTQ individuals so that their lives and contributions are left out of the official US cultural fabric). In fact, silence has been used to deny an individual's—or group's— existence in the social world (e.g. a transgender individual does not exist in the gender binary system upon which our thinking, vocabulary, social relations, and cultural institutions are based). But silence has also been a powerful tool for personal and collective resistance (e.g. LGBTQ persons refusing to give their names or those of other patrons in gay bars when the police routinely harassed them in the 1950s and 1960s).

Susan: I concur with your assessment of pivotal connections between silence and power, and it is this connection that I see at the center of the US DOS. While the power of heteronormative violence has silenced LGBTQ identities, perspectives and contributions, the US DOS provides an opportunity for these to be "heard" through a silence that violates expectations. It is this violation, as well as the explanations that proceed and follow the silence, that calls attention to violence that ordinarily goes unrecognized and unchallenged.

Gust: It is ironic that a group that has a long history of being silenced in US culture is using silence to increase awareness of heteronormative violence and sexual oppression. However, silence, on this day, is not simply used as a device to draw attention to these conditions but also to provide an opportunity for participants—regardless of their sexual orientation—to experience life, even if it is only for a few hours, as devalued, stigmatized, and unintelligible members of society. In this sense, silence is an intervention in the social world (i.e. to highlight sexual injustices in US culture), as well as an opportunity to experience an inner world with greater mindfulness (i.e. to focus on feeling marginalized and oppressed).

Susan: Thank you for your reminder of the multiple and powerful functions of silence in the event. Persons participating in the event have noted that observing supportive silence throughout their community increased feelings of safety and validation. The silence of resistance and agency draw attention to the silence of oppression, but this empowering silence is also paired with discourse that proceeds, accompanies, and follows the event (e.g. website postings, notices to others, cards of explanation made to distribute during the silence, press releases, curricular materials, buttons, t-shirts, "breaking the silence" after-gatherings). Here, silence and voice have a symbiotic relationship—the discourse might not be heard except for the silence that captures attention and the silence might not be understood except for the discourse.

Purposeful, physical silence also provides an opportunity to reflect on oppressive power in a way that transcends merely thinking about it. In the words of a heterosexual high school student, through the act of physical silence one begins to "to understand the burden of stifling one's voice" (De La Torre, 2008) and the silence provides an opportunity to initiate an extended dialogue that will hopefully lead to a safer environment where multiple voices are heard and respected.

Gust: Yes. The US DOS is not simply about silence; it is really more about the interplay between silence and voice. The meaning and the power of this day is about such interplay—silence becomes more meaningful through the explanations preceding and proceeding it and such articulations become more powerful when accompanied by a visible and sustained silence. In many ways, the US DOS is providing us with an alternative discourse about silence.

Continuing our exploration

Using a queer methodology, we reported on our participation in the 2008 US DOS and engaged in a dialogue to examine the complexities and politics of silence in this chapter. As LGBTQ ideas, identities, and events in the US expand—unevenly and unidirectionally—flowing mostly from the US to other cultural systems and minimally from the other direction, the US DOS has the potential to become an international day of observation and protest against anti-LGBTQ violence around the globe. For example, some schools in Australia have adopted this event. In these moments of possibility, US ideologies, politics, and cultural conceptions of silence will inevitably interplay and collide with local conditions and cultures to produce different meanings, discourses, and politics. How would cultures with different discourses on silence, such as those privileging silence over voice and speech, make sense of the US DOS? How might these cultures use this event to highlight anti-LGBTQ bullying, harassment, and other forms of violence? How is silence experienced and rendered meaningful by same-gender loving individuals in other cultural systems? What are the potentials of silence for social change, particularly in our age of globalization and empire?

As we contemplate the above questions, we imagine that our understandings of silence will continue to circulate in a world of new possibilities. As Cheryl Glenn (2004, p. 160) reminds us, silence is "an imaginative space that can open possibilities between two people or within a group. Silence, in this sense, is an invitation into the future, a space that draws us forth."

Notes

Please direct all correspondence regarding this chapter to Dr Gust A. Yep, Communication Studies Department, San Francisco State University, 1600 Holloway Avenue, San Francisco, CA 94132. Gust dedicates this essay to Tyler (1993–2008) and Dino (1993–2010), my beloved fluffy Pomeranian companions, whose loving presence I feel during moments of deep silence. Susan dedicates this essay to Alex (1995–2008) who showed me the value of love, voice, and silence.

1. Recognizing that we live in an era of Western domination, unprecedented US military power, and uneven transnational flows—what critical theorists such as M. Jacqui Alexander, Henry Giroux, Peter McLaren, Jasbir Puar, and Arundhati Roy, to name only a few, have aptly characterized as "the age of empire"—we mark the event as US-based to avoid its possible universalization. To highlight their multiple forms and expressions, we pluralize sexuality and silence, and to recuperate silence from its common associations with passivity and powerlessness, we wish to call attention to its potential connections with agency and resistance.
2. We use the gerund for our sections to emphasize that our journey in this project was an active, fluid, and ongoing process.

References

Achino-Loeb, M. (2006). Introduction: Silence as the currency of power. In M. Achino-Loeb (Ed.), *Silence: The currency of power* (pp. 1–19). New York: Berghahn.

Adam, B. D., Duyvendak, J. W., & Krouwel, A. (Eds) (1999). *The global emergence of gay and lesbian politics: National imprints of a worldwide movement*. Philadelphia, PA: Temple University Press.

Agathangelou, A. M., Bassichis, M. D., & Spira, T. L. (2008). Intimate investments: Homonormativity, global lockdown, and the seductions of empire. *Radical History Review*, 100 (Winter): 120–143.

Altman, D. (2001). *Global sex*. Chicago, IL: University of Chicago Press.

Browne, K. & Nash, C. J. (2010). Queer methods and methodologies: An introduction. In K. Browne, & Nash, C.J. (Eds), *Queer methods and methodologies: Intersecting queer theories and social science research* (pp. 1–23). Farnham: Ashgate.

Campbell, K. K. (1989). *Man cannot speak for her: A critical study of early feminist rhetoric* (Vol. 1). New York: Greenwood.

Carbaugh, D. (2002). "I can't do that!" but I "can actually see around corners": American Indian students and the study of public "communication." In J. N. Martin, T. K. Nakayama, & L. A. Flores (Eds), *Readings in intercultural communication: Experiences and contexts* (2nd ed., pp. 138–149). Boston, MA: McGraw-Hill.

Clair, R. P. (1998). *Organizing silence: A world of possibilities*. Albany, NY: State University of New York Press.

Cvetkovich, A. (2003). *An archive of feelings: Trauma, sexuality, and lesbian public culture*. Durham, NC: Duke University Press.

Day of Silence (2008a). *Day of Silence home page*. Retrieved from http://www.dayofsilence.org on 25 April 2008.

Day of Silence (2008b). *Frequently asked questions*. Retrieved from http://www.dayofsilence.org/content/getinformation.html on 5 June 2008.

Day of Silence (2008c). *The history of the Day of Silence*. Retrieved from http://www.dayofsilence.org/content/history.html on 5 June 2008.

Day of Silence (2008d). *The truth about the day of silence*. Retrieved from http://www.dayofsilence.org/content/truth.html on 5 June 2008.

De La Torre, V. (2008). *A day of silent empathy: Conard joins effort to help understand gays' plight. /Hartford Courant/*. Retrieved from http://articles.courant.com/2008-04-26/news/whdsilence0426.art_1_gay-straight-alliance-straight-education-network-school-day.

Duncan, P. (2004). *Tell this silence: Asian American writers and the politics of speech*. Iowa City, IA: University of Iowa Press.

Glenn, C. (2004). *Unspoken: A rhetoric of silence*. Carbondale, IL: Southern Illinois University Press.

GLSEN (Gay, Lesbian and Straight Educational Network) (n.d.). *More than silence: Organizing a breaking the silence event*. Retrieved from http://www.dayofsilence.org/downloads/r118.pdf on 10 June 2008.

GLSEN (2008a). *Students from record 7,500 K-12 schools registered for national day of silence*. Retrieved from http://www.glsen.org/cgi-bin/iowa/all/news/record/2291.html on 5 June 2008.

GLSEN (2008b). *Lesson plan for the 2008 annual day of silence*. Retrieved from http://www.glsen.org/binary-data/GLSEN_ATTACHMENTS/file/000/001/1139-1.pdf on 10 June 2008.

Greene, B. (n.d.). Lesbian couple behind national day of silence. *Oasis Magazine*. Retrieved from http://www.oasisjournals.com/Issues/9803/profiles.html on 5 June 2008.

Gullapalli, D. (2000, April 11). Muffled day of silence barely audible. *The Cavalier Daily*. Retrieved from http://www.cavalierdaily.com/CVArticle.asp?ID=3994&pid=568 on 9 June 2008.

Halberstam, J. (1998). *Female masculinity*. Durham, NC: Duke University Press.

Hemmelgarn, S. (2008, April 24). Pink is in for day of silence. *Bay Area Reporter, 38*(17), 1, 15.

Jaworski, A. (1993). *The power of silence: Social and pragmatic perspectives.* Newbury Park, CA: Sage.

Kurzon, D. (1995). The right of silence: A socio-pragmatic model of interpretation. *Journal of Pragmatics, 23,* 55–69.

Lee, Z. (2004, April 21). Silence won't bring about equality. *The Daily Cougar.* Retrieved from *Lexis Nexis Academic* 9 June 2008.

Prokosch, M. & Raymond, L. (Eds). (2002). *The global activist's manual: Local ways to change the world.* New York: Thunder's Mouth Press/Nation Books.

Seidman, S. (2002). *Beyond the closet: The transformation of gay and lesbian life.* New York: Routledge.

Yep, G. A. (2003). The violence of heteronormativity in communication studies: Notes on injury, healing, and queer world-making. In G. A. Yep, K. E. Lovaas, & J. P. Elia (Eds), *Queer theory and communication: From disciplining queers to queering the discipline(s)* (pp. 11–59). Binghamton, NY: Harrington Park Press.

Yep, G. A. (2009). Gay, lesbian, bisexual, and transgender theories. In S. Littlejohn & K. Foss (Eds), *Encyclopedia of communication theory* (Vol. 1, pp. 421–426) Newbury Park, CA: Sage.

Yep, G. A., & Elia, J. P. (2012). Racialized masculinities and the new homonormativity in LOGO's *Noah Arc. Journal of Homosexuality. 59*(7), 890–911.

Zepeda, S. (2009). Mapping queer of color methodology. *GLQ: A Journal of Lesbian and Gay Studies, 15*(4), 622–623.

Part III

Recovering Silences: Community, Family, Intimacy

12
Keeping Quiet: Performing Pain

Della Pollock

> The critical self-reflection of the loving eye is a reflection of a full not empty space, a reflection that is communicated not on a smooth hard resistant surface of a mirror, but in the tissues of the flesh of the world.
>
> (Kelly Oliver, 2001, p. 221)

In this chapter, I address one dimension of a larger project concerned with speaking pain against the grain of its presumed unspeakability.[1] Here, continuing to think through one interview encounter, I'd like to consider that not-speaking or keeping quiet in the particular sense of *tending silence* may be a way of realizing the relational subjectivity of pain. In this account, pain shares with language a certain fickleness. Speaking pain is dangerous. It may cause more pain by, for instance, inadvertently contributing to discourses that tend to dismiss it or by inviting others into a relation of practical suffering. Accordingly, speaking pain is a performative correlate for what happens between subjects facing pain whether "on a smooth hard resistant surface of a mirror" or "in the tissues of the flesh of the world" (Oliver, p. 221). The space between must then be carefully kept, swept and brushed, maintained, not so much against the unspeakability of pain but against the potential excesses of speech, the possibility of overspeaking it and violating the tender space it opens.

In the course of this study, friends and colleagues have regularly assumed that by pain I mean emotional hurt or anguish. Their assumption is consistent with a normative division of the affective and material body, when both falter against cultural preferences for calm speech, whole utterances, language lodged in the presential rationality of the word as *logos*. But the assumption also suggests a subordinate denial.

Corporeality is divided against itself in the abjection of physical pain, even from the already forsaken realms of loss and hurt, when these are sublimated as psychic effects, part of a feeling-mind that leaves the body doubly othered: *cut away* from both rational-mind and feeling-mind, affect now allied with reason in *mind* against their sensuous other, the body of flesh, bone, blood, and nerves.

This double exclusion has many implications, not the least of which is to identify pain with unthought, even prediscursive experience, and experience in turn with a kind of crude materiality. In this alignment of *body, pain, experience*, pain cannot speak. It is a figure of dead weight. Of the twice-disowned body (consciousness of which my back surgeon once remarked: "oooh! I don't want that"). Pain stands in for the troublesome regions below the head, whose mouth is then by shame: it cannot speak what the surgeon's, friend's, lover's ears and eyes—for many and various reasons—cannot or will not recognize. If it isn't or cannot be heard, pain has no sound then except those yowls and wails by which we—the one who looks at the wailing "other" and the wailing one now so distinctly othered—name pain *humiliating*.

In this work, I am consequently not so much interested in the experience of pain, because "pain" has already been measured and marked by various objectifying mechanisms and because it has so often been identified with "experience" as unreflexive, sensate, flesh-being in the world that to repeat concern with the pain-experience threatens to redouble that identification. Part of the problem I want to address in opening a space in which pain may be heard is that pain, the flesh-body, and experience have been so consistently and effectively collapsed that:

1. Pain is commonly understood as a limit experience; it is, as we say, shaking our heads in sullen resignation, *leveling*; it's what brings us all to our knees—and proves us all terribly, stupidly mortal.
2. Accordingly, it marks a linguistic horizon beyond which there are no words, only inchoate noise, cries, and moans that are incompatible with civil discourse.
3. In turn then, as David Morris has made so painfully clear, people in pain may be identified with—or may identify themselves with—a kind of precultural corporeality or feral, infantile state that is and often has been dangerously raced and gendered. To feel pain is to fail to rise above it.[2]
4. Pain therefore becomes at best a figure of incivility; at worse, an object of shame and disgust that, one way or another, has to be gotten rid of—even if only by cultivating more pain, as the new gym

credo (apparently adopted from military training)—"pain is weakness leaving the body"—would suggest. While by the 1980s motto, "no pain, no gain," pain signified a kind of fullness, a form of body-capital promising profit, the marine slogan recommends pain as a way of purging the lack it signifies—the lack of words, lack of strength, lack of pride and dignity. "Pain" cleanses the body of weakness; it performs the double negative work of *voiding lack*.

And so to talk about the experience *of* pain is to participate in a discursive inversion. It is to perform its construction *as* due muteness, emptiness, lack of moral and physical strength, and repugnant savagery—and so potentially to cut up wounded subjectivities all over again.

So, I shift registers from the *experience* to the *performance* of pain, imagining with my interview participants a performative subjectivity composed of, or rather in, processes of talking-but-not talking or what I will call *not* not talking about the pain of pain.

I begin by asking:

Why is it that we are so ready to accept that pain can't be spoken, to locate it outside the symbolic order, with those conditions of mute disorder or at best Kristevan semiosis, that make the pained subject a figure of lack or lassitude?

Why is it moreover that we fail to recognize that even feminist mandates to "break the silence" around sexual abuse and violence, for instance, may (even simply following Foucault's logic of the confessional) be part of the disciplinary regime of gender performatives they are meant to "break"?[3] Subjecting the person in pain to breaking the double bind of silence in which he/she is caught constitutes a kind of compulsive violation, if not exactly violence. If silence is the discursive terrain of pain, then speaking it exposes the embodied subject to renewed exile—to wincing embarrassment for a subject apparently too incivil to feel it herself, to exhausted sympathy yielding to the wish that the person in pain would just go back to her cave, to mandates for "management" that correct ill-begotten behavior on the promise of a ticket to the show—dis-incorporate the body and come on in.

We are privileged to assume, as bell hooks taught us long ago, that what we don't hear doesn't exist—and yet simultaneously to fear that what we *can't* hear may harm us. Silence is suspect. Where there is silence, it seems, there is the hidden transcript, the opaque threat—and, as Page duBois has observed, the warrant to break that silence, to commit the kind of violence apparently necessary to make animal flesh transparent, to excavate the truth. The presumed secrecy of the flesh (especially in its already suspect female or feminized forms) ostensibly justifies torture.

Pain is unspeakable. Silence is unacceptable. These are the pillars of Elaine Scarry's remarkable study, *The Body in Pain*. A landmark in studies of the body politic, *The Body in Pain* has even been underestimated in its contributions to understanding the colonizing power of torture. And yet there's the problem. Scarry argues that torture "unmakes culture," that it breaks down cultural identification and so identity and agency, at the root level of the performative capacity even to name one's self and body. The obscene, violent infliction of pain reduces its object to a gurgle. To a figure without cultural bearings and so without the language necessary to say as much. Accordingly, Scarry calls pain itself pre-linguistic (when even *post*-linguistic, beyond given speech resources, might be a better descriptor). And it is this claim, largely separate from its context in torture as itself a form of "breaking silence," that has gainsaid her larger argument and helped to secure the now widely reified claim that pain is not so much before as below language.

Against this claim, and compulsions to confess whatever it is one is hiding—even if that is, paradoxically, *pain*—I want to wonder about how to hear tenuously preserved silence, and about how to understand the bodily investments that stake it, by winding my thoughts through those of one participant or "co-witness" in the project, someone I'll call Alexa.[4]

Alexa did not want to talk about pain. But she did not *not* want to talk about it either. When I introduced my own concern about the communicability of pain, she came back hard with an ethic of invested relationality:

> pain *is* communicable
>> not necessarily before words
>> but in the sense of
>>> "feeling someone's pain"
> "if someone you love is hurt, you hurt"

For Alexa, pain is communicable almost in the sense in which we say a disease is communicable: it is contagious by affective contact or by relay on currents of what Alexa calls "love."

In the same vein, Talal Asad argues that "pain is not merely a private experience but a public relationship." It specifically comprises what, following Austin, I would call a performative rather than a constative relation of address. "Addressing another's pain," Asad continues, "is not merely a matter of judging referential statements. It is about how a particular kind of relationship can be inhabited and enacted." This is for Talal Asad, like Alexa, a relation of love:

> An agent suffers because of the pain of someone she loves—a mother, say, confronted by her wounded child. That suffering is a condition of her relationship, something that includes her ability to respond sympathetically to the pain of the original sufferer. The person who suffers because of another's pain doesn't first assess the evidence presented to her and then decide on whether and how to react. She lives a relationship. The other's hurt—expressed in painful words, cries, gestures, unusual silences (in short, a recognizable rhetoric)—makes a difference to her in the sense of being the active reason for her own compassion and for her reaching out to the other's pain. It is a practical condition of who she and her suffering child are. [This applies equally, of course, to the pleasures the two may share.]
>
> (Asad, 2003, pp. 81–82)

Asad translates ostensibly private or individual pain into public and practical suffering. He at once dismisses a deliberative response to pain ("the person who suffers because of another's pain doesn't first assess the evidence presented to her and then decide on whether and how to react") and insists on primary relationality: "the person who suffers because of another's pain...lives a relationship." Accordingly, compassion is not a collapse of difference into identification or what may amount to flaccid sympathy.[5] To the contrary, the difference between the one who hurts and the one who finds the rhetoric of her pain "recognizable" or who recognizes her pain makes a practical difference: it ignites "the ability to respond" particularly in the form of "reaching out" to another's pain across persistent difference. In other words, relationality is a condition of difference that makes responsiveness to pain possible. Pain thus demarcates the space between subjects who are subjects in part because they are in relation. They "inhabit the relationality of love" and so each *become[s]* one who loves, one [who] suffers in and through love." The relationality of love is dynamic. It defines the transitive subject of address for whom the "practical condition" of love precedes subjectivity or the unfinalizable process of becoming "one who loves."

Asad's mother-figure responds to a "recognizable rhetoric": "painful words, cries, gestures, unusual silences" that make a difference to her "in the sense of being *the active reason*...for her *reaching out* to the other's pain" (emphasis added). The relation catalyzes "reaching out," presumably across the space/time defining subjects variously inhabiting the affective and spatial relation Asad and Alexa call "love." That the mother recognizes a peculiar rhetoric of pain and reaches out toward rather than rejecting it (or abjecting, containing, or otherwise disciplining it into normative submission) suggests a distance she feels driven to overcome but that remains, defining the very act of "reaching out." Even in the fullness of "reaching out," each one and the other, "you" and "someone you love," remain distinct. Recognizing the rhetoric of the loved one's pain enjoins the mother/lover to performativities of "reaching out," and in turn then "becoming" *one who loves*. The relation is mobilized. It becomes active. Accordingly, when Alexa says that "if someone you love is hurt, you hurt," she is not saying that the someone who loves and the someone who hurts are somehow the same—or that they collapse into each other in flat empathy. Following Asad, following Alexa, pain does not target an individual or denote injury as much as it draws *you* and *someone you love* into a performative incarnation of a relation by which pain travels back on circuits of recognition, cutting back into the "one who loves," who loves now *more* because she hurts and must then continue reaching out across the ineluctable difference that defines relationality, only to be hurt *more* in an irresolvable and unsolicited relay of love and pain. Alexa doesn't solicit this transfer. It, like her own chronic pain and who she is or has become within the repertoire of pain and the relationality of love, *just is*.

The communicability of pain thus has less to do with content utterance than with the conditions of relation in which it is spoken or given to be heard. Performatively, the question becomes not whether pain can be spoken but whether and when it can be heard or, more to the point: recognized. What are the "practical condition[s]" of pain that make it peculiarly legible, whether conventionally worded or not? As Alexa notes, pain has a skewed relationship to language. It is, as Alexa says,

> not outside the realm of discourse
> but it is   not   always worded
>
> maybe it doesn't take as many words

On the other hand, in a fabulous turn to the erotic, she compares pain to sex. Like sex, she says, "we don't talk about [it] and so we're always talking about it!" Even in Alexa's syncopated reflection, pain lingers just behind ("it is not always worded") or runs boisterously ahead ("so we're always talking about it!") of what she has to say about it.

In speaking, Alexa vigorously talks back to a host of presumed interlocutors, especially those who would insist that she needs therapy, the "talking cure," in order to remember her trauma more precisely and then to "work through" it appropriately. She flat out insists that this is not, for her, a habitable relation of being:

> I don't want a more precise memory
> > I don't think it's restorative
> > > healing
> I don't need to go into it
> > to heal it
> I do think of it as a foundational wound
> > on the one hand, I wish I didn't have this
> > > pain
> > > > this
> > > history
> > but
> > I wouldn't be who I am
> > I wouldn't *be*
> > > without that.
> > this is
> > > it just is.

Refusing a therapeutic model of address and release, Alexa claims her pain for *herself*, for her being: she wouldn't *be who she is*, she wouldn't *be*, she wouldn't *be* without *what is*. In this ontological alignment of self with pain—"I wouldn't be... it just is", pain is radically unothered. In this slight reckoning with an obscure "history," Alexa recovers pain from those conditions of therapeutic redress that would divide the I who *is* from the pain that *is*: "... this/pain/this/history... this is/... it just is/" and "I wouldn't be who I am/I wouldn't *be*/without that." Quietly trailed through Alexa's elliptical gaps and pauses is an insistent, conscious, and unsentimental refusal of the kind of "healing" that would paradoxically, even perversely, cut into her phenomenological claim on a definitive relation between what is and who she is.

You may be wondering what "this history" is to which Alexa so sparingly refers. After about an hour, maybe an hour and a half of conversation, I was in fact panicking, thinking I'd missed something of critical significance. *The start of the story. The expository details.* But

it wasn't until then that Alexa recalled the "cause" of her pain—and
even then she offered only a few words as if in an aside, invoking and
immediately putting *aside* an early car accident only in order to explain
a scar that lingers, almost imperceptibly (quietly) in the lower crest of
her eye socket. Caught in the careful attention to hush and rise to which
she called me, I wondered about my own power to represent—and the
representational power of dominant narrative forms in which I was/am
located. Scientistic forms of cause/effect; linear forms of a then b then c;
tragic forms of flaw and demise; heroic forms of triumph over the monstrous "other." Ethnographically and relationally, how do I *hear* Alexa
and listen to her here, now, with you? How do I perform the relationality
of recognition and response to which I am called—without overtaking
her performance with a narrative of origin: an as-if already worded story
that flows from a causal moment, a beginning breach or tragic flaw that
would in turn betray the chronic nature of her pain—the synchronicity
of subjectivity and pain—she so forthrightly claims and that is in, in
so many ways, at odds with formal commissions of "history"? To the
extent that I recognize the rhetoric of Alexa's pain or adequately receive
what is given to be heard within the frame of our peculiar relationality,
I realize that Alexa's pain is not *in* the car accident she was in when
she'd "just turned 4," when she was "very little" (descriptive phrases in
which she at once seems to cradle and to speak her younger self). To the
extent that she even, briefly *refers* to the accident, she does not *defer* her
pain to it.

I realize that I cannot *lean away* from Alexa's astructural account
into the ready arms of narrative structure, and the sense of order and
competency they would confer—on me, if not Alexa. Narrative and
the performance of pain are proving, in this instance among others,
incommensurable.[6] And so I *lean into* what Alexa cannot remember and
I imagine into the gaps in her speech, the resolute space between us,
the time expanded and collapsed in the quick reference to "history":
an instantaneous *crash, smash, break, bang, whip, twist, rip, wrangle, of
tin, glass, flesh, bone,* arrested forever in an uncomprehending "very
little" person, who "wouldn't be" who she is, who "wouldn't *be*" without it. This origin is not outside the subject, fixed out there in time,
space, or narrative like a starter's gun always already about to go off;
nor is it singular. Alexa describes her spinal issues "as a result" not of a
car accident *per se* (which would easily slip this account into the mass
repertoire of car accident stories) but of "being twisted around"—and
when she does so, she skips between verb tenses and time frames as

encompassing as *all my life* and as elusive as "when I was very little."
She says:

> I've had
> > I had
> > spinal issues *all my life*
> > as a result of being twisted around
> > when I was very little.

Alexa's spinal issues may be "a result of being twisted around." But the
pain she feels off and on, more and less acutely, exceeds both a definitive
causal logic and the foreclosures of narrative sequence. Alexa's emphatic
all my life at once collapses and expands the time of pain. If the car
accident is the origin of her pain, and is the would-be origin of something like a story about it, it is dispersed concentrically and unevenly
throughout her life, through *all* her life, including that part of it which
is *not yet* or yet to come. The accident, held within the whisper of a
scar, is synchronous with the chronic discontinuity of pain. *The origin
of the pain is diffused within it; the pain is suffused with its origin*, making
the pain itself forever original—surrogating the pain for the traumatic
event to which it refers only in forever belated, insistent, and delicately
shattered repetition—thus making narrative difficult, if not impossible,
even wrong.

The beginning is the end. Alexa speaks quietly, sparsely, at the place
where the diachronics of linear history cross the synchronics of imme-
diate telling/reflection. At that crossing is an emergent, alternative
chronicity: a sense that what has been will be again and again in new,
not entirely imaginable forms. I am tempted to call this performative
time. Pain pierces the narrative project with its own implacability.
It answers to expectations for a clear beginning, middle, end, and/or
subject-action-object formality (whether the "subject" is pain or the
embodied self) with narrative surplus. However much we may wish to
contain and/or rationalize it within given narrative forms, it escapes.
It stakes its ground in *persistent originality*.

Cathy Caruth answers to the logic of origins by arguing for what she
calls the performativity of trauma in memory.[7] What cannot be assimilated, indeed, *experienced* or absorbed into given cognitive structures of
meaningfulness upon occurrence, emerges later, *as if for the first time,*
albeit in a perverse form of repetition. As the first emergence, the repetition is the original. Remembering inaugurates experience. Through the

work of unbidden recall, the remembering subject performs beginnings into being. Caruth counters the displacement of subjectivity by narratives of origin by displacing origins into the performance of memory. She thus provides critical leverage on Alexa's account, supporting her resistance to the vortical claims of origin; claims by which Alexa would be sucked into a history that otherwise rests beside her.

But Alexa's account of pain takes yet another turn away from origins—whether in the past or belatedly performed. Unplaceable, irredeemable, but having lasted *"all my life,"* Alexa's pain is chronic beyond chronological. It has an ontological veracity in and beyond linear time; as she insists, it "just is." Alexa's "just is" may suggest an ideological collapse, perhaps a stoical deferral to the "tyranny of the indicative" and its renewal in commonplace repetititions of "the way things are" (Fiske, 1993). I would suggest, to the contrary, that the quick point of this "just is" presses at the jugular of discourses dedicated to effacing pain and its irreducible presence. It "just" is makes a homely claim on pain's *unheimlich* materiality. It just "is" asserts its vital currency. Alexa's pain no more goes away with time or management than does she sublimate it in narratives of medical or personal redress (self as patient(-)victim *of,* self as triumphant hero *over*). However infelicitous, this is the reality by which the *all* of her life is defined without which she wouldn't—with equally emphatic simplicity—*be*.

So why not talk about it? or why not-*not*-talk about it? Alexa had offered to speak with me, knowing I knew she lived with chronic pain—from what and of what kind, I really didn't know. It was particularly remarkable then that, in the course of our conversation, Alexa offered several reasons why talking about pain or going "into it" was not such a good idea:

> Because I don't think it's restorative
> > healing
> I don't need to go into it
> > to heal it
>
> I guess I'm saying "what for"
> > right?
> For me there has to be a
> > what for
>
> I don't think that for me
> there's a reason in itself
> > to remember pain

Because, she says,

> it's not likely to lead to less pain
> but to more pain

Talking and healing are not companionable; "I don't need to go into it/to heal." The conditional relationship of talk must be purposeful and promising: "For me there has to be a/what for." Talk is performative. It creates that which it names. Not only does it not dispel pain by (perhaps impossibly) pinning it down with a word nor does it "lead to less pain"— as if (faux) compassion might about absorb it: it makes *more*.

To the extent that Alexa *doesn't not* talk about pain, however, she slips the grip of talk that reproduces itself in "more pain" through what Eve Sedgwick calls periperformatives: here, in reiterative negations that "cluster" around the performative utterance of pain and break its constitutive spell (Sedgwick, 2003, p. 68). *I don't think it's . . . I don't think that . . . It's not likely to lead.* For Sedgwick, the "mock-constative form of the periperformative" offers a "powerful spatial warping" of the authorized or normative felicities of performative speech (Sedgwick, 2003, pp. 77–78). It does not necessarily diminish the force of the conventional performative as much as it *puts it aside*, effectively disowning its claims on the performing subject (for Sedgwick, specifically in the context of chattel ownership whether by marriage or slaveholding).

Speaking as yet cautiously with me, Alexa rejects the possibility that there's a reason "in itself" to talk about pain to those who don't already hear her or others' pain on currents of love. A colleague with whom I was talking about Alexa's circumlocutions suggested that *not*-not-talking may itself be a language of love, a form of vernacular intimacy. It is the hush between referential language and its conventional other, dead silence. It is a reflection of what Kelly Oliver calls "a full not empty space, a reflection that is communicated not on a smooth hard resistant surface of a mirror, but in the tissues of the flesh of the world" (Oliver, 2001, p. 221): in embodied relation, sensuous play-relay, in the accumulation of breath, syllables, sound, touch, and asides that does its work *beside* compulsory forms of witness and *between* subjects becoming loving subjects by diligently not-not-talking.

In the spatial register of the periperformative, the poetics of not-not-talking is also a refusal to participate in a symbolic order composed of the "hard resistant surface[s]" of words as mirrors—shiny surfaces reflecting light back onto the one who looks *hard* for precisely for that which he/she cannot see, that which language will not disclose: the truth for which it metonymically stands in. Soften the gaze and you can see that the mirror is only posing as a window, offering the seduction of a transparent view onto the obstinate world of pain.[8] Accordingly, talking does not so much "give voice" to pain as it gives authority to the linguistic systems in which "pain" is encoded: systems often at odds with being in the soft "tissues of the flesh of the world" or, even beyond trauma, in freefall histories of *the accident*.[9]

Not-talking thus also actively resists displacement by experts who seem to possess a diagnostic alphabet, who make the body legible through a kind of mimetic naming, or even mimicry in the form of those happy/sad face emoticons that now substitute for numerical scales in many physicians' offices.[10] In the social drama of diagnosis, pain is a breach in the social order, traded in for the satisfactions of medical redress that nonetheless often prove weaker than the persistence of pain and trauma and that may foreclose, as the anthropologist and occupational therapist, Cheryl Mattingly, has argued, on dialogic possibilities for alternative identity making. (Now, I love a diagnosis as much as the next guy but I am troubled by the extent to which its representational work may vacate subjectivity altogether. A pain specialist I know says that the most frequent question he's asked is, "am I in pain?" By the time his clients get to him, the gap between the body and the word has grown so wide that it comprises at least a secondary breach, another wound.)

Talking about pain, participating in the noise of its exacting translation, may thus involve:

1. "cutting up" the chronic diffusion of pain, paradoxically reiterating wounding in performances that, in the constancy of their repetition, acquire a chronic aspect in their own right and comprise a secondary series of *cuts*;
2. defacing the sensory landscape of invested affect that opens before the pained subject, what another participant described as a radical intersubjectivity (such that her partner monitored her symptoms and "did the rage"), and most evoke as a sense of *becoming embodied* or sliding—however inconsolably—into the register of body-knowing;
3. effectively un-remembering the body to itself, surrendering it instead to ready codes of legibility and transparency (that often counter remembering with dis-membering the body, particularly by isolating the pain to segmented body parts);
4. practicing the debilitating self-alienation initiated by medical militarization of the self against the body-stubborn, variously regaled in discourses of "fighting."

Alexa witnessed her mother's lifelong struggle with pain, and concludes:

> seeing someone spend their life
>
>> fighting pain
>
> I don't want that to be my life.

In another variation on not-talking, Alexa substitutes "someone" for "my mother," a common slip into generalization that here, secures a relation of loving witness at the same time that it allows Alexa to mark her difference and distance from her mother now figured as an example of one way of living with pain. After the wide-open ellipse following "pain," Alexa adds a link to the periperformative chain of what she doesn't want or think: "I don't want that to be my life." Alexa proposes her mother's life as a model of "fighting pain" which she can then choose not to follow—"*I don't want that to be my life*"—without breaking bonds of affiliation with her mother. The gaping spaces surrounding "fighting pain" remain full, even as Alexa disengages from the implicit mandate—*fight pain*—that separates nonetheless loving subjects.

For Alexa, pain is not an alien other she might fight or even heal (fighting and healing are not so uncommonly aligned here). Nor is it a figure for the effluvia of an abject self, trying to purify itself of an internal, unwelcome stranger.[11] Rather, she identifies it *as*, and herself *with*, an as-yet open wound.

As-yet-open, this cut in her body-history is a place of possibility. It opens into a temporality beyond chronic repetition. By not-not-remembering, Alexa never arrives at *the* pain, the definitive ache of the other within. She holds off arrival even as she projects departure, arguing that:

> you can spend your whole life fighting that...
> or you can look at it
>> as a departure
>> a point of doing something different.

With exquisite tact, Alexa visits pain: she comes as close to pain as stepping up to the top landing and speaking through a screen door held briefly ajar, as if asking for directions, and yet then heading off without street names or landmarks—to where, neither of us seems to know.

I have vowed to be a kvetch. A vow is an Austinian performative, in this case contracting me not necessarily to complaining a lot but to a parodic projection of a fantastical future filled with yiddishkeit noises about aches and pains. I like to think of this as an ironic performative that marks, for instance, a friend's stoic silence, a silence that is less about maintaining the WASPish protocols of containment with which he might have preferred he'd grown up than about being identified with his pain and so being overdetermined by it—identified, over-identified, even overwhelmingly identified as disabled, unable, incompetent, and without "a departure/a point of doing something different."

Outed, chronic pain *appears to be* lack. It is the token of something— some propriety, some degree of control or self-management, or even of wholeness itself—that is *missing*. Pain as visible absence invites us to avert our gaze, to turn away, perhaps out of a sense of polite *regard*, but even so with the likely effect of shaming *disregard*. Eve Sedgwick tracks shame to a "disruptive moment in a circuit of identity-constructing identification communication" (Sedgwick, 2003, p. 36). Shame is not defined by taboo or repression as it is the effect of the break in a chain of reciprocally confirming *looks*: prototypically, the child's look into the face of the caregiver returned as a form of gratifying mimesis. Shame erupts at the moment the caregiver (the beloved?) breaks the circuit of reciprocal recognition, when he/she "fails or refuses to play [his/her] part in the continuation of mutual gaze." In this moment, the child experiences herself as un-recognized, as bereft of recognition: at a loss for the identity found in the image of the mirroring-self. In this moment, "shame floods in," filling pale cheeks with the pink flush of unworthiness. And the averted gaze is met with a second aversion: the one from whom the look was initially withdrawn now drops her head in shame, turning away her eyes in what Sedgwick calls the "double movement shame makes: toward painful individu- ation, toward uncontrollable relationality" (Sedgwick, 2003, p. 37). Losing the identificatory connection intensifies desire for/dependency on it.

In this silent communication of shame where identity should be is the production of self as lack—a self that is then feminized or defined "feminine." Or, as Joan Rivière suggested in early forays into psycho- analysis, what we call "womanliness" is a masquerade, a performance, surrogating lack (Rivière, 1986). It is the full face of lack. Unlike Butler's performative feminine, Rivière's woman has always already failed condi- tions of substantial identification by phallic or *phal-logo* absence. To the extent that the word and its logics are masculine-identified, *she* cannot speak. What she *is* is speechless. Without the capacity to signify intel- ligibly and effectively within the symbolic order, "woman" becomes a semblance of herself: a masquerade only, a representation without reference, an empty signifier. Such a performance requires vigilant maintenance or it will undo itself as camp, potentially producing a disintegration of even the semblance of subjectivity.

Rivière's "woman" has been subsequently, significantly recast. But it remains salient if only for Rivière's identification of speechlessness with the feminine and the feminine with speechlessness. To the extent that pain is identified with a lack of language, it is feminized and subject to similar compulsions of compensatory performance *across gender*, even if that simply means, for instance, answering family members' *how are you?* By the letter of family lore-law: "okay," another participant consequently consistently responds, although translating this in the family tongue to mean "barely breathing."

Alexa slips the compulsory regime. She insists that she *has* a "foundational wound," even if by subjunctive disavowal:

> I wish I didn't have this
> pain
> this
> history

She claims the cut in the flesh of her history as definitive. It is a corporeal schism that lingers as wholly invested trauma. Not "just" pain, as it were. Not a body-object or alien physiological phenomenon culturally ideally subject to executive control, medical-corporate "management," or masculine dismissal.

Alexa's wound *is*. Against loss by shame and translation into the social/symbolic order as lack, Alexa tucks her pain into an archive of vital refusal. Housed in a performance of don't wants and don't needs— I don't want a more precise memory, I don't think it's restorative, I don't need to go into it; slung between approach and departure: Alexa holds her pained self in a kind of continuous incipiency that is, nonetheless, vulnerable to just cause:

> For me there has to be a
> what for
>
> I don't think that for me
> there's a reason in itself
> to remember pain
> because it's not likely to lead to less pain
>
> but to more pain

Answering to a good reason (what she previously defined as someone else's need), is likely, ironically, to generate "more pain." For Alexa, remembering pain creates pain. The performance of pain makes *more*. It creates a surplus. Following Rivière, it would amplify what is culturally designated "lack." Worse, it would hurt. Implicated now as a kind of authorizing witness to Alexa's performative claims on keeping quiet, I can only think that if she is going to give away this homely quiet, if she is going to break this ample silence: she had better have a damn good *what for*.

In the end, it seemed that Alexa risked speaking with me in order to stipulate and to claim rights to quiet. Alexa spoke in, around, and through pain against the tide of its unfolding in discourses of health, relays of hurt, and the production of lack, ultimately keeping it to herself, for her *self*, to tend quietly until something like the relationality of love into which she at least provisionally called me calls for something else or *more*. Then she will reach out across ineluctable difference and become "one who loves," who hurts, who recognizes and responds to the practical condition of pain. And so she will make a difference out of difference "in the tissues of the flesh of the world."

Notes

1. With thanks to Mark Olson, Brian Rusted, and Evan Litwack.
2. Alternatively, as suggested, for example, by Harriet Jacobs in *Incidents in the Life of a Slave Girl*, the slave was presumed to be so inhuman as to not be able to feel at all. Thus, any protestation would be histrionic and further proof of untrustworthiness.
3. See Linda Alcoff and Laura Gray's essential critique of talk show talk, drawing on Foucault's exegesis of the confessional: "Survivor Discourse: Transgression or Recuperation?" *Signs* 18 (2): 260–290, 1993.
4. All quotations offered with written and oral consent. All quotations are offered in the form of ethnopoetic transcription, based on Tedlock's foundational model on which I have relied throughout related work. See, for example, Pollock, *Telling Bodies Performing Birth* (New York: Columbia UP, 1999).
5. See Patrick Anderson, *Against Empathy* (forthcoming), Lauren Berlant, (Ed.), *Compassion: The Culture and Politics of an Emotion* (New York: Routledge, 2004).
6. See Michael Bernard-Donals and Richard Glezjer, *Between Witness and Testimony: The Holocaust and the Limits of Representation* (Albany: SUNY Press, 2001) on the related incommensurability of witness and testimony, and its attendant forms of silence.

7. Caruth marks an intersection between performance and memory studies by which scholars have been troubled, especially in part because of the apparent confluence of both with trauma studies. While there is much to be said about the rise of trauma in ethnographic writing and what increasingly seems the claim of trauma on performance/memory studies, here "trauma" usefully signals the immediately *unassimilable* that accents the plane of performance on which Alexa's "experience" becomes part of an active relation of witness.

8. Thanks to Ali Ezraghi for his provocative observation that Oliver's form of loving witness entails "a look evacuated of the gaze."

9. It seems important at least to note possible ways in which Alexa's vernacular poetics might engage Paul Virilio, with Sylvère Lotringer and Mike Taormina, *Art of the Accident* (Semiotexte, 2005).

10. Note that some pain specialists have moved on to the still less quantifying, image-centered use of a color spectrum.

11. See Julia Kristeva, "Approaching Abjection," in *Powers of Horror* (1980), abridged version collected in *The Portable Kristeva*, Kelly Oliver (Ed.) (New York: Columbia Press, 1997), pp. 229–247.

References

Asad, Talal. (2003). *Formations of the Secular*. Stanford, CA: Stanford University Press.

Butler, Judith. (1990). *Gender Trouble*. New York: Routledge.

Caruth, Cathy. *Unclaimed Experience*. Baltimore, MD: Johns Hopkins University Press, 1996.

duBois, Page. *Torture and Truth*. New York: Routledge, 1991.

Fiske, John. *Power Plays, Power Works*. New York: Verso, 1993.

Mattingly, Cheryl. *Healing Dramas and Clinical Plots*. Cambridge: Cambridge University Press, 1998.

Morris, David. *The Culture of Pain*. Berkeley, CA: University of California Press, 1991.

Oliver, Kelly. *Witnessing: Beyond Recognition*. Minneapolis, MN: University of Minnesota Press, 2001.

Rivière, Joan. "Womanliness as Masquerade." In Victor Burgin, James Donald, and Cora Kaplan, eds, *Formations of Fantasy*. New York: Methuen, 1986, pp. 35–44.

Scarry, Elaine. (1985). *The Body in Pain*. New York: Oxford University Press.

Sedgwick, Eve. *Touching Feeling: Affect, Pedagogy, Performativity*. Durham, NC: Duke University Press, 2003.

Tedlock, Dennis. *The Spoken Word and the Work of Interpretation*. Philadelphia: University of Philadelphia Press, 1983.

13

3210 S. Indiana: Silence and the Meanings of Home

Francesca Royster

I come from a family of women who know the power of silence. My mother's great grandmother, Big Mama, had a glance with the power to wither roses, and could stop couples from kissing in the movies in front of her with a simple shake of the head. My Aunt Teensie needs only raise a solitary eyebrow to get tables cleared, beds made, dishes done. These women,—dignified women—could cuss and snap their necks at you, too, if required, but they also knew how to polite you into silence. Silence is a tool of protection, respectability, and rebellion. But what of the stories and experiences that have shaped this silence? As generations die, and the landscapes of home change, we are threatened with the loss both of those stories and of the significance of what isn't said. In this essay, I will consider the power of home, the material matter of memory, to explore the power of silence—and story—for black women.

Here I am exploring the role of silence in terms of the politics of respectability for black women by using memoir and women of color feminism. In particular, I hope to explore the absences in stories about black women's lives by using memoir as a tool to explore what is sometimes left unsaid, or else is deliberately, even strategically erased. As I circle around the space of home—here our family home, 3210 S. Indiana on the south side of Chicago, I use my own memories of domestic spaces and the still and silent objects that occupied those spaces, as well as the stories embedded in them—to recover lived embodied experiences and feeling, the lessons learned by everyday living and ways of viewing the world, following Cherrie Moraga's "Theory in the Flesh" as "one where the physical realities of our lives—our skin color, the land or concrete we grew up on, our sexual longings—all fuse to create a politic born out of necessity" (Moraga and Anzaldúa 1983, p. 20).

Black women have used their bodies, standing, present and accounted for, to show, not tell, how to survive: the authority of a finely laced-up leather boot, unscuffed. The elegant Billy Holiday upsweep, kept neat with its many pins, day after day, year after year, in the face of changing styles. A way of conducting oneself with quiet dignity on streetcars, forcing "Yes, Ma'ams" from white storekeepers; adults harried with bundles, children in the midst of their private chatter stop and nod hello. Audre Lorde (1982) captures this quiet power in her description of her own mother, navigating the streets of Harlem in the 1920s and 1930s, in *Zami: A New Spelling of My Name*:

> To me, my mother's physical substance and the presence and self-possession with which she carried herself were a part of what made her *different*. Her public air of in-charge competence was quiet and effective. On the street, people deferred to my mother over questions of taste, economy, opinion, quality, not to mention who had the right to the first available seat on the bus. I saw my mother fix her blue-grey-brown eyes upon a man scrambling for a seat on the Lenox Avenue bus, only to have him falter midway, grin abashedly, and, as if in the same movement, offer it to the old woman standing on the other side of him. . . . I became aware, early on; that sometimes people would change their actions because of some opinion my mother never uttered, or even particularly cared about. . . . As a child, it made me think she had a great deal more power than in fact she really had. My mother was invested in this image of herself also, and took pains, I realize now, to hide from us children the many instances of her powerlessness. (pp. 16–17)

Silence itself tells its own story. It marks a site of struggle and strategy. One of the chief catalysts of silence for black women, especially as it takes place in migration stories, has been around sexuality and the abuse of sexuality. Speaking of the erasure of story, Hortense Spillers has famously described black women as

> the beached whales of the sexual universe, unvoiced, misseen, not doing, awaiting their verb. Their sexual experiences are depicted, but not often by them, and if and when by the subject herself, often in the guise of vocal music, often in the self-contained accent and sheer romance of the blues.
>
> (Spillers, 2003, p. 153)

Indeed, we might think of all of the ways that black performance traditions, from the Blues to Eartha Kitt's claim that she "Wants to be Evil" to the rhythm and blues oral histories of Mary J. Blige, are provocative negotiations of confession and absence of explicit verbalization. What do we make of those moments when words slip into a hum, or better yet, when the singer steps back from center stage and lets the horn or the piano do the talking for her?

But we might also consider silence not just as the erasure of information by others, but also as a strategic response, in particular in the face of past violence. In her essay "Rape and the Inner Lives of Black Women in the Middle West: Preliminary Thoughts on the Culture of Dissemblance," historian Darlene Clark Hine suggests that one of the primary but unspoken forces shaping the black migration of black women from South to North in the early twentieth century was the threat and fact of sexual violence: "I believe many black women quit the South out of desire to achieve personal autonomy and to escape both from sexual exploitation from inside and outside of their families and from the rape and threat of rape by white as well as black males" (Clark Hine, 1995, p. 281). In the struggle to reinvent themselves in their lives in the North, women cultivated a protective shield, a culture of dissemblance that often took the face of confidence, laughter, and sexual knowing. E. Frances White (2001), in *The Dark Continent of Our Bodies: Black Feminism and the Politics of Respectability*, suggests that such messages of dissemblance can be passed along intergenerationally by "suppressing certain narratives or omitting key facts" in stories about surviving white racism and or sexual violence, in favor of more heroic, or perhaps just plain less painful, humiliating versions (White, 2001, p. 14). The culture of dissemblance can be loud, distracting us from things not said. But it can be silent, too.

In the aftermath of violence, witnessed and felt, black women have built fortresses out of their own bodies, and out of the brownstones, tenements, cold-water flats, and rented rooms of Northern cities. On the stage of the city, they show their children how to stand tall in a crowd, and how to make oneself invisible. With their own hands, they have built gardens from junk heaps, pulling out the broken bottles and rocks to grow fragrant vines and hardy flowers: marigolds, zinnia, geranium, morning glory, and to bury other things deep enough not to be found by their children in their loam. The old stories, the legends and the haunts, change shape in these new cities, they become refashioned into song, into pots of hot soup, into something written on paper, faded, and slipped between nightdresses at the bottom of bureau drawers.

Black pain has also been sculpted into black aspiration, the mortar that holds the bricks of hard earned homes and striving neighborhoods. And this pain gets transmogrified bodily, too, into stiffened posture, legs crossed at the knee and not the ankle, heads held up high. The cult of True Womanhood and domesticity, a Victorian aspirational model of quiet, calm black womanhood revised the idea of black women as loud, sexually aggressive, and otherwise immoral, the stereotype circulated in white culture as a justification of black women's sexual exploitation. Early black feminist activists, such as Anna Julia Cooper and Maria Stewart, struggled between the need to speak out against oppression and violence and the need to be polite, to rise above the fray. In her 1831 pamphlet "Religion and the Pure Principles of Morality," Stewart mourns that black women have been subject to sin and corruption, and seeks as a model a quiet strength and righteousness:

> O ye daughters of Africa! What have ye done to immortalize your names beyond the grave? What examples have ye set before the rising generation?.... Where is the maiden who will blush at vulgarity?.... Did the daughters of our land possess a delicacy of manners, combined with gentleness and dignity; did their pure minds hold vice in abhorrence and contempt: did they frown when their ears were polluted with its vile accents, would not their influence become powerful?" (p. 27).

Stewart encouraged her readers to become the models of virtue and piety in the face of violence and vulgarity as a means of leadership of the race. But this advice leaves a very small and often constraining space for truthtelling. In the twentieth century, the performance of quiet, and therefore virtuous black womanhood, becomes even more explicitly linked to goals of class mobility and aspiration. As feminist cultural critic Lisa B. Thompson (2009) suggests, the performance of the stereotype of a middle-class black lady, from pianist Hazel Scott to Condoleezza Rice, "relies heavily upon aggressive shielding of the body; concealing sexuality; and foregrounding morality, intelligence and civility as a way to counter negative stereotypes" (p. 3). Black women have policed their words and bodies to create a new morality for the eyes of whites and for each other. This has irrevocably changed the quality of the stories that we tell about ourselves. We must learn to hear the stories that are not said out loud, the stories in the silence.

In her essay, "The Site of Memory" (compiled in the essay collection, *Inventing the Truth: The Art and Craft of Memoir*, 1987), Toni Morrison describes her role as a novelist, as one who must lift the veil from the real lives that were often kept protected by secrecy and silence. Morrison notes that while black autobiographical storytelling is an important contribution to US literature—especially the slave narratives of the late nineteenth century—these narratives were often fraught places to seek the truth of the inner lives of the people writing them. As eloquent as they are as defenses of black humanity, these narratives are also fraught with silences. Indeed, such silences were an aspect of the defense of black humanity:

> Over and over, the writers pull the narrative up short with a phrase such as, "But let us drop a veil over these proceedings too terrible to relate." In shaping the experience to make it palatable to those who were in a position to alleviate it, they were silent about many things, and they "forgot" many other things. There was a careful selection of the instances they would record and a careful rendering of those that they chose to describe. Lydia Maria Child identified the problem in her introduction to "Linda Brent's" tale of sexual abuse: "I am well aware that many will accuse me of indecorum for presenting these pages to the public; for the experiences of this intelligent and much-injured woman belong to a class which some call delicate subjects, and others indelicate. This peculiar phase of Slavery has generally been kept veiled; but the public ought to be made acquainted with its monstrous features, and I am willing to take the responsibility of presenting them with the veil drawn [aside]."

> But most importantly—at least for me—there was no mention of their interior life.
>
> (Morrison, 1987, p. 110)

For Morrison, the life's work of the writer—memoirist or novelist—is to grapple with these silences, to both remove the veil and to help readers understand the worlds that are unsaid. It means, in part, attempting to bridge shared memories. It means a lot of guesswork. It means invention, improvisation, and conjuration: "If writing is thinking and discovery and selection and order and meaning, it is also awe and reverence and mystery and magic" (Morrison, 1987, p. 111). But Morrison does so, not by simply removing the veil of silence, but by examining its patterns, and the stains and places where the weaving is unraveled; examining its place in the everyday lives of the people that she loves. The stories that we need are in the physical world; objects and bodies that give shape to our lives. They hold the shape of the narratives that are sometimes unspeakable.

Which brings me to 3210 S. Indiana our family home. The house itself was a form of dignity and protection—not only from the elements, but from the judgments of others, a guarantor that our family was part of a striving black middle-class. As a boarding house, it was a source of income and community. But it was also a keeper of secrets. The objects of our everyday lives hold the shape and the energy of the stories that we don't always tell out loud. 3210 S. Indiana was an old Victorian brownstone that my great-grandmother owned and ran as a boarding house when she came from Louisiana to Chicago in the 1920s. That house, which stood in the Bronzeville neighborhood, on Chicago's South Side, has been torn down in the midst of neighborhood gentrification. The property was bought by Illinois Institute of Technology in the 1980s, a few years before I graduated from high school. But the history of losing and rebuying, scraping and hocking and "making do" goes so much deeper. I've researched the history of the house's ownership and I've seen that it has had several owners, even while it was the "family house"—husbands and then ex-husbands, the bank, a "holding company," my great-grandmother and then the holding company again. I see reflected in that history the unspoken fact that the house's presence as sanctuary, as a safety net for others in the family to rest when they lost *their* homes, could never be taken for granted.

I remember Christmases spent there as a child, and the dark corridors that took you to back bedrooms. On the other side of those walls, in the second half of the house, once lived the boarders who came up from Mississippi and Arkansas and Louisiana and the Carolinas, and they had their own music and food smells and fights and loves, too. And sometimes it was family who lived there. Uncoupled uncles. Even my mother and sister and I when we were on the run and needed a place to land.

Sometimes I dream of roving these spaces. In sleep I find hidden rooms, forage closets full of old furs and dressing gowns. Or I sit on the lap of my great-great-grandmother, Big Mama, who also lived there, but who died before I was born. A few years ago, armed with my first video camera, I took shots of the neighborhood, and the gaps that were left. For a few years, the vacant lot where 3210 S. Indiana once stood was used as a parking lot. Now it stands vacant, a field, with unbelievably lush green grass, unused. I yearn for the stories held by that house—the lives of my great-grandmother and the rest of my family, the boarders who lived there, the interactions, for business and pleasure that may have happened there.

The ghosts of past violence hover over this house, unspoken but present. The key story, the one that I'd most like to know, is how we got there: how my great-grandmother, Lucille Williams ("Cillie") and her mother ("Big Mama") came to Chicago. That story was never told to me, and told in contradictory versions to my mother, but each time, there is a suggestion of violence, implied, and sometimes explicit. They came from Louisiana—New Orleans—and I've been told that they *had* to leave. In fact, there's a legend that my mother told of how Big Mama's mama (known only as "Mama," maybe because she didn't need the "Big" for people to fear her) held white men at bay with a gun at the front door while Cillie and Big Mama fled out the back. I see this scene in my mind's eye as if I was there, but I don't know if it really happened. I think of the ways that this fighting story must have empowered my family, shaping a future with hope, limits, and all. Presenting a possibility when things get too hot. My family held on so tightly to the image of us as homeowners in that period of struggle and risk, even as the promise of the neighborhood faded.

Another version of the story is that Cillie came to Chicago alone, pregnant with her green-eyed child, John, sending for her mother later. Did Cillie come with the help of John's father, a man whose name she never told even her son? Or did she leave New Orleans to flee him? My grandfather John, nicknamed Toodles, spoke with a stutter from a bad tonsillectomy that he got as a child, he explained to me once. He was handsome, Cillie's undisputed favorite, and seemed to be followed by a cloud of love by the women who forgave him his short temper and distance, including my grandmother, who he left for an Army nurse when he returned from World War II, and my mother, who missed him despite the green apples he brought when he'd come to visit. My macho grandfather, with a taste for the better things in life, like the Lincoln Town Car that he always drove. He always had 20-dollar bills in his pockets for his granddaughters and was the first man I ever saw with an Afro toupee. My grandfather, even in his late sixties, was hotheaded enough and spry enough to jump out of that Lincoln Town Car, brandishing a gun at two young men who were not moving fast enough through the dark alley behind the building that he owned. My grandfather, unlike his darker-skinned brother, Bobby, had café au lait skin.

Oral histories of the Bronzeville neighborhood, such as Timuel Black's (2003) *Bridges of Memory*, document the ways that this neighborhood and its mixture of grand houses and tenements, labors, doctors, teachers, all living side by side hold stories of loss and survival. And in many of these stories, too, there are gaps, things the teller doesn't quite know how to explain: hazy birthdates, mothers who died in childbirth, lost siblings, lost farms, missing family lines, repeated jokes whose punch lines are left unexplained to them. Speaking about her search for the missing facts of her mother's story, interviewee Mildred Bowden's determination becomes its own story: "Oh yeah, it takes patience, but I'll be able to do it. I know that" (Black, 2003, p. 243).

Bronzeville's borders span the South Side of Chicago from 22nd Street to 63rd, North to South, and Wentworth and Cottage Grove East to West, and it was for a time *the* place of settling for black people up from the South. St Clair Drake and Horace Clayton wrote in the famous study of the neighborhood, *Black Metropolis*, that Bronzeville was "a city within a city, the second largest Negro city in the world" by the 1940s, after Harlem (quoted in Stange, 2003, p. xiii). It was the first black neighborhood in Chicago, and until the 1960s was, thanks to the pressures of racial covenants, one of the few places that blacks were allowed to own their own homes in Chicago. The nickname Bronzeville was made famous by poet Gwendolyn Brooks, who was born and raised there; it could be both tough and nurturing; a place of lively cultural life: black and Jewish-owned stores dotting 47th Street, blues clubs and speakeasies, the restaurants like Gladys's (one of the only original soul food restaurants from that earlier period that is still standing). It has been praised as the birthplace of the Chicago Blues. (Chicago Blues banners now grace 47th street, in this period of renovation, revitalization, and out and out gentrification.)

By the time I arrived on the scene as a child in the early 1970s, Bronzeville had definitely seen better days. Many of the large Victorian brownstones had been carved up into cramped apartments, and then managed spottily by absentee landlords, though some homeowners, like my great-grandparents, remained. Cillie's house kept its glow of prosperity, even after she became too old to take care of the boarders, or do the housekeeping in others' houses that kept her afloat. The gray wooden steps were repainted periodically, the yard worked, and fallen parapets replaced, in part because her bachelor son, Uncle Bobby moved in, managing the house and the yard until he broke his back in a car crash with his girlfriend's Volkswagen bug. While no one said it out loud, I knew that to some of the kids who lived in the neighborhood, Cillie was rich. When we'd come to visit from Nashville, Cillie would send my sister Becky and I to the candy store across the street, and the kids would look with envy at the dollars in our hands. The store was always a little dim, and was actually the front room of somebody's basement apartment. You could crane your neck beyond the store to see kids playing in worn pajamas and hear someone watching TV. I felt my difference from the kids who lived there, but I envied them the boxes of Bazooka and chocolate cigarettes, Red Hots and Blow Pops and Lemonheads that they got to live with every day.

Cillie's house seemed so different from our newly constructed place in Nashville, in the Fisk faculty apartments, with its sliding door patio and faux wood paneling. At Cillie's, there was stained glass above the big picture window in the front room, and above each doorway, as if each was once the door to a tiny apartment (or maybe a church, I thought). Of course, there was a nice, contemporary bathroom and kitchen, and a big TV/stereo component set on which my sister and I watched *The Flintstones* and *I Dream of Jeannie*. But along the walls were older things on shelves that seemed to have been there forever, or at least from an era clearly different from our own: a dusty jazz quartet that looked like it had been made from wooden matches, porcelain blue and gold candlesticks and a cuckoo clock that were given to Cillie by the Silvers, the family that Cillie once cleaned for, and who lived in Wilmette. And my favorite: a small Chinese cabinet, painted yellow and red, with flowers. There were six delicately knobbed drawers, and when you pulled them open, they smelled, it seemed, of spices from far away. I'd check the drawers every time I came to visit, and mostly they were empty. But once I remember finding a bird's nest in the bottom drawer, carefully wrapped in yellowing newspaper. I always thought of this as Cillie's New Orleans cabinet and imagined that it had come from a ship docked there from somewhere else even further away, smuggled in, maybe. Shooed away from the adult gossip and storytelling that would happen in the kitchen, I would daydream on the big dalia-ed couch in the front room, imagining Cillie walking up the road in pigtails, and my grandfather John right behind her, just a toddler, pulling the cabinet in the back of a wooden wagon, on their way to Chicago.

Without the people to tell me the truths of these stories still alive with me right now, I am left with the objects of home, and the untold stories that *those* objects hold. If home is made of the people and places that we remember, it is also made up of these silences, absence, pauses—the shadows around corners. The stories of who we are wait to be unpacked from the everyday objects around us, wait for us to listen to conversations that aren't said: a yellowing taped dictionary, teacups, chipped but still displayed proudly on a mantle, the grease-dotted recipe for red-eye gravy. Stories await in the water-stained ceiling above the bathtub, or in the plastic slipcovers on the couch that are removed for visits from one uncle, but not for the other.

In her narrative of her geneological research into the white and black sides of her family, in her book *My Confederate Kinfolk: A Twenty-First Century Freedwoman Discovers her Roots* (2006), African American journalist, novelist, and dramatist Thulani Davis describes her own thwarted struggle to understand the emotional lives of the people that she discovers—the unseen, unheard feeling behind their actions:

> At the heart of my story are people I have come to know largely by their actions. It is interesting to try to understand people without any of the reasons given for what they did. After transcribing nearly one hundred pages of personal documents for the white family, I began to have opinions about each family member—likes, dislikes, amusements, pity. Still, they rarely gave reasons for choices and stuck to stating the facts. So many issues in life were not discussed that the actions taken became the road to the emotional life. For those who were in bondage, I have no pieces of paper that bear their thoughts. With the freedmen and women, any actions, choices, or decisions made after 1865 seemed huge. They had enormous significance if only because they could not be made before and may represent long held desires or impulses, but they were all initiations of self-determination. As such, they are still compelling. (p. 4)

The silences in our geneologies might be shaped by lack of access to privacy or to the tools of writing; ideological ideals that favor action and accomplishment over feeling; past historical conventions that favor facts over details, public life over private, men's lives over women's, white lives over black. These silences might reflect fear, modesty, humiliation, shame, resistance, triumph, thoughtfulness, perseverance.

My quest is to tell the stories that are left in silence—not just the actions, but the emotional heart of the stories, the residue of which I think can be found still in the objects of home. I am driven to do so because I want to know the women I love better. I know that their stories are a part of mine. I want the world to know the beauty of their lives and their struggles. But in reverence to these women who also understood silence to be a source of dignity, I have to ask what work has this silence done? How is it, too, a part of the interior life of the women that I love, and who I keep attempting to know?

If it is my job as a writer and as a daughter to plumb the objects of the home that I have shared with these mothers and grandmothers, it is also my job to explore the meanings of their silence: to respect and understand their silence as being about their pain, remembering how loss can be a physical thing, nestled deep between your lungs so that you feel it every time you breathe; to respect the desire to keep one's own counsel, even in an age of party lines and club meetings and kitchen table chat; to keep the world of children and adults separate. Perhaps these silent stories protect us as black children, keep us in the glow of lemon yellow and sky blue for a little longer. The lessons of racism, or poverty or sexual abuse in the 1940s for my mother, or in the 1970s for me, unfortunately come soon enough. Or maybe these silences are a claim to an adult world in the life of a mother, to have something of your own, something sad, something delicious, when dinner means sharing your plate with the sticky fingers of the child sitting on your lap. My father tells me that he never knew that his mother liked the breast of chicken, because his whole life, she had given the breast, the leg, the juicy, dark meat of the thigh to her children, leaving the stingy-meated back for herself. He was an adult before he saw her eating white meat, and he was thoughtful enough to ask her about it.

Perhaps this silence is the claim to the right to mull things over, to not have the answer (even when the bills are piling high), to admit, through words unspoken, that some things are bigger than you are.

Silence might prolong a state of grace, or it might be a response to beauty, a way to hold on to the sublime, like the smell of lemon verbena that hovered around my great-grandmother. Its source I could never find. One visit, while Cillie and my mother talked in the kitchen, drinking chicory coffee and finishing the Parker House dinner rolls from the night before at the blue enamel table, I set out to find it. I remember sneaking a footstool into the bathroom and looking through her medicine cabinet, even the highest shelf (I was already a skilled finder of hidden Christmas presents, at age six), trying to locate Cillie's smell in a puff of talcum powder or a shiny diamond-cut bottle of cologne, and to sneak a bit behind my ears like I did with my mother's bottle of Jontue at home. ("Sensual, but not too far from innocence.") I found a mysterious rubber bulb contraption, a bottle of Woolite, even the almost-gone bottle of Chanel No. 5 that we gave her for her birthday, but never located the source of that smell that suggested viney gardens, a green elsewhere, far away from the stacked wooden skeletons of soot-gray back porches, and a Chicago sun that never quite seemed to come close enough to turn the rough weeds of Bronzeville lots into blooms. This was the smell that flowed and hovered from my great-grandmother's skin—cool and fragrant and moist—when I kissed her hello on the cheek, and that came from her apron when she held me to her thin, still-strong body.

Despite her hipness (and at 73, she was hip, with smart wash-and-wear pantsuits and a stylish shag wig for the days when she headed downtown to shop at Sears and then Hillman's, for groceries)—it made her seem from another place and time. When she hugged me, suspending me with her in that lemony state of grace, I was home.

References

Black, Timuel.D. (2003). *Bridges of memory: Chicago's first wave of black migration. An oral history.* Evanston, IL: Northwestern University Press.

Davis, Thulani (2006). *My confederate kinfolk: A twenty-first century freedwoman discovers her roots.* New York: Basic Books.

Drake, St Clair and Clayton, Horace R. (1945/1962/1993) *The Black Metropolis: A Study of Negro Life in a Northern City.* Chicago: University of Chicago Press.

Hine, Darlene Clark (1995). "Rape and the inner lives of black women in the Middle West: Preliminary thoughts on the culture of dissemblance," *Words of fire: An anthology of African-American feminist thought.* Edited by Beverly Guy-Sheftall. New York: The New Press, pp. 380–387.

Lorde, Audre. *Zami: A New Spelling of My Name. A Biomythography.* Freedom, CA: The Crossing Press, 1982.

Moraga, Cherríe and Gloria Anzaldúa (Eds) (1983). *This Bridge Called My Back: Writings by Radical Women of Color.* New York: Women of Color: Kitchen Table Press.

Morrison, Toni. "The Site of Memory," in *Inventing the Truth: The Art and Craft of Memoir.* Edited by William Zinsser. Boston, MA: Houghton Mifflin Company, 1987.

Spillers, Hortense J. "Interstices: A Small Drama of Words," in *Black and White and in Color: Essays on American Literature and Culture.* Ed. Hortense Spillers. Chicago, IL: University of Chicago Press, 2003, pp. 152–175.

Stange, Maren. *Bronzeville: Black Chicago in Pictures, 1941–1943.* New York: The New Press, 2003.

Stewart, Maria Miller. "Religion and the Pure Principles of Morality, the Sure Foundation on Which We Must Build," in *Words of Fire: An Anthology of African-American Feminist Thought.* Edited by Beverly Guy-Sheftall. New York: The New Press, 1995, pp. 26–29.

Thompson, Lisa. *Beyond the Black Lady: Sexuality and the New African American Middle Class.* Urbana and Chicago: The University of Illinois Press, 2009.

White, E. Frances (2001). *The Dark Continent of Our Bodies: Black Feminism and the Politics of Respectability.* Philadelphia, PA: Temple University Press.

14
Fences, Weapons, Gifts: Silences in the Context of Addiction

Kris Acheson

Through the years, many have struggled to understand silence as a phenomenon and as a communicative tool, and the result of this struggle is a multi-disciplinary body of literature full of more contradiction than agreement about the definitions, values, and uses of silence (Acheson, 2007). In much of this work (e.g. Anzaldúa,1987; Foss and Foss, 1991; hooks, 1989; Lakoff, 1990; Olsen, 1978), silence is juxtaposed against speech in a binary of power, with silences and the silenced perceived as less powerful while the spoken and those who speak are deemed more powerful. However, continued scholarly disagreements over silence make it clear that the relationship between silence and speech, as well as the relationship between each of these and power, cannot be explained by a simple binary, and that one's perception of these relationships is often dependent upon one's paradigmatic perspective (Acheson, 2007).

Adam Jaworski's (1997) response to disputes over definitions of and boundaries surrounding the term "silence" was the suggestion that silence(s) may be best studied metaphorically. I agree, not only because metaphor begins to reach outside of the precision of language—which is, in fact, never quite precise enough to capture an experience of silence (Acheson, 2008a), but also because we humans live, think, and experience the world metaphorically, perceiving phenomena in terms of other previously experienced and/or culturally constructed phenomena (Lakoff and Johnson, 1980). Metaphor can help us tease out complex relationships, especially those between silence and speech, and silence and power.

With regard to the paradoxical juxtaposition of voice and silence, the very fluidity and multiplicity of metaphors allow for a post-modern, both/and understanding of silence as *both* opposite of language *and* part of language (see Acheson, 2008a, for a fuller discussion of this paradoxical relationship). More topical to this current edited volume of work, though, is the issue of silence as it relates to power. Because all metaphorical mapping is partial (i.e., the similarities between source and target domains extend only so far) and compound (with source domains applied to various targets and targets understood with numerous source concepts), metaphorical analysis provides the freedom to consider and accept multiple, overlapping, incomplete, and even contradictory understandings of what silences *represent* and *do*.

In this chapter, thinking about silences metaphorically not only provides an avenue for understanding how silences are intertwined with power, but also allows for actual shifts in power in interpersonal relationships when silences are used to communicate. The particular context for silences in the research discussed here is addiction, and communication in families who live with addiction. As participants in the study move back and forth between various metaphorical understandings of silence—such as fences, weapons, and gifts—the power dynamics within their families fluctuate. In the case of addiction, metaphor makes it clear that silences are not always negative, not always unhealthy, and, perhaps most importantly, not always imposed.

> *lullabye hushed*
>
> i wish i
> could be sure
> you took comfort in my
> presence.
>
> i wish i
> knew exactly why
> you ache.
>
> if your
> hands could open
> wide enough
> i'd share
> the hope that burns
> inside me.
>
> you could
> use it for a
> crutch
> or a bedtime
> lullabye

or slap it
on your face to form a
smile.

but the silence is a
chain-link fence
between us
teasing me with diamond-shaped
glimpses of your heart
but leaving only room
to poke through
fingers.
no toe-holds to
climb.
my shoes too
wide
and your spaces too
narrow.

i hope when i
rattle that fence
that the silence
vibrates and
hums you to sleep
because you won't
let me do it
and
you so badly need a
lullabye.

I have lived with addiction. It ruled my home; it shaped my world, and my body knows its language. I know how it can permeate a family, creeping into every fold in the fabric of daily life, coloring communication until the line dividing addict from non-addict shimmers and melts and fades, and the one becomes indistinguishable from the other. I know how it can breed silences, how silences can both foster the addiction and wage war against it, how families with addiction woven into their very being long for silences, rail against silences, take comfort in silences, feel trapped in them. My body knows these things, for I have lived through addiction.

Most of this knowledge, however, was preconscious—a survival skill that helped me to navigate daily life but was never subject to examination. For that reason I have devoted the past two years to a phenomenological study of silences in the context of addiction. I wanted more than to merely know the silences of addiction. I wanted to be able to articulate how people in that context experience silences—what silences mean to them and what communicative effects those silences achieve. And so, through various ethnographic and autoethnographic methods, I developed a set of 33 poems to analyze metaphorically. These poems are composite descriptions of many people's (myself, those I interviewed, and the people who participated with me in Al-Anon family groups) experiences of communicative silences in the context of addiction; they are drawn from interview transcripts and fieldnotes and from my own journals. As a collection, they represent a range of possible experiences of silence within that context. Here in this chapter, I offer a slice of the metaphorical analysis from my dissertation to you, layered with several examples of the poetry that came from this project.[1] Listen to the silences in the poetry, and watch them metamorphize from fences, to weapons, to gifts, for this is how people who live with addiction have storied their silences to me. . . .

Silences are fences

When addiction lives with a family, it doesn't sit comfortably inside, lounging in the den or round the table. Although it may sometimes seem a palpable presence in their midst, addiction is not nearly so benign as "just another member of the family." In fact, addiction can become an enveloping presence; it can settle over and around family members as a silence that contains them, restrains them, and separates them from each other and the rest of the world. People quickly perceive that some topics are off-limits; some things are simply not-to-be-said. In this way, silences can become fences—deceptively strong chain-link fences that tease with the connection that could be (and perhaps once was) there between family members. And, between family members and people on the periphery, people removed from the immediacy of life with addiction, that fence of silence can seem to be built of concrete.

> *the hardening*
>
> in the silence
> my tongue begins to move
> and i say the words that comfort
> because

because
my mother's hands are moving
picking
at the lace on the sleeves
of her Sunday dress.
my mother's hands are
plucking
pulling the lies from my throat.

they unravel
quickly
leaving behind their
skeletons
and a certain
acid
taste that must be
rope-burn

but the silence doesn't
shrink
it settles around the lies and
hardens
into a wall.

my mother's hands are
still
behind the wall
now
but so is the beating
of her heart
to me.

Such walls of silence can serve well. They protect people on both sides—those on the outside from the pain of seeing the havoc that addiction can wreak and those on the inside from the shame of being seen. But they also sever bonds. They segregate and isolate and suffocate.

And not all of them are built by choice. Some silences are constructed by the absence of someone to listen, or out of the sheer inadequacy of language to express the horrors of living with addiction.

mute

he goes out
slams the door
on my prose.

he doesn't need them.
it's not them
he steals away
to use
but he takes my words along
anyway.

he slices the sounds
right off my tongue
leaves it hanging there
dry
with a hush too thick
to spit
out.

that kind of betrayal
spins you so fast
you lose your bearings.
pin the conscience on the
lying bastard
doesn't work when
he's not around to
stab.

and even if i found a
voice
to protest
i wouldn't know
how to pack enough
consonants
into a curse
to make it as
sharp
as the crack of his
relapse
splitting my hope.

Silences are weapons

Members of families where addiction is present can become seduced by the power of silence. They know the pain that they experience when they feel silenced, either by pressure not to burden others by speaking about the addiction, by the shame of exposing addiction's symptoms to bypassers and onlookers, by crises that shock them into silence, or by abandonment, which removes from them an audience for their words. And, knowing this pain, people learn to use silences themselves, to achieve specific communicative goals. They wield silences like weapons, and with them they resist addiction and retaliate for the pain it causes them.

treatment

i think he needs
to taste
his own remedy.

i think he has
no clue
how it feels
to be with someone who's
alone
to be shut out shut up shut down.

i'm tired of
watching him
looking through me.

so i dole it out:
his treatment.

he'll ask me,
what's wrong?
why so quiet?

and i'll fade away
shut myself
into my head
like he does
in his bottle
hoping my retreats
cut as deeply
as his do.

Weapons of silence do indeed cut deeply. They are powerful tools in the constantly waged battle for power called family dynamics. These struggles for control are complex, although not necessarily unhealthy, under any circumstances. They become treacherously complicated by addiction, though. In families that include one or more addicts, the power struggle becomes bitter because *no one* feels in control. Everyone, addicts and non-addicts alike (if those labels that we commonly use are even valid for distinguishing one type of communicator from another in families affected by addiction[2]), feels tossed about in the maelstrom of addiction. They are bombarded by competing desires—to use and to abstain, to stay and to leave, to speak and to remain silent—and the aftermath of each storm rarely seems to be a matter of choice.

Silences are gifts

But some do learn to choose. In the struggle for power, some people who live with addiction learn to stop fighting each other, shifting from a battle for control over each other to a struggle for self-control. They stop simply reacting with silences and start performing them purposefully, in ways that honor their own health and ultimately can benefit the entire family. Such silences become weapons of a different kind, not the slicing, stabbing knives of retribution or manipulation but instead a sort of arsenal of lullabies; they constitute a music of healing.

breaking habits

you told me
i was worthless
a fucking cold-blooded bitch
but this time
i didn't give back
as good as i got.

you told me
you had fucked up
as if i didn't know
but this time
i didn't give in
and tell you
i was disappointed.

you told me
you were sorry
that you hadn't meant
to hurt me
but this time
i didn't give up
and say
it was alright.

i'm breaking habits
even if you aren't
and winning my battles
if only
against myself.

This poem documents a journey, taken in silence, toward a new self—a chosen self. It is not an easy journey, for the habits formed in the context of addiction, those behaviors developed as coping mechanisms, can feel quite comfortable despite the harm they cause. Breaking programmed reactions of speech (the destructive cycles of criticism and mollification that become second nature for many who live with addiction), requires both time and effort. When people in the context of addiction undertake such a journey, however, they enable themselves to reconstitute their old familiar weapons of silence, not only into tools used for a purpose other than inflicting wounds, but also into something quite new and different.

The speaker in the first poem performs that magic act, transforming imposed silence into chosen silence. Hope and desperation take another's fence of silence and make it a lullabye. The silence folds back on itself, simultaneously comforting both the one it was meant to protect and the one who has learned to hum its tune. Silence, in essence, can become a gift, a benediction offered to those who may only know silences in other forms: as weapons raised in anger and pain, or fences built by fear and shame.

With this last poem, I return to that transformation found in the first. It, like the other poems and the analysis here, is my gift to you—you who have lived with addiction, too, and know these silences as well as I, as well as you who have not, but who might catch a glimpse of that world through these words.

giving silence

if you haven't lived
a life like mine
you might just see
an empty box
but
the silence i bestow
on the people i love
is a treasure
bound
with invisible tape.

i offer it
to my partner
when he drinks.
i offer him
space and
freedom and
the right to fuck things up.
i always did think
laws against suicide were
absurd.
people in that much
pain
are the last ones
who need to be punished
and they certainly won't
change course
just because
someone tells them
it's wrong.

i offer it
to my parents
though their hands are
buried shut.

speaking their sordid stories
is a settling of scores that
leaves me unsettled
and i am no longer

caught
so tightly in their
web of needs
that i have nothing but
to hang there
squealing and
calling them names.

i offer it
to myself
an outward sign of
an inner calm
that won't be
ruffled or
shaken
by any of them
by what they have done
or can no longer do.
a measured refusal
to react.
a firm grip
on the only thing
that's mine to control
in the chaos
of others' choices.

i offer it now
to you
like a benediction.
may you travel it
fully
may its fruits fall into
your open ears
without my noise
littering the
journey.

Notes

1. See my dissertation (Acheson, 2008b) for a fuller analysis (Chapters 4–6)
   and/or for the entire set of poetry (Chapter 3).
2. I argue, in fact, in my dissertation (Acheson, 2008b), that they are not valid.
   With regard to communicative behaviors, addicts and non-addicts living in

the context of addiction are often indistinguishable from one another, and specifically in the case of silence, they experience their own and others' silences in similar ways.

References

Acheson, Kris (2007). Silence in dispute. In C.S. Beck (Ed.), *Communication yearbook 31* (pp. 1–58). Mahwah, NJ: Lawrence Erlbaum Associates.

Acheson, Kris (2008a). Silence as gesture: Rethinking the nature of communicative silences. *Communication Theory*, 18: 535–555.

Acheson, Kris (2008b). Relative silence: A phenomenological study of silences, families, and addiction. Unpublished dissertation, Arizona State University.

Anzaldúa, Gloria (1987). *Borderlands/La Frontera: The New Mestiza*. San Francisco, CA: Aunt Lute.

Foss, Sonja and Foss, Karen (1991). *Women speak: The eloquence of women's lives*. Prospect Heights, IL: Waveland Press.

hooks, bell (1989). *Talking back: Thinking feminist, thinking black*. New York: South End.

Jaworski, Adam (1997). "White and white": Metacommunicative and metaphorical silences. In Adam Jaworski (Ed.), *Silence: Interdisciplinary perspectives* (pp. 381–401). Berlin: Mouton de Gruyter.

Lakoff, George and Johnson, Mark (1980). *Metaphors we live by*. Chicago, IL: University of Chicago Press.

Lakoff, Robin T. (1990). *Talking power: The politics of language in our lives*. New York: Basic Books.

Olsen, Tillie (1978). *Silences*. New York: Delta/Seymour Lawrence.

15
My Monster and My Muse: Re-Writing the Colonial Hangover

Kimberlee Pérez

Silence. For me, not the absence of sound, but a point of entry into deep listening. What I hear and feel in silence is precisely what renders it complex. I have been conditioned to think of silence as alone. Lonely. Vulnerable to the companions that sometimes accompany silence who want blood, seek vengeance, and wreak havoc on my insides. I draw my breath in. As I listen to silence, silence in the ways the editors of this project engage it—as a space of possibility, resistance—my mind drifts to the weight of imposed silences. The kind of silence one leverages against another, uses as violence, that withholds or suffocates voice. Abject, ugly, lack—these are the places I am quick to turn as I con-template (in) silence. The world and my place in it, I anticipate and imagine. In this space I tune into familiar narratives: I don't want to (go). They won't like me. I don't know/where/to whom do I belong. Something/someone isn't right, shouldn't be trusted. Don't move, stay home, stay still, go. Go now. Run. Something deep inside, something old, something I learned early, leads me first to what might do harm. To remain silent/ly watching, waiting. Locked in a posture of suspicion of people, places, movements. My learned life-body posture looks like this: hands stretched out in front of me, muscles tense, eyes aware. I want to maintain focus on the multiple expressions of silence as a communicative phenomenon and practice, as simultaneously occurring as well as *interdependent* with voice and the conditions that give rise to silence. In order to get to resistance, we must recognize and attend to our suffering. Suffering is in relation to resistance. Therefore, given my tendency to anticipate and dwell in loss and fear, I am interested in look-ing deeply into their interdependent arising to understand their relation as practice, strategy, and healing.

Silence born of fear. Fed with rage. Silences of empire. Inherited through multiple generations, passed down like heirlooms to be guarded, protected, and least of all spoken. Empire, from the belly of the beast with its many facing heads, forms the contours of a shifting subject. Look at me. I am the half-breed, transracial, light-skinned queer. Although quite uncertain of where I belong, I do not walk alone. I walk in relations of tender love and cautious alliance. I brace for a fight. The bastard children of empire walk lightly together. We negotiate our paths with trepid and light steps, raging silences,[1] with yearning hearts and hopeful, ever-cautious, gazes. We who travel in this way, wondering when and if we will be swallowed whole, chewed up and spat out, find ourselves exhausted at the end of the day, sometimes at the start of every day. When I am weary, my silences have razor edges; edges that are as apt to slice through my heart and yours as they are to be smashed by the weight of the hammer of colonial tactics and neoliberal practices, whether in the university among colleagues and students, on the train, or on the street. Agency incomplete, illusory, conditional. You think I choose this silence? You. Think. I. Choose. This. Silence. Ask yourself why not. Even with the sweet curiosity that sometimes comes with a sustained practice of prayer and meditation, steady breath, the edges of my wondering are laced with barbed wire.

Into this meditation creep fear and shame as I imagine you imagining me. Do you find me pathetic? Do you see Charlie Brown? Do you not like me? Am I like you? Do I reflect you? How do you, how do I, feel anger, touch longing, read pain, and know suffering?[2] Over time I sharpen the blade of these narratives on the stones of experience, on yours and mine, on the ghosts that linger, whisper their curses, prayers onto those left behind. What else to do with the weighted load? On the uses of anger and tending to pain, Audre Lorde (1984) writes, "It is painful even now to write it down.... And how can we expunge these messages from our consciousness without first recognizing what it was they were saying, and how destructive they were?" (p. 165). In other words, to transform our *suffering* we might have to endure further *pain*. We may have to look in the mirror, to rip open scars. For those of us who feel the trace of our scars from the surface of our skin to the depths of our souls this idea is terrifying, haunting. Why would I want to go there again? Urging us onward, beckoning us toward healing, Lorde continues, "I HAVE LIVED THROUGH IT ALREADY, AND SURVIVED" (capitals as original, p. 172).

There is often a distance, then, between what one lives through (what one survives) and healing it. However far we move from pain, our suffering moves through our bodies and relations. W.E.B. DuBois haunts narratives of movement, progress, as he writes that "the nation has not yet found peace from its sins" (p. 11). In cultures produced through the machinations of empire, prevailing discourses—and here I want to specifically mark discourses of whiteness—exacerbate, insist, and rely upon that distance that keeps us from peace. Of course, the kind of peace that DuBois is referring to—the peace of accountability, forgiveness, social justice, and change—is inconsistent with empire. For empire depends on inequality, dominance, and hierarchy. And that premise both depends upon and shapes our narratives, embodied performances, and our relations. The Western subject must get over it/her/himself, get on with it, be silent about our pain and get back to work. While the traces of our suffering may linger in our bodies, speech, and relations, in order to maintain discourses of progress, our proximity to feeling, touching, and transforming that pain remains outside our collective grasp.[3] Whiteness compels narratives that move us forward in space and time. It promotes ideologies of an unwillingness to heal, and our bodies follow. And it governs us all; from privileged subjects who are threatened by difference (xenophobia, racism, and sexism) to the subjects of difference who seek normative belonging and invest in whiteness (assimilation, conformity, and other investments in whiteness).[4] The active production and maintenance of distance from the past and an investment in progress and future is what I would like to name here as *white temporality*.[5] It is my argument that white temporality materializes in multiple sites: it structures relations, our belongings and understandings of them, it compels certain embodied performances, and produces certain narrative structures including the perceived disconnect between silence and voice.

The order of whiteness, the logic of colonial knowledge structures that emerges in modernity, depends on the construction of relations in terms of binary separations. Voice and silence emerge in this formula as a hierarchical split. To remain silent is to be outside the democratic processes of the public sphere (Herakova, Jelača, Sibii, and Cooks, 2011), to risk being dependent on others to represent you, to be misread or misunderstood, to be without voice. In the binary relation of voice and silence, voice is everything. Silence is to voice as absence is to presence. To have voice is to utilize the agency to speak for oneself.[6] Voice is agency, visibility, location, determination, and power. The current turn in critical studies is to challenge the reliance on silence as dependent to voice by delving into silence, knowing it deeply, knowing it differently.[7] In an effort to move away from binary constructions, I find Buddhist philosophy and practice instructive. Here I integrate the

Buddhist concept of *interdependence* in a move to suture the binary of voice and silence into a different relationship.[8] Thich Nhat Hanh (1998) explains interdependence as the phenomenon where "cause and effect co-arise (*samutpada*) and everything is a result of multiple causes and conditions. The egg is in the chicken, and the chicken is in the egg. Chicken and egg arise in mutual dependence. Neither is independent. Interdependent Co-Arising goes beyond our concepts of space and time. 'The one contains the all.'" (p. 221). Rather than distinct modes of communication, strategy, and practice, the conditions of silence and silences as a condition arise together. While one might be favorable to the other—certainly resistance and possibility are more desirable then oppression and suffocation—these two conditions give rise to one another. To understand silence in this way I see a means of resisting the trappings of white temporality. As I enter the silent reflection of meditation and writing, I wonder at my narratives that emphasize, that cling to my (sometimes silent, other times not so much silent) suffering. Questions emerge. Where did I learn to anticipate loss while I watch others (seemingly) expect to gain? Whereas I feel lost, others appear to know exactly where they are going, what will come to them, as normal as anything else. While I sometimes develop relations that bring me closer to power through predominately white people, and therefore have material gain (Lipsitz, 2006),[9] I have not yet adapted (assimilated?) fully into the kind of *expectation* that I identify those with privilege enacting.[10] If I expect anything, the expectations are situated in a chain of repetition embedded in my psyche and bodily performances mired in suffering.

Toward healing and transformation, in this essay I address the tendency of white temporality to produce narratives that structure our relations in the service of empire, to rewrite our colonial hangover.[11] As one who has devoted a great deal of time to arguing the power of narrative to resist the forces of empire, I want to reflect for a moment on what might be seen as a contradiction with, or departure from, personal narrative. My investment in narrative compels me to look closely at its relations to power which hold the potential to reinforce discourse, enforce a certain order of relations, and invest in normativity just as much as it holds the potential to resist these things (Langellier, 1999; Langellier and Peterson, 2004). We must carefully tend, then, to the structures, to the doings of our narratives, their conventions, and relations to power. Under what conditions do narratives emerge? For whom? From what? With what effects?[12] The risk that power hails narratives in the service of white temporality warrants our suspicion and care.

Lest I fall into further binary trappings that would urge me to abandon narrative, rather I am interested in how we might utilize silence as a practice to think through narrative differently and follow Lorde's mandate to enter into our suffering.[13] The practice of silence, I argue here, is one that would allow us to listen to the narratives we hold onto, as well as to listen to the silences embedded within them. Rather than the prescribed direction of white temporality, these practices hold potentiality that we have yet to know. In the sections that follow, I enter into the kitchen in my family's home. The kitchen is often understood as a feminized, privatized site of familial gathering, of noisy talk, multiple generations, and the preparation and sharing of food. In my home, the kitchen where we eat is also a site wrought with tension, and sometimes silence. In the kitchen, I encounter narratives that place me in relation to history, empire, and men who have anchored my understanding of family, who have provided me with both access to and denial of identity, and of the multiple performances of Latinidad in the USA. The first narrative is one I have told before in multiple contexts. It is one story of my grandfather and the politics of inheritance and language. I tell the story in much the way I have always told it, although each telling is its own (re)making. In revisiting this story it is not my intention to rewrite *this* story for a different ending, an alternate ordering, but rather to ask in what ways the narrative as I have known it serves and is compelled by white temporality. Following a reflection on that narrative, I attempt to put into practice a narrative that confronts and reroutes the direction of white temporality through a story of my father. I've written a lot about my relation to my father in an attempt to resist him, to reinvent him and us, and as a means to imagine myself closer to him. Here I narrate a recent experience with him through mindfulness of the interdependence of silence and voice. Finally, I conclude the essay by reflecting on silence as a practice and tactic for reading and producing narrative and relation.

Kitchen story no. 1

A US flag covers the shiny wooden coffin. The raised dais displays the body of the immigrant turned patriot interpellated into the promises of the nation. The nation that switched places with the signing of a treaty, the borders crossed and crossers. Inside was my grandfather. My round, bald, gentle grandpa. He held onto the edge of an accent in the softness of his speech. The bottle of whiskey in the freezer he nipped every day. In the years since his death I nurture memories, invent new ones, and lionize a man that I likely know little about. For some time I held onto the Mass card from his funeral in my wallet.

I would take it out and hold it in my hand, memorizing this narrative of my father's father. My dad never had much to say about my grandfather. My mother told me once that he was angry with him for leaving my grandmother. But he never told me that. The spring before my uncle died we drove for a whole day around the Arizona desert talking. He told me that after my grandfather died he had night visitations from him where they would sit and talk for hours. It wasn't a spectacular story, but it was beautiful. And he missed his father. He adored his father. I drank my uncle's stories down, quenching a thirst so dry and old that I didn't know was there. Maybe in the desert we knew better the need for water. The night my uncle died he came to me. He comes when I ask and sometimes when I don't. Somehow I knew to tell my father of these night visitors would be a betrayal so I held my tongue. My grandfather is a little more stubborn with his spirit. Sometimes I see him, but we don't speak the same language.

When I did see my grandfather he was tender, loving. With age I never lost my tendency to lean into him. It did get more complex. I didn't want the tootsie rolls from the pockets of his Knights of Columbus vest any more. I was no longer satisfied with the food on his table. I knew he must have stories. I somehow got the idea that if only I learned Spanish the unnamed need would be satiated. So I signed up in my junior year of high school with the goal of impressing my grandpa. While he spoke English, Spanish was his first language. And I never learned. My dad yelled at us in Spanish here and there. My brothers taunted me singing "La Cucaracha." And there was always Speedy Gonzalez. But I wanted my grandfather. In high school Spanish, I remember the teacher, who was new, took one look at me from his roster in a sea of German names in my Lutheran school and began to speak to me in Spanish. Surely I must know it already. Shame fueled my resolve to reach toward my grandpa. I would soon meet the creases of our belonging.

One day, alone at our kitchen table, I take in a breath. I am ready. The time is now. Listo. Ahora. I have never remembered, or even dared to create what I might have said. It's too painful, what happens next. And that's what I remember. Carefully and quietly, nervous and proud, my speech is first met with silence. The doting grandpa I have come to depend on turns into a stranger. "Never speak to me in that book Spanish again," is all he says and we are done. The magic is over. At that moment and into my body seeps a hesitation around my right, my longing, my desire to learn Spanish. Shame. Distance. Loss. I thought the stories were rightfully mine—Mexico, the crossing, the marriage re-consecrated on the other side. Texas, Iowa, Chicago, Flint. How did we get here? Who are we? Who am I? I thought the stories would sound different in Spanish. He met me with silence. We never spoke of it again and I tell this in a story I have written for strangers. Later that year my grandfather died. I don't remember any Spanish spoken at his funeral, just the image of the coffin, the roses we threw on top if it at the gravesite, and the food and booze later in his kitchen.

This narrative—written, told, told again—is one that has served me well. In receipt of the narrative, I have absorbed gasps, clicks, nods, and gazes of sympathy. This narrative functions in one way as a coming out, an anti-passing, linking language and visibility to a body that resists easy or certain identification, a body that is often read in context and in relation. Stories prompt responses. In one telling, a Chicana that I had been with in an extended performance context offered that she never would have talked to me, meaning that she previously saw me as white. And why wouldn't she? There was no reason for her not to; last names disappear after introductions as we slip into the significations of our bodies to communicate with one another. As we continue talking through the night, she shares her own stories of tensions across generations and we ally ourselves together against our ancestors in contempt, in pain, in distance. And in one way I get exactly what I want. I am no longer white. I am no longer in question. I belong to her. I, and then we together, locate myself in a legacy of assimilation, one to which I am neither accountable nor active participant. It is a legacy that I indeed resist. But here I would also like to suggest that as I revisit this narrative in silence, to read its silences, I find in this particular telling, the structure, the order and the telling locate me at the intersection where the forces of assimilation and white temporality meet. As I introduced above, it is my argument here that white temporality produces and structures certain investments and materializes in narratives that feed it.

As I reflect on this telling, I do not want to erase or overlook the hurt I experienced as a teenager who wants to connect across a generation. The gaps between my grandfather and I are heavy with different experiences, different yet shared histories, and different relations to empire. They are real, felt, meaningful. Yet to the conditions of the production of this memory, of this telling, we must attend. What I ask myself is this: What happens if I read his silences differently? What if I strike an alliance with, rather than against him? What if I understand my speech to not resist, but to participate in the direction of white temporality, against the past, and in preservation rather than healing of my own pain? If white temporality insists that we march swiftly forward, there was no reason my grandfather would want me to know Spanish. The conditions of his own existence meant that he spoke in private. The culture demanded his compliance—in English—and that he looked a certain way. Though my grandfather's silence does not *protect* me, instructs Audre Lorde (1984), I think his was about protection. Himself. Me. Silent, unequal agreements of assimilation. There is a gesture of protection that accompanies certain silences—a hope that the next generation's loss will be their guarantee against difference. *Una ofrenda* laid down on the altar to the future.

Though the future might be constructed as one that is compliant with white temporality, I do not read the gesture of care and protection in the same way. Further reading into his silence, past his frustration, additional readings emerge. Was his a refusal of *book Spanish*? In an effort to preserve his language as he understands it, not in the hands of empire but passed down through family, was he performing his own shame and his own anger that my speech was routed through school? Could it perhaps be a silent admonition against my father for not keeping his language, for not teaching me Spanish himself?[14] I cannot know my grandfather's intention, his meaning, his life. And this is more an attempt to understand the conditions of my understanding and narration as much as it is to reach toward him from a different stance, from a different direction. A return to this narrative offers a healing of that pain, opens the door to compassion, forgiveness, and a loving, a political alliance rather than a turning away from the past. His silence prompts my narrative. My silence finds his voice. At the interdependence of silence and voice, white temporality is curbed, slowed, visible. Silences swirl through generations, waiting patiently, deeply, until we can sit still enough to listen. To take the time to linger in the slowness of the silence, listen for the instructions and the invitations to heal. To transform.

Kitchen story no. 2

From the position of suffering, of tending to my pain, I often cast my father in the same light as my grandfather, and inside of our relationship I often push at him. Actually, punish him. And he punishes me right back. Rarely satisfied, through narrative I imagine into what he is really thinking. It's not that he doesn't tell me what he's thinking; in some ways my father is a man of few silences. He's often loud, sometimes mean, he continues to scare me, and there are many times in my life that I don't like him at all. Yet he is my father. He is largely silent around matters of race, of ancestry, and of history. At least with me he is silent, the daughter who doesn't match his skin, who is just as apt to be read as his date than his daughter. I have long turned toward his approval, his recognition of me. In my identity construction, he is my link to brownness. Paternally brown. And so my desire for what he is always brings me back to stories of him. My father taught me to be brown, to be Mexican. He did it silently, often through his relation to whiteness.

Over the past few years something shifted with my dad. He has started talking with me in a way that I have learned to call racial bonding—shared knowledge brings us together. We are not they. They are different than us. It started when I came to him after a student of mine called me names, prompting anger, fear, and hurt. But through that speech I was able to meet my father's silence with a different visibility. Hailed into visibility by my student's violent speech, I was now brown in my father's eyes. It opened a space for him to speak, to share stories, offer advice. "Those white guys giving you a hard time?" he'll ask, either of my colleagues or my students. "Stupid white guys," is one of his favored retorts. These are quick exchanges, a performance of alliance. Us against them. Yet he is just as quick to name me white, depending on his mood, on the context. Maybe when I push too hard, too quickly. Bolstered by the rhythms of the white temporality that pervade my life, I over-step, cling too tightly. When I say something about Mexicans, when I look too much like my mom when he's angry. Then to him I'm "white bread" and maybe even the milkman's kid. Do I represent a silent distance from whiteness that is mine and not his? Am I the stupid white guy? Am I not his? The pain of these remarks cut, even with an armory of literature. At the same time, I see my interdependent investment in a white temporality even in my quest for brownness. I insist on his pronouncements, even *depend* on them, as if without the paternal blessing my brownness would be erased, invisible. Masculine authority, feminine submission, and ever-present tension reside through the years. Again, like with my grandfather, I don't want to dismiss my pain. When I sit alongside the pain, I take comfort in thinking through the spaces where I resist the speed of whiteness, the possession and care of brownness, and dwell in the silences that I do share with my father, generate stories I haven't told.

Sitting at the kitchen table, tired of fighting with him, I learn to rest in silence. Take refuge in mantras in my head, I trace my breath, and convince myself that it's important to maintain our relationship, to foster it. He is now the only one left in his imme- diate family, likely the last of his generation. This scares me, the loss of my uncle, as I watch my cousins cling to my father's voice and body, their father so similar to mine. I used to fantasize that I was my uncle's daughter. I saw no other explanation for the blue eyes that mirrored his, that were so distant from my own father's brown eyes. I wanted to be the gentle soul I saw in my uncle but I would always catch the uncanny resemblances that are distinctly my dad in other ways. We are the same. Sometimes I wonder if he'll come to me after he dies like some of the other men in my family. I think it might be easier to commune with the dead. But I have not yet lost a parent and my cousins' pain—their longing for one more day, one more conversation—propels me out of that fan- tasy of future. I have committed to be present to my relationship to my father. I call. I visit. I speak. I figure the reality is that we haven't got much time. I pray for grace, for forgiveness. My anger seethes at my inheritance, his silence: assimilation, monolingual, pride laced with shame, violences (un)bound by fear. In silence, I have learned to make space around these trappings of empire that reverberate through generations. Making space and slowing time I sink into the pain, feel it deeply. Know that the wounds are just that and reach beyond the pain I have learned to repeat. I smell the spices he teaches me to reach for, long for the heat on my tongue alongside the tangy bubbles of beer. I open my arms to the unabashed affection he doles out without hesitation. Hugs, kisses, the arm around my shoulders. "I love you" never slips past any conversation.

We sit together in silence eating the eggs that we drown in hot sauce, cover with beans and join with spicy meat. There are no forks along- side our plates, just a bag of heated up tortillas kept warm with a towel. We are at breakfast. The only sounds are the chews and the tears as the dog salivates in the corner. In a moment that surprises me, he begins a story. He rarely, if ever, tells stories of his family. "I remember my grandfather," is where he begins. My body stills, stiffens just a little. I have no idea where this is going and so I assume the posture of uncertainty, ready for anything. But my anticipation is laced with curiosity. He tells me of another breakfast, a breakfast with his grandfather. "My grandpa and I were sitting there eating eggs and beans sopping them up with tortillas. My dad walks in and tells us that we should be using a fork." Clearly agitated now, righteous against his father, my father becomes my great-grandfather. "Why use a fork? God gave us hands and he gave us tortillas." Now he laughs out loud, a glimmer of the boy from his story. We laugh together as we eat, enjoy the tortillas from that side of town, tortillas that I crave when I am away and don't ever have to ask for when I return; tortillas that I leave with by the dozens to place in my freezer and on my table.

My dad continues with a story about his grandfather that I have heard before. This story usually feels leveraged, threatening, aimed from a distance somehow. But this time it feels different. He begins, "You look just like your great-grandfather. He was tall with the bluest eyes. My grandmother was short like your grandfather, but he was tall and had blue eyes." I love the idea that I look like my great-grandfather. The pictures I have in black and white never color in the image of his eyes. But in this moment I see myself differently. My father has brown eyes, dark skin, shiny black hair that's now peppered with grey. "We come in all colors, that's for sure." And that laughter again. And all I hear is "we." We come in different colors. I belong. Drifting back to my grandfather, I fear I have engaged in yet another alliance against the past. This time with my father. There are conditions to our belonging. Borders crossed and crossers once again. In my silence I reach for them all, this lineage of men. In the kitchen I want to gather us together. My silence feels light, welcome. I have no words.

In quiet contemplation

These stories provide portraits of assimilation, recall unspoken movements and denials, and can be archived only in unspoken ways. My *ofrenda* is not an end in and of itself but a means of listening to assimilation—enforced silence—and attempts at sense making are dependent on the modes of their telling, receiving, and historical and contemporary flows of time. I would like to pause for a moment in the temporal dimensions of silence. At the intersection of cultural theory and spiritual practice, the relation between silence and voice might be entered into through silence as a methodology, as practice. On the one hand, silence as contemplative practice might provide us with refuge from the speed and direction of white temporality. In meditation, we slow down our relation to time, imagine, narrate; feelings come rapidly. Silence allows us space to listen. As stated above, Audre Lorde (1984) uses the word *transformation* to describe the relation between voice and silence. For Gloria Anzaldúa (2002), a spiritual practice leads us into the sacred space of nepantla. A retreat from the forces that define us otherwise, in nepantla we are changing, shifting, moving, feeling deeply. While the violence of imposed silence might have been the cause of holding my breath in, silence might also be the conditions under which I am able to release it. And breathe *freely*. When we shed old skin the process may indeed be excruciating, but we emerge, Anzaldúa writes, through it to conocimiento.[15] Perhaps as a condition of our capacity to move beyond suffering, into and beyond survival, is the practice of silence to recognize and honor pain as that which brings about healing, into living conocimiento.

These sites are dependent on our willingness to travel, to move, to be in time. Therefore, silence and voice are interdependent phenomenon. While we must attend to their causes and conditions, the experiences of both, each is a temporary site from which something else can and will emerge. If we approach silence from a different perspective, we can attend to its shifts in fluid ways. In the service of resisting the white temporality of empire, I turn to Maria Lugones' (2005) discussion of subjectivity and relationality. Through recognizing the production and limitation of agency from Western thought—that which is individualized, separated, and an ambition that watches out for one's self—she thinks of agency differently. We are interdependent, she argues. What happens to me is dependent on you. When I listen to you, I change; we are bound. She moves us toward relationality (see also Carrillo Rowe, 2008). While we must do our own work, then, to move into our pain, we do our work in and through one another. Therefore, silence operates here not only as a meditative and methodological practice but also as a decolonial and relational approach to silence.

Through silent practice, I learn to still, to slow down the pace of my narrative, to contemplate what other meanings might emerge when I am silent. In my silence, I hear differently. I feel differently. And the interruption of the quick paced expectation of a white temporality, of the chrono-politics, of the rehearsed narratives that emerge out of silence imposed, I offer that this practice of silence is a healing one: a healing that works across generations, across relations, and across communicative practice. At the edges of these travels, of representation, I sit in silence, often confounded, sometimes hopeful. I move with tense ambivalence toward silence. In discrete moments, through the repetition of learned habit, silence flows through my body as rage, terror, invisibility, hypervisibility, shame, recognition, longing, learning, pleasure, and potentiality. Its rhythms—sometimes cacophonous, sometimes harmonic—are as likely to soothe and open as they are to haunt and foreclose. Silence is my monster and my muse. In the stillness of silence is where the visions come, where memories that are mine and not mine shift into words and phrases, where stories take shape.

Acknowledgments

The author offers special thanks to Rae Langes, Karma Chávez, and Marita McLaughlin for their comments, conversations, and care. The author also thanks Sheena Malhotra and Aimee Carrillo Rowe for their invitation and feedback.

Notes

1. Dalia Rodriguez (2011) argues that there are raging silences experienced by people, particularly in academic settings. Drawing on Lorde's (1984) discussion of the uses of anger, she works through the ways in which silence can be productive.
2. In distinguishing between pain and suffering, Audre Lorde (1984) is particularly insightful. She describes pain as the experience of a moment, in response to an assault or onslaught, something that harms us physically, mentally, spiritually. Suffering, on the other hand, she describes as what happens when we hold on to pain. When we choose, or are unable to let go of pain, it is a constant memory, ever present companion. Suffering is the carrying of, the caring for our pain without healing it. She urges us to tend to our pain, to release it. In Buddhism, the reality of suffering is a primary tenet, the First Noble Truth. The second is that we participate in the creation of our own suffering, or look deeply into the conditions under which suffering occurs (Nhat Hanh, 1998). However, Thich Nhat Hanh explains that through the practice of meditation, of sitting in silence, the Third and Fourth Noble Truths offer that the cessation of suffering and a path that leads to removing the causes of suffering from our lives are also possible (see also Chögyam Trungpa, 1984, the Tibetan Buddhist lineage holder who brought the teachings of Shambhala to the West in the 1970s). Lorde's distinction between pain and suffering is insightful here, and neither text denies that pain won't continue to occur.
3. Mab Segrest (2002) theorizes the effects of whiteness and its costs in her discussion on the souls of white folks. Following W.E.B. DuBois' (2003) writing on the effects and legacies of slavery on Black subjects, Segrest turns the gaze to white people. She interweaves narratives from multiple time periods (slavery, academia, family, and the Truth and Reconciliation hearings in post-apartheid South Africa) and argues that we might locate the effects of power on those who inherit and benefit from racist and sexist systems

in our distance from our unwillingness and/or inability to face these systems directly. She refers to this as the anesthetic aesthetic of whiteness, or the performative and embodied cutting off of oneself from that pain. This manifests, Segrest argues, in the sites of our bodies and relations, including alcoholism, mental illness, and more.

4. In *The Possessive Investment in Whiteness*, Lipsitz (2006) argues for an understanding of whiteness as property, and therefore whiteness has material as well as social and cultural value. See also Ruth Frankenberg's (1994) seminal writing on whiteness and gender, and David Roediger (2007).

5. There is a recent and productive turn in queer theory that links attitudes toward the future with heteronormativity (see Halberstam, 2005; Edelman, 1994; Freeman, 2010). Other discussions of queer temporality push at these ideas to integrate an intersectional approach, particularly race and class, to dimensions of futurity (Muñoz, 2004). While these emerging theories are productive and challenge the absence of queer and non-white bodies and voices, I want to draw on them here to focus more specifically on the productive force of discourses of whiteness. While it might well be argued that white temporality has taken precedence over, and is embedded in ideologies since modernity and colonization (see in particular Freeman's (1994) discussion of chronopolitics), here I would like to begin to develop an argument for the naming and practices of what takes place, and how it informs speech communication (in voice or silence).

6. Maria Lugones (2003) describes the markers of agency (voice, certain types of labor, certain invitations to dialogue) as located in Western logics of individualism. Here, we understand that the very agency that one might find in and through empire as a response to it, is defined through it.

7. Silence as a communicative phenomenon, as opposed to silence as the absence of voice and therefore irrelevant, continues to gain traction across different disciplines. In feminist theories, from Adrienne Rich, Audre Lorde, and Cherie Moraga, silences are often read as imposed by power, and therefore something in need of resisting. In feminist and qualitative methodologies, scholars are beginning to encourage us to *read* silences for what they may communicate and/or indicate, as a site of reflection and understanding. For example, Kamala Visveswaran (1994) encourages us to read silences as sites of responses to uneven exchanges between researcher and researched and that we might learn something from attending to what silences might indicate. Maggie MacLure, Rachel Holmes, Liz Jones, and Christina MacRae (2010) follow Derrida's theorizing of silence as wholly unanalyzable, and therefore open to multiple analysis; silence is therefore never closed. In their article on silence as that which *resists* analysis, the authors read against the grain of dominant understandings of a situation for the multiple meanings and insights that a posture of incompleteness might open into readings of silence in qualitative contexts. Similarly, tracing the reflective components of silence, Liliana Herakova, Dijana Jelača, Razvan Sibii, and Leda Cooks (2011) describe their own experiences of silence in qualitative and uneven dialogic encounters and mark different kinds of silence that occur. Silence in pedagogical contexts also continue to be explored, in how to read and evaluate student silences, how students of color especially in predominantly white contexts might use silence, etc. (for a discussion of students being

silenced see Freire's seminal text *Pedagogy of the Oppressed*, 2000. For a more recent example of reading silence in pedagogical contexts see also Johnson, 2004; Johnson, Rich, and Cargile, 2008; Hao, 2011). The continued treatment of silence as communication leads to more complex understandings of its trappings, uses, and as sites of resistance. I begin this essay by thinking through the ways in which I have experienced and learned to understand silence largely as imposed upon me and how that leads to perceptions of the world.

8. Critical cultural theories identify the function, limitation, and effects of binary logic systems and practices. Alternatively, dialectical approaches and other correctives offer broader and less rigid understandings of culture and speech.

9. In *The Possessive Investment in Whiteness*, Lipsitz (2006) argues for an understanding of whiteness as property, and therefore having material as well as social and cultural value. See also Ruth Frankenberg's (1994) seminal writing on whiteness and gender, and David Roediger (2007).

10. For a fresh and honest discussion and theorization of the politics of relation between women in academia, Aimee Carrillo Rowe's *Power Lines* (2008) is instructive here. In her qualitative study on the relationships women develop, she argues that our relationships are never outside of power, and that we often look *up* power lines in order to develop those relationships that can help us negotiate the complexities of academe. Some relationships, then, are deliberate. This does not negate the meaningfulness of the relations that we develop, rather that our relations are often strategic in that they can also perform the kind of bridgework necessary for survival as well as to hold the potential for conscious-raising and institutional change. Here, I am not interested in diminishing or reducing my relationships to especially white people as seeking access to power, yet, the reality is that these relationships aid in the ease of negotiation as a woman of color.

11. While the use of the term colonial hangover is often used to depict the hangover of the presence of a colonial force in a colonized land and people, here I follow Segrest's (2002) and Frankenberg's (1994) leads and consider the ways in which colonization and its modern legacies in the dynamics of neoliberalism and whiteness effect white people. The colonial hangover I am referring to, therefore, is the *suffering* that is likely present in white bodies. I read the suffering alongside, rather than separate from, the privilege that white people gain, the material benefits of whiteness. The colonial hangover indicates the blockage of healing that comes from not attending to the costs of privilege. Further, the colonial hangover that I mean to argue here is present in the narrative production of all people who continue to navigate its legacies.

12. Yasmin Nair (n.d.) cautions us against structures of power and the ways they produce certain narratives from different groups. She focuses on the intersections of queerness and immigration to look at the conditions of survival and belonging in certain spaces. Narratives insisting on belonging— pleas to recognize or insist upon humanity, citizenship—she argues, potentially undermining agency and interfering with the movements aimed at structural change. Thanks to Karma Chávez for introducing me to Nair's

cautionary argument and for challenging me to think critically about a romantic relationship with personal narrative.

13. The Audre Lorde essay, "The Transformation of Silence into Language and Action" (in Lorde, 1984) is often cited as an argument for resisting the oppression of one's voice. These kinds of imposed silences and their correction, she writes, are rendered a particular urgency in times of crisis or in the finality of death. When we read this essay alongside "Eye to Eye" in the same volume, where Lorde writes of the role of power and oppression as they mediate relations between women of color, I am drawn to her emphasis on and her use of transformation. What I would like to suggest here in support of my argument about the interdependence of the conditions and uses of silence is that transformation depends on an ongoing relationship.

14. Thanks to Marita McLaughlin for her insightful read on this potential meaning, as a condition of Mexican American families' relations to the past and to language.

15. For her insights on the paths of nepantla and conocimiento, I am deeply indebted to my relation and ongoing conversations with Karma Chávez. The idea that I take up here on this point is credited to her. Though her comment was not related to this essay in particular, her timing and its fit are as usual, impeccable. Anzaldúa develops these points in both *Borderlands/La Frontera* (1999) as well as in the edited volume *This Bridge We Call Home* (2002).

References

Anzaldúa, Gloria. *Borderlands/La Frontera: The New Mestiza*. San Francisco, CA: Aunt Lute Books, 1999.

Anzaldúa, Gloria E. "Now let us shift ... the path of conocimiento ... inner works, public acts." In AnaLouise Keating (Ed.), *This Bridge We Call Home: Radical Visions for Transformation*. New York: Routledge, 2002, pp. 540–578.

Carrillo Rowe, A. *Power Lines: On the Subject of Feminist Alliances*. Durham, NC: Duke University Press, 2008.

DuBois, W.E.B. *The Souls of Black Folk*. New York: Fine Creative Media, 2003.

Edelman, Lee. *No Future: Queer Theory and the Death Drive*. Durham, NC: Duke UP, 2004.

Frankenberg, Ruth. *White Women, Race Matters: The Social Construction of Whiteness*. New York: Routledge, 1994.

Freeman, Elizabeth. *Time Binds: Queer Temporalities, Queer Histories*. Durham, NC: Duke UP, 2010.

Freire, Paolo. *Pedagogy of the Oppressed*. New York: Continuum, 2000.

Halberstam, Judith. *In a Queer Time and Place: Transgender Bodies, Subcultural Lives*. New York: NYU P, 2005.

Hao, Richie Neil. "Rethinking Critical Pedagogy: Implications on Silence and Silent Bodies." 31:3 *Text and Performance Quarterly* (2011): 267–284.

Herakova, Liliana L., Dijana Jelača, Razvan Sibii, and Leda Cooks. "Voicing Silence and Imagining Citizenship: Dialogues about Race and Whiteness in a 'Postracial' Era." 62:4 *Communication Studies* (2011): 372–388.

Johnson, Julia R. "Universal Instructional Design and Critical (Communication) Pedagogy: Strategies for Voice, Inclusion, and Social Justice/Change." 37:2 *Equity and Education* (2004): 145–153.

Johnson, Julia R., Marc Rich, and Aaron Castelan Cargile. " 'Why Are You Shoving This Stuff Down Our Throats?': Preparing Intercultural Educators to Challenge Performances of White Racism." 1:2 *Journal of International and Intercultural Communication* (2008): 113–135.

Langellier, Kristin M. "Personal Narrative, Performance, Performativity: Two or Three Things I Know for Sure." 19 *Text and Performance Quarterly* (1999): 125–144.

Langellier, Kristin M. and Eric E. Peterson. *Storytelling in Daily Life: Performing Narrative*. Philadelphia, PA: Temple UP, 2004.

Lipsitz, George. *The Possessive Investment in Whiteness: How White People Profit from Identity Politics*. Philadelphia, PA: Temple UP, 2006.

Lorde, Audre. *Sister Outsider: Essays and Speeches by Audre Lorde*. Berkeley, CA: The Crossing Press, 1984.

Lugones, Maria. "From Within Germinative Stasis: Creating Active Subjectivity, Resistant Agency." *Entre Mundos/Among Worlds: New Perspectives on Gloria Anzaldúa*. Ed. AnaLouise Keating. New York: Palgrave MacMillan, 2005, pp. 84–99.

Lugones, Maria. *Pilgrimages: Theorizing Coalition Against Multiple Oppressions*. New York, NY: Routledge, 2003.

MacLure, Maggie, Rachel Holmes, Liz Jones and Christina MacRae. "Silence as Resistance to Analysis: Or, on Not Opening One's Mouth Properly." 16 *Qualitative Inquiry* (2010): 492–500.

Muñoz, José Esteban (2007). Cruising the Toilet: LeRoi Jones/Amiri Baraka, Radical Black Traditions, and Queer Futurity. 3 *GLQ: A Journal of Lesbian and Gay Studies*: pp. 353–367.

Nhat Hanh, Thich (1998). *The Heart of the Buddha's Teaching: Transforming Suffering into Peace, Joy, and Liberation*. New York: Broadway Books.

Nair, Yasmin. "What's Left of Queer? Immigration, Sexuality, and Affect in a Neoliberal World." *Yasmin Nair*. n.d. Web. 10 Jan. 2012.

Rodriguez, Dalia. "Silent Rage and the Politics of Resistance: Countering Seductions of Whiteness and the Road to Politicization and Empowerment." 17:7 *Qualitative Inquiry* (2011): 589–598.

Roediger, David R. *The Wages of Whiteness: Race and the Making of the American Working Class*. New York: Verso, 2007.

Segrest, Mab. *Born to Belonging: Writings on Spirit and Justice*. New Brunswick, NJ: Rutgers, 2002.

Trungpa, Chögyam. *Shambhala: The Sacred Path of the Warrior*. Boston, MA: Shambhala Publications, 1984.

Visweswaran, Kamala. *Fictions of Feminist Ethnography*. Minneapolis: University of Minnesota Press, 1994.

Part IV

Legacies of Silences: Memory, Healing, Power

16
The Silence in My Belly

Sheena Malhotra

As we go for one of our evening walks, Kimberlee asks in a quiet voice, "What does it feel like to be 'Sheena, who has cancer?'" I breathe in sharply, trying to remain calm on the surface as I reflect on her question. Her question pierces the quiet exterior I've built like a cocoon. It breaks the silence. The silence of my experience of living with cancer. The silence of someone recently diagnosed and operated on for ovarian cancer.

I think about it for a moment. "It feels exaggerated and crisp all at the same time," I tell her. Everything. It's like the channel suddenly switched from the generic morning show (news, interviews, easy chatter, and weather), which was my everyday life as a young academic, to a high-stakes HBO drama with one unexpected twist and turn after another. You can't predict the ending, and every move, every decision builds to a cliffhanger. A series where the writing is ironic and sharp.

The exaggerated and crisp new drama that is now my life has taught me about silence in a new way as I come to terms with my walk with cancer. "It feels like there is a silence," I tell her. "A silence *here*," I say, rubbing my hand over my stomach. Here, in my center, where my womb used to be. Here, in my center, I am coming to know silence in a more embodied way than I have ever known before. I grew up in India, spending my teens as a competitive national swimmer, training my body hard. Three to four hours a day, we'd lift weights, stretch, and swim. So much time spent under water; my relationship with silence was already complex. Culturally, I had learnt to utilize silence as a strategy to navigate complicated interpersonal relationships. Personally, I had come to appreciate the act of swimming as interplay between breath and silence. I often found solace for my thoughts and emotions in the silence of the water, in the midst of the grueling physical training. It became a retreat and a strategy for handling difficult emotional terrain when I was not ready to disclose and discuss troubles with friends. However, even though I was familiar with silence as being part of my physical life, it feels qualitatively different to discover the silence actually residing within my body. Kimberlee and I are quiet for a time as we walk. We do not speak, absorbing the full weight and meaning of that silence.

Silence, agency, and possibility. These lie intertwined at the heart of this chapter. When I began working in the Western feminist academic tradition, I struggled with the Western compulsion for voice and speaking.[1] Words fill the Western canon. Speaking is valorized: speak your position; take a stand; speak, speak, speak! This, of course, is about agency. The need to speak also comes from a fear of not being heard, of being invisible. And it is a valid fear. Silence equals invisibility as vividly described in literature by women of color (in feminist classics, e.g., *This Bridge Called My Back,* Moraga and Anzaldúa, 1981). The erasure of voices materially and symbolically in this society is critical. As a postcolonial, diasporic subject myself, I understand the importance of agency and voice in terms of reclaiming space and exercising our power. In fact, I believe silence as a strategy could extend Homi Bhabha's (1994) ideas about the many forms of subversive resistance utilized by colonial subjects.[2] Evoking Gayatri Spivak's (1988) haunting question about whether the subaltern can speak reminds us that the other side of the equation of being able to speak is really about engaging our ability to listen and the silence necessary for that listening.[3]

A few days after our silent walk, a gift from Kimberlee arrives in the mail. It is Audre Lorde's (1980) *The Cancer Journals.* The book is a collection of Lorde's writings (journal entries and essays) through and after her diagnosis of breast cancer. Flipping through the pages, I find much connection and life-affirming wisdom in Lorde's words and experiences. Her strength and her vulnerability are inspiring. As a person of color, as someone who is not a citizen, I relate to her positioning within the Western medical establishment, which I now am forced to navigate, while being across the globe from my family. I am ever grateful for the medical insurance that my job provides. But I run full-tilt into my biggest unconscious fear about living in the USA—the fear of facing a serious illness alone. For me, like Lorde, it is a community of friends that steps up in very embodied, daily ways to help me traverse my fears and the alienation of examination rooms and surgical release forms. My mother drops everything and flies from India to be with me through the surgery and the months of chemotherapy that will follow.

But Lorde speaks about silence in a way very different than I feel it. She warns us about silence, "May these words serve as encouragement for other women to speak and to act out of our experiences with cancer and with other threats of death, for silence has never brought us anything of worth" (Lorde, 1980, p. 10). Read in the context in which she was writing, which was to break the silence about breast cancer and its treatments, her words are powerful. I remain grateful that she and other writers and activists[4] have found ways to give voice to their experiences of reproductive-system cancers, to break those silences that had separated women from one another's journeys with the disease. Lorde wrote about silences that are imposed from the outside and must be broken. I agree that when silences are imposed and oppressive, they must be dismantled.[5] I agree that giving voice to our lived experiences, as women, as women of color, as feminists, is key. But I find in her work a conflation between agency and voice that I am suggesting should be unpacked. I would like to take up silence in a different way, to consider silences that have complex relationships with agency.

The physicality of silence

When Lorde was writing in the late 1970s and early 1980s, breast cancer was not spoken about except in hushed tones, and women were pressured to have reconstructive breast surgery after undergoing a mastectomy so that they could appear "normal" again. Lorde rejects that notion, calling on women to break silence, to become visible to each other. She says,

> But I believe that socially sanctioned prosthesis is merely another way of keeping women with breast cancer silent and separate from each other. For instance, what would happen if an army of one-breasted women descended upon Congress and demanded that the use of carcinogenic, fat-stored hormones in beef-feed be outlawed? (1980, p. 16)

Three decades later, breast cancer research is one of the most highly funded forms of cancer research (Parker-Pope, *The New York Times*, 6 March 2008), precisely because women have spoken out, and organized.[6] Of course, more work remains to be done as breast cancer continues to impact women's lives in very significant numbers.[7] However, awareness about breast cancer, and organizing around treatment and funding research have grown immensely since the time of Lorde's writing.[8]

I want to draw attention to the fact that Lorde recognized the physicality involved in silencing breast cancer. Literally, the way to "silence" women who underwent mastectomies—and keep them from coming together as a group—was to recreate the appearance of the missing breast(s): an attempt to make the surgery and the disease invisible. There was a very physical dimension, deliberately forged, to the silence, and indeed, to the agency that Lorde advocated reclaiming. She was asking women to reject the silencing surrounding breast cancer by making different choices around the physicality of their lives and their bodies.

Like Lorde, I have often experienced silence in a very embodied manner: in my throat, as a stillness in my bones. During the time of my cancer the materiality of the silence in my body impacted those around me. That summer, it felt like silences moved our beings, and filled in the spaces between the buzz of friends in my life who formed a chemo-care relay team, flying in from different parts of the country to be there for Mom and me. Silence surrounded the shock of facing the stats, of being told I had an "average" five-year life expectancy at 35! I watched the silence of that fact sink into my mother's face, and then a few hours later, watched the fight return to her spine as she reminded me with quiet determination that I have never been "average." After that, I noticed her refusal to ever repeat that statistic, as if she could drown out the specter of its possibility with her silence. She took refuge in her silence. Maybe I could too? Perhaps it is all a part of the drama of dealing with the idea of cancer, the Big "C" that remains unspoken outside this close circle of friends. I thumb through thirty-three "get well" cards that never call the "C" word into being. Another silence. But it is already here. In my body, in my womb and in my stomach. And I sit with that. Especially in the afternoons....

I am particularly drawn to the possibilities that reframing silence opens up for fluidity and resistance.[9] The fluidity of silence is reminiscent of the gender fluidity that accompanied my chemotherapy. To walk in the world for some time without hair, without eyebrows and eyelashes, which delineate and define our faces, our humanity, I find myself moving into new realms, isolated, almost animal, beyond gender, walking in another world.[10] People were met by my silence or my dimpled smile when they called me "Sir" during my "baldy days." Such ambiguous moments created new ways to play with gender fluidity because of the moment of hesitancy it engendered in the other person; a discomforting moment of being unsure. Silence as possibilities can also translate to a space of unsettling possibilities.

I came to a new relationship with silence in a very real way through the embodiment of having undergone a radical hysterectomy. It was a part of my body, my "belly," that fell silent. A silence wrought by having many of my organs (ovaries, uterus, gall bladder, omentum, and all the "stuff" surrounding them) evacuated. And so I am left with a physical silence, caused by the absence of all that used to inhabit my abdominal cavity. It is a silence that I did not expect. Over the years since, I have come to regard as a miracle: the ability of the human body to heal itself, to reclaim evacuated spaces. It is a miracle that has allowed me to resume my everyday life. Most days I forget that I ever had cancer, or underwent major surgery. But in the moments of quiet, when I reckon with the silence in my body, my belly reminds me there might be other ways to know silence; a meditation and a breathing through that is also part of my truth and my learning. I learn to respect that silence just as much as I respect the voice I had begun to exercise as a woman of color within a Western, feminist academic space. I sit with a silence that is my uninvited teacher and learn to give it respect. And I find it profound, the abundance that is generated from this space of loss.

Impositions and reckonings with silence and agency

But what of silences that are not actively chosen? The silence in my body was surgically imposed. It was deemed a medical necessity to save my life. And that raises the question of agency. Within the Western approach to medicine and healing, I had to do the surgery, and do it quickly, in order to stop the spread of the cancer. It resulted in a silence with real lived consequences to it (no ovaries equals no more possibilities of childbirth), and metaphysical implications as well. So when considering the question of agency, and choices one might make around silence, I find that agency is a complicated prerequisite to silences that might be empowering or profound.

I had agency in particular ways in this situation. The fact that I had medical insurance meant that I had access to health care and was able to get the medical attention I needed. I also had agency in that I was empowered to make choices around my treatment and care. However, the choice I faced boiled down to: *do the surgery in the next few days, followed by chemo, and you might have a small chance of stopping the cancer,* or *don't do the surgery, and you will probably die from the cancer soon.* Faced with these stark choices, it became very clear that this was a fight for my life, so I exercised my agency by choosing to go with the recommendations of my doctors. I did the surgery and six rounds of chemotherapy. However, the silence in my belly is a consequence of that choice. That part was "imposed" in some ways, in the sense that my resultant missing womb was not what I had necessarily invited or wanted.

I have learnt that the silence I find residing in my body, even though it was not fully chosen, can still be profound. Yes, agency is a part of this equation, because I had agency in making the originating choice that resulted in the silence I am grappling with. And agency is involved in the choices I am making around how I am positioned today as a result of that original choice. So I believe that when rethinking silence as a space of possibility, agency must always be a factor. We have learnt from our feminist forerunners that silence without *any* agency is oppressive, particularly given the material conditions of the lives in question. There are too many examples of those proliferating our literature, particularly when it comes to women, the working poor, queer folks, and bodies of color. Women of color writing against the silences imposed by patriarchal systems have significantly advanced our understanding of how lack of agency functions as a key source of oppression. But the converse is not a straightforward equation either, wherein silence + agency = empowering silence. When we do have some degree of agency, and then find ourselves at unexpected points in the road of life, I believe that the equations between silence and agency become more complex.

I grapple with what feels like a lack of agency in the "silence" in my body and womb. The silence in my belly now means an absence of choices about whether or not I want to birth children. There is no fluidity about that question any longer. I breathe into the emotions thrown up by a lifetime of regressive gender conditioning (that I'd intellectually rejected a long time ago)—one that equates being a woman with having children. I recognize that it is a very different proposition for me than it might be for other women who have always wanted a child. I somehow knew I would never actually birth a child of my own, believing the presence of any children in my life would come through siblings, a partner, friends, or adoption. But now that the silence in my belly translates to an absolute and irreversible reality—one that means that I cannot birth a child whether I want to or not—I am taught in harsh sunlight about the luxury of soft choices.

However, the longer I sit with it, I learn that even if a silence is not chosen, it can still be profound. I start to imagine into expanding definitions and new gender plays. And I keep thinking about the "silence in my belly" as I read Lorde. I wonder about how our frames differ, and how those differences might be tied to the historical points in time we occupy vis-à-vis the feminist and critical studies movements. Without her call for voice, my contemplations of silence would have no meaning, no ground on which to stand. It is only now that we have some degree of agency that I can write about agency's complexities. I realize, when it comes to silences we inhabit, perhaps the more important form of agency is in the response we bring to wherever we find ourselves standing.

Silence as a space of possibility and transformation

In the end, I see silence as a space of possibility and transformation. I question the ethnocentric assumptions underlying US academe, which privilege voice as the only form of intelligible communication. Too often, our impulse is to talk through, talk over, talk ourselves out of spaces of discomfort. Conditioned by a positivist-oriented culture, we are often taught to trust only that which we can see or hear, to value the linear and the logical rather than the whole and the intuitive. Language too is a form of expression wherein one word necessarily builds on the next in order to be intelligible.[11] But since words within language come pre-loaded with unspoken or underlying histories and meanings, they often get contained through the dominant reading (as Hall, 1980, reminds us) of the word itself. Indeed, words fix us into the moment of their utterance, and often into the dominant meanings they contain. Silence, on the other hand, allows a space that reaches beyond linearity: the linearity to which words limit us. I consider silence a space of possibility because thoughts, ideas, explorations do not have to flow in one direction or the other. They can move and morph and change directions and hold more than one thing at once. Like the oxygen that feeds a fire and indeed allows the rhythm of its expression to change form, as flames dance differently by its very presence, silence breathes and meanings can shift, perspectives can be revealed. Just as fire signifies the transformation of form from matter into air, silence too opens the space to imagine the unimaginable, allows us a place for reflection, re-articulation, and unarticulation so that we can come into another way of communicating that is beyond language.

I will not lie. There are times that I have hidden behind my silence, my shyness, usually to provide myself with the space to think through a position, to tease out the nuances of how I believe in my own mind at a pace that seemed more "natural" to me than the rapid-fire instantaneous knowing and speaking expected of me in many academic settings. Working in Western academe and more particularly, working within Western *feminist* academic settings, I realized I was fast becoming "invisible" through my chosen silences. I cannot say that I have yet found effective ways of making myself visible that do not capitulate to Western academic norms (i.e. I know I must use my voice, or my words, to be validated). Simultaneously, even as I contemplate choices around speaking out, I have harbored the secret fear that I am a coward; a coward for not speaking, for not clearly defining and declaring who I am, for not taking a stand because I have not spoken in a way that is intelligible within this tradition. I am learning to distinguish for myself the instances when my silences originate in a space of contemplation and agency, as opposed to other silences that might be rooted in my fears. It is internal work that brings about its own reckoning and growth. But being able to discern between the two allows a more active choosing of silences that have meditative qualities and expansive possibilities, choosing the space it gives one to breathe and reflect.

I am drawn to Anzaldúa's writings in *Borderlands/La Frontera* (1987), which challenge these more linear forms of knowing and logic formation. She encourages a consciousness that entails a "shift out of habitual formations: from convergent thinking, analytical reasoning that tends to use rationality to move toward a single goal (a Western mode), to divergent thinking, characterized by movement away from set patterns and goals toward a more whole perspective, one that includes rather than excludes" (p. 101). I am convinced that any such holistic perspective must include silence *alongside of* voice. Indeed, it is often silence that opens up the space for the emotional and deeply transformative work to occur. Silence, and sitting with the silence, allowed me to reframe and reorient my experience with cancer into teachings that have a profound and powerful impact on my life. It was by entering the silences that accompanied the surgery that I was able to explore the new dimensions of voice that were being birthed in my belly. This form of silence feels similar to the expansive breathing in yoga. It can be quite different from our everyday or aerobic breath. All are necessary.

I return to my original question: What might I birth from this silence in my belly? For one, I already know that I have birthed a new voice. Or is it my old voice with a new clarity to it? I narrate every moment with a clarity that simultaneously sees that moment in close magnification and from afar. I am learning to more fully inhabit the HBO drama series that is now my life. I am finding a voice filled with the silences of all that remains unspoken. As I move locations—from competitive swimmer to young professor to cancer survivor—I am forced to move forward and back. I depart from a purely intellectual existence and return into a much more embodied and spiritual one. Suddenly, the urgency of understanding the differences between the silences that nourish us and those that slowly kill us has become one of the biggest gifts of this silence in my belly.

Perhaps the question is one of context, physicalities, intentionality, and agency. There are moments when speaking, speaking out, voicing one's truth, claiming the space of visibility is of greatest importance. However, there are different contexts in which silence can be an act of resistance, when silence can open up spaces that words would have closed out. Understanding the complex interplay between agency and silence is key to embracing the silences we engender, or that we encounter. Silence transforms. I enter the silence and continue to imagine new spaces of fluid possibilities, even when certain realities seem fixed around me. In the years since my original diagnosis, I have learned to breathe in a yogic way. To be present to the exhilarating transformations wrought by the silence in my belly. I've learned to dwell in silence more deliberately, so that I could ultimately speak and live with clearer voice. I come to realize the silence in my belly has been absolutely key—to the healing in my life, and to the birthing of this book.

Acknowledgments

I thank Kimberlee Perez and Kathryn Sorrells for their careful reading and editorial comments on this essay. Their insights have been key to its development.

Notes

1. Jonna Kadi's essay, "Speaking (About) Silence" (2002) critiques the mostly white, upper-class space of her graduate program and the ways in which it felt silencing to her as a queer, person of color. She urges us to listen to the silences to really understand nondominant experiences of dominant spaces. While she aligns with a more traditional reading of silence as being oppressive, she offers insight on the importance of listening within academic spaces, repeating, "If there is a hesitation with which I speak, it is because I am surrounded by spaces filled with my silence. If you want to hear me, listen to my silence as well as my words" (p. 545).
2. Homi Bhabha (1994) has written extensively about the complicated relationship between colonial subjects and their colonizers. He writes about ambivalence as a love–hate relationship between colonizer and colonized. Mimicry and hybridity emerge as both imitation and mockery of the

colonizing powers, sometimes working as complicity and others as forms of resistance. I believe that we could also explore the ambivalence of silence as a strategy of resistance within that context; however, that is outside the scope of this essay.

3. See the introductory chapter to this volume for a more detailed discussion of Gayatri Spivak's question.
4. There is significant critical scholarship on breast cancer, particularly about the activism and politics that surround breast cancer research. See Ulrike Boehmer (2000); Maureen Hogan Casamayou (2001); Mary DeShaze (2005); Maren Klawiter (2008); and Barron Lerner (2003) for more detailed discussions of breast cancer research, politics, and activism.
5. The irony is that ovarian cancer is often considered a "silent killer," because it is often (80 percent of the time) discovered in later stages when it is more likely to be fatal (National Cancer Institute, 2012).
6. There is an argument that breast cancer is funded partially because it is about the most objectified part of a woman's body, that it is visible, that it signifies femininity, and that we, as a society, put a high value on women's breasts.
7. It is estimated that 230,480 women will have been diagnosed with and 39,520 women will have died of breast cancer in 2011 (National Cancer Institute, 2012). In terms of lifetime risk, the research shows that one in eight women will be diagnosed with breast cancer during their lifetime (National Cancer Institute, 2012).
8. Breast cancer has now become one of the most highly funded forms of cancer research when considering the ratio of dollars spent on research to the numbers of women diagnosed with breast cancer (Parker-Pope, 2008). This growth in funding is largely due to the activism around breast cancer research by women in the last few decades, as it used to be one of the most under-funded forms of research, even though it was one of the most prolific killers of women.
9. See Keating (Chapter 2), or Clair (Chapter 6), in this volume.
10. From *National Women's Studies Association Journal* (NWSAJ). Special Issue, "Moving Locations: The Politics of Identities in Motion," 17 (2).
11. Of course, living in California, it is impossible to speak of language and silence without also mentioning the ways in which the ability or inability to speak a particular language (English in this case) is used as a tool of discrimination and oppression against large populations.

References

Anzaldúa, Gloria (1987). *Borderlands/La Frontera: The New Mestiza*. San Francisco, CA: Aunt Lute.
Bhabha, Homi K. (1994). *The location of culture*. London: Routledge.
Boehmer, Ulrike (2000). *The personal and the political: Women's activism in response to the breast cancer and AIDS epidemics*. Albany, NY: SUNY Press.
Casamayou, Maureen Hogan (2001). *The politics of breast cancer*. Washington, DC: Georgetown University Press.
DeShaze, Mary K. (2005). *Fractured borders: reading women's cancer literature*. Ann Arbor, MI: University of Michigan Press.

Hall, Stuart (1980). Encoding/decoding. In Stuart Hall, Dorothy Hobson, Andrew Lowe, and Paul Willis (Eds), *Culture, media, language*. London: Hutchinson (original work published 1973), pp. 128–138.

Klawiter, Maren (2008). *The biopolitics of breast cancer: Changing cultures of disease and activism*. Minneapolis, MN: University of Minnesota Press.

Lerner, Barron H. (2003). *The breast cancer wars: Hope, fear, and the pursuit of a cure in twentieth-century America*. Oxford: Oxford University Press.

Lorde, Audre (1980). *The cancer journals*. San Francisco, CA: Aunt Lute.

Moraga, Cherrie and Gloria Anzaldúa (Eds) (1981). *This bridge called my back: Writings by radical women of color*. New York: Kitchen Table Press.

National Cancer Institute (2012). *Surveillance epidemiology and end results*. http://seer.cancer.gov/. Accessed on 13 February 2012.

Parker-Pope, Tara (2008). "Cancer funding: Does it add up?" *New York Times*. 6 March 2008.

Spivak, Gayatri (1988). "Can the subaltern speak?" In Cary Nelson and Lawrence Grossberg (Ed.), *Marxism and the interpretation of culture*. Chicago, IL: University of Illinois Press, pp. 271–315.

17
Standing in the Wake of My Father's Silence (An Alternative Eulogy)

Bryant Keith Alexander

> It would be erroneous to say Sohrab was quiet. Quiet is peace. Tranquility. Quiet is turning down the volume knob on life. Silence is pushing the off button.[1] Shutting it down. All of it. Sohrab's silence wasn't the self-imposed silence of those with convictions, of protesters who seek to speak their cause by not speaking at all. It was the silence of one who has taken cover in a dark place, curled up all the edges and tucked them under.
>
> (From the novel, *The Kite Runner*[2])

> It was the first time that I had ever slept on the shores, and I began to understand why people said of the lake, that there was no end to it, even though it was bounded by rocks. There were rivers flowing in and flowing out, secret currents, six kinds of weather working on its surface and a hidden terrain beneath. Each wave washed in from somewhere unseen and washed out to somewhere unknown.
>
> (From the short story, "Shamengwa"[3])

Silence in human social engagement is not only the absence of talk, it is also a strategic rhetoric used to emphasize the said and the unsaid. Hence, in the absence of words, silence speaks volumes about the relationship of its engagement or the impulse of its in/action. In this short piece I am using the occasion of eulogizing my father as both a commentary on our life together, and as a critical component of my own recovery from that life. But more importantly, I am engaged in a reflection on how my father used silence as parental stratagem and social agency. In the process, I am made more aware of the effects of my father's silence, the legacy of that silence, and the psychology of silence that circulates like complicity in my blood.

Wake—to be or to remain awake

I have written about my dad before—about my struggle to negotiate the class-based guilts of his profession in relation to mine—the garbage man and the professor.[4] As a gay man, I have written about the tyranny of his disciplinary impulse in the enculturation of masculinity. As a relatively insecure adult/child I have written about the dominance of his parental regime, as well as his privatized moments of displayed care and concern for me, and my love for him. These are not competing narratives, as much as they are stories circulating in the constellation of culture, family, and the dynamism of a Black father/son relationship. And like many, I feel that I may have slept through most of my childhood, taking the everydayness of family life as a given. Yet in my adult life I am fully awake, and the luxury of childhood assumptions has given way to the necessity of critical reflection; the need to understand the realities of my current predicament based on a culturally specific lived experience. In the death of my father, and in the moment of giving his eulogy, I am alert to the necessities of the occasion. The memories flow, and I am in a process of actively constructing a particular image of my father, salvaged from the hubris and umbrage that comes in the processes of sons talking about their fathers. Such a process promises that I will never again sleep my way through the realities of his life or the legacy of my life with him. Now, I stand vigilant over his corpse and memory, trying to give voice to silence.

Wake—to hold a vigil over the body of someone who has died

My father's disciplinary impulse was often swift—in the manner signaled by the pull of his belt off his pants, the crack of a switch from a tree, or the manner in which his heavy hand landed on my face or backside. My parents believed that to spare the rod was to spoil the child, and I believe the same (but then again I don't have children). Yet, no matter how hard my father could hit, his worst form of punishment was his silence—the absence of his voice on issues that mattered—the death of his mother, my brother's death from AIDS,[5] my gay identity, another brother's incarceration, my sisters' pregnancies, siblings dropping out of high school, his own health—and the ways in which silence was used as an act of punishment. In the absence of words, there is only speculation about intention and the curious mind fills in the space with only the most negative of possibilities—disappointment, disgrace, disapproval, disillusionment, dismissal—a lack of care. Hence silence is sometimes the most severe criticism.[6]

During this time in which I *stand* shemira—*waiting, watching, and comforting the soul of my father in his journey forward,*[7] I am taking the opportunity to speculate on his life. I begin to wonder if my father's silence was always intentional, or was it his inability to find the words to express thoughts and feelings? I wonder if a lack of education and the legacy of his own enculturated masculinity as "the strong silent type," prevented him from the type of intimate engagement with his children that would have released us from the prison of his silence. And even now, as I speculate, I know that this speculation is only a polite gesture that tries to contextualize my father in time and circumstance, for that is what a eulogy must do. I know that in some cases, the practice of voice as a politicized expression of desire is not volitional but structured and suppressed in systems of circumstance—of race, class, and power. But I also know that my father had a particular facility with language that made his desires very clear—angry public tirades, violent name calling—all tempered at times with privatized apologies as performances of care and comfort. So my father's use of silence was rhetorical and strategic—an intentional not saying that cut deeper than words of derision. But even as I try to shed light on his behavior, I know that I will always stand in the darkness, on night watch; waiting and wanting for him to tell me his truth.

Wake—to come back, or bring somebody back to a conscious state after sleeping

Time and the memory of loss have a way of dissipating the inheritance of the living. Eulogies operate in that tropological space of tethering memories in death to the resolve of the living to remember. In the eulogy, voids of silent grief are filled with ceremonial talk, making the absent present and forcing the one giving the eulogy to stand for the one who cannot. During the eulogy, I am standing in the silence of family and I realize that they expect me to resurrect my father with words. To make conscious and not only awaken in them the memory of who he was, but to color memory with a tone of civility, establishing an impulse of kind remembrance that will linger for a lifetime. And I must oblige. It is a command performance of exemplary son, a repayment of a life given for a life now gone. It is a moment of return—for in the absent possibility of awakening the deceased, the eulogy becomes an act of awakening truths in the mind and hearts of family and friends; truths that lay shrouded in the darkness of hurt feelings, of wrought emotions, and the necessity in the moment to place such thoughts aside, or douse the wounds with the sanitizing agent of rhetoric. Knowing, of course, that such wounds sometimes leave scars that are soul deep and spirit strong. In this since, memory in the moment of death is not contested, yet the articulation of memory in the context of the eulogy is contestable; and the eulogy becomes the site for both revenge and reconciliation.

Wake—to become alert and active or make somebody alert and active after being inactive, in a daydream or preoccupation

In waking my father, I must break my silence. There are moments of remembrance that influence the act of the eulogy. Like those literal moments of trying to awaken my father after falling drunk asleep in the corner chair of the living room. As a child, those were moments of tentative unexpectedness. Moments when I did not know if he would wake up swinging—like from a childish nightmare or simply open his blood shot eyes and stare at me like I had committed some cardinal sin; disturbing a momentarily self-induced amnesia. Yet in either case, there would be a moment of dysphoria (or was it dystopia?), a disoriented haplessness of my father and a moment of benign befuddlement on my part. These were moments of dis-recognition and disdain from both the person being awoken and the person awaking. There were very few benefits in awakening my father in that situation, other than fulfilling my mother's request to ease him from public view and lay him comfortably to bed. And maybe in the eulogy, this is what I am doing again.

In his death, I am made alert. I come to acknowledge my own addictions and avoidances. They are at times less visible, but serve as coping mechanisms that help validate my sense of self and allow me the strength to endure as a private person in the protocols of public life; avoidance of unnecessary social activities, the quest for privacy, the controlled response to tensive situations, or the lack of immediacy in expressing anger and disappointment. I have tracked these defense mechanisms back to my father. And I am not so sure that his preoccupations and my own are not masking the same things in the mixture of identity politics as a generational legacy. In reading my father's silence, I have come to forge an alliance with him in understanding myself.

In the eulogy, my father's biography becomes my own. I am both talking about him and breaking his silence to talk for him, as much as I am engaged in a moment of confession and self-revelation.

Wake—the rack left in water by a vessel or any other body moving through it

Maybe I have always been standing in the wake of my father's life; who he was and how he lived his life. This is all clear to me as I stand in this moment of eulogizing him. I am both the result of his being and the active possibility of who he was. In this sense, I have always struggled to find myself in relation to him—sometimes running away from the waves of his shifting currents: serious and silly, hard and gentle, introspective and shallow, stoic and gregarious—fleeting and mercurial; each leaving waves of combustibility strong enough to move me to tears, for differing reasons. I struggle to temper those currents in myself, erring on the side of compassion and humility, also knowing that there are often limits to these particular performances of sociality. Such moments of explosion or implosion in my own performances of patience, care, and forgiveness often lead me closer to understanding my father—even as I continue to hold him at arms length. I begin to hear his voice and he speaks to me through his silence, through my own voice. And just when I think I understand him, his *wave is washed away, somewhere unseen and somewhere unknown*, and I am left wet and wondering.[8] And as I try to understand the wave, I realize I have missed him all together, for the wave was just the effect. And now I am only feeling the rippled after turbulence of him, having been, here.

Wake—a position behind somebody or something that is moving ahead fast; the aftermath or after-effects of a dramatic event or powerful thing: quiet, silent

After my father's death, I stood in the wake of his life. I was forced to reflect with more serious intention on the ways in which I am my father's son, an after-effect of his being. I had to acknowledge that even though a part of my professional career is about being "public" and "speaking," the more meaningful aspects of my life are really about "privacy" and "silence" (a not saying, and a not doing); a desire for loneness that is both the reflection of lingering insecurity and the aftermath (or effect) of being the fifth child of seven children in a house where privacy was at a premium. Mine is sometimes self-induced silence as a performance of tempering the allocated power that has been given to me as a man, as a Black man, as a Black male academic and how those are modulated by racial and gendered politics of my being. My father taught me the possibilities and limitations of such racial performatives. His lessons were specific to whiteness and performing to White people; situations in which my articulate voice is seen as challenging White authority, and is thus characterized in terms of the monolithic construct of the "angry Black man" against the vulnerability of whiteness. Such a social binary only exists in the White imagination as marketing tool, social defense against blackness, and the sustainability of White power. In these situations, my silence, as a performative engagement, is not always a successful restraint against the anger-filled verbal violence that has often stripped people bare; especially when they have carelessly made me the executor of their happiness or the scapegoat for their unreflected privilege or negligence. Times when they have expected me to care more than they, and do more than they, do, to maintain social relations. Times in which whiteness claims the privilege to speak, displacing and silencing the voices/thoughts/feelings of the other—as a ritual practice of divine order.[9]

My silence is sometimes a very directed performance *of not saying, of not speaking up, of not expressing*—as a self-restraint against a potential torrent of invective that, like my father's own performances of silence and non-silence, leaves its own devastation. For you see, while my father was often silent, he was never quiet; a distinction that is made in the strategic absence of voice in the power of presence, in which silence speaks at a deafening volume. This is not a prideful admission on my part, but one that serves a purpose in its iteration. Like the eulogy, speaking a truth allows for a particular level of critical reflection and possible recovery for others and more importantly in this case, my own recovery and my own realization of the dramatic effect that my father has had in the man that I have become.

I know that silence is also a strategy of nonresponse that can be an act of violence, a doing. And maybe, unlike my father, I know the difference, though at times the results are the same. Such admittance on my part is a form of resurrecting my dad. It is an act of breaking through my own wall of silence. It is my vow to do, and be, better.

Wake—to make somebody aware of something

As a kid and young adult, I used to wonder whether my father ever really wanted children. (I know that sounds sad.) I wondered if he kowtowed to my mother's desire; one of two children, and a good Catholic girl, my mother wanted a large family (seven children and one miscarriage). I never doubted that my father loved us, it was just that he never was seen in public with us—few visits to church, no parades, no fairs, no malls—mostly privatized home events. I wondered if he was aware of the impact of his actions, and whether his silence as absence was an act of revenge or recovery. In my eulogy for my father, I strategically remind my siblings of this aspect of my father and begin to ask them to remember him in loving yet critical ways, for he has provided us with a template of being that we must all claim, and should we choose, subvert.

Through a lifetime of written and unwritten ethnographic research on my family culture and my father as the primary ethnographic subject (with me as his doppelgänger), I have been able to capture only glimpses of who he was, and consequently, who I am in relation to him. And while ethnographic practices should not be about capture but illumination—for my own selfish purposes, I have tried to capture and study these performances of family culture for my own self-knowledge. In his death, my father has now moved ahead fast and deep into memory. So fast and deep that the project of the eulogy, like archeology, becomes an excavation of memories against time; a process of digging up and trying to piece remnants of experience in a field of reflection and refraction that only becomes increasingly sedimented yet demands a particular evidence of effort in the days between death and burial, the aninut. In which time, the cultural performance of the eulogy is invoked as a ritual act to sustain memory in community using the tropes and figures of prayer, commemoration, and apologia to bridge the limenal gap of being departed and being gone; making us all aware of his absence and our present, and our own mortality. We comfort each other; we who are left behind.

Wake—a stream of turbulence in the air left by an aircraft or land vehicle passing through it

Memory is not a silent place. The process of remembering is loud with reverberations and banging against the recesses of the mind and heart. This is particularly raucous in the process of family eulogy. In the family eulogy there are competing voices, competing narratives and recollections that seek to suture wounds as well as those spaces between fantasy, reality, and nightmare—utopia and dystopia, vying for space in the pantheon of family remembrance where memory has to be a livable space; a refuge in/from the reality of loss and regret.

Silence, though a powerful rhetorical tool and a frugal escape from reality, is not a performative option in giving a eulogy.

My father's death caused *a stream of turbulence,* a disruption in a plane of peace or complacency to life with my father. Each of his children and my mother were forced to deal with the reality of the loss and to do a quick inventory of things said and unsaid, and the resulting impact of his passing. As the chosen child to speak, I was asked to make my private processes public. In the eulogy I wade through the competing forces of desire and regret; I stay off currents of resentment and retaliation; I shelter myself from the debris of emotions made airborne in the swiftness of his departure.

So while I am standing in the wake of my father's silence, both then and now, I am talking about him. And for a son, that is a sacred rite and a daunting task.

In spite of my father's ways, I stand in his silent absent presence, loving him, still.

Notes

1. The actual eulogy for my father titled "He Fell Down" is included in Bryant K. Alexander (2006). " 'Were/Are, Fort/Da': The Eulogy as Constitutive (Auto)biography (or Traveling to Coalesce a Public Memory)." In *Performing Black Masculinity: Race, Culture, and Queer Identity.* Lanham, MD: AltaMira Press, pp. 161–187.
2. The first epigram that I use to frame the text is taken from the novel, *The Kite Runner* by Khaled Hosseini (2003). I read the narrator of this novel as yet another boy standing in the wake of his father's silence and making sense of his life, as both eulogy and apologia (New York: Riverhead Books, p. 361).
3. The second epigram is from a short story by Louis Erdich (2002, p. 5) titled, "Shamengwa." In seeking answers about my father this text reminds me of the complicated family histories that always unknowingly inform our own personal histories. The role of water and the pond in this story serve as a source of renewal and remembrance as I play with the metaphor of wake. "Shamengwa" was written by Louis Erdrich, posted 25 November 2002 (www.newyorker. com), republished in Walter Mosley and Katrina Kenison (Eds) (2003). *The Best American Short Stories.* New York: Houghton Mifflin, pp. 173–188.
4. See Bryant K. Alexander (2000). "Skin Flint (or The Garbage Man's Kid): A Generative Autobiographical Performance." Special Issue: The Personal and Political in Solo Performance. *Text and Performance Quarterly,* 20: 97–114.
5. My brother, Nathaniel Patrick Alexander, died from AIDS in October 1994. I write about the occasion of this loss in a piece called "Standing at the Crossroads," *Callaloo,* 22 (2): 343–345, 1999. The piece was republished in

Edwidge Danticat (Ed.) (2000). *Beacon Best 2000: Best Writing of Men and Women of All Colors.* Boston, MA: Beacon Press, pp. 72–75.

6. The construction that "silence is sometimes the severest criticism" is most often attributed to Charles Buxton.

7. The terms, *aninut* and *shemira*—are part of the Jewish customs of death and mourning. The aninut *is* considered the earliest phase of mourning, which occurs between death and burial. Shemira refers to the act of guarding or watching the dead from the moment of death to the moment of burial.

8. This is an allusion back to Erdich's short story, "Shamengwa."

9. See Bryant K. Alexander (2004). "Black Skin/White Masks: The Performative Sustainability of Whiteness (with Apologies to Frantz Fanon)," *Qualitative Inquiry,* 10 (5): 647–672.

18

Stitching Survival: Revisioning Silence and Expression

Laila Farah

> The country is gone. There is no money and there is not a very
> bright future ahead, but what we do have is our stories from
> our parent's time which we can pass down to our children; this
> is all we have left in the camps...but we have our hands and
> are not going to sit idle....
>
> (Zahra, *Ein el Helwe* Palestinian Refugee camp)

The *Nakba* (catastrophe) that ensued at the advent of the creation of
the state of Israel created a Palestinian exodus of mass proportion. It has
been revised and diluted, primarily by the Israeli and the US governments, but also by host governments still contending with the longest
standing refugee population in the world. Such is the case with Lebanon.
The media, many Arab nations, and the imperial expansion of Israel,
both in terms of land grabbing and military development and aggression, have all exploited this diasporic community for sixty years. Since
1948, Palestinians living in Lebanon have been multiply displaced
through years of war, military invasions, and a decimated physical
infrastructure within the camps they are relegated to. The Lebanese government is no less culpable for the abysmal living conditions on the
ground in the camps than other Arab nations who purport to support
the Palestinian people as a political stance against Israel. Israel, on the
other hand, refuses the fundamental right of return to these nearly half
a million refugees, despite UN resolutions and the tenets laid out in
both the Human Rights Doctrine and the Geneva Convention.[1] There
are now three-and-a-half generations of Palestinians in the camps in
Lebanon, with no hope of bettering their lives, unless they are mirac-
ulously accepted as *émigrés* to European nations. They are forbidden
from building permanent homes and are refused employment in over

sixty-four professions; they do not possess citizenship or official travel documents and have virtually no human and/or civil rights in their current status. They are a people whose nation exists purely in their bodies, hearts, and minds, and thus, in the embodiment of their culture and history.

In this essay, I offer multilayered narratives through intergenerational responses to the violence done to and the continued oppression of Palestinian refugees in the thirteen camps across Lebanon. In a larger version of this research, I explore the lives of Palestinian women from all camps in Lebanon to understand how oral histories function as a resistance to the final erasure of this refugee population. I examine how the collective and individual memories of the elder women create the basis of a national identity in the absence of a physical nation. For the purposes of this piece, I solely focus on the second layer of exploration. I examine how these narratives are internalized and creatively embodied by younger generations, who, in turn, continue to break the deadening silence around the world toward their plight. The creative means of voicing their life histories take on many forms, but I shall focus only on embroidery, or *tatreez*. While the preservation of oral histories is more traditionally viewed by Western feminists as breaking silences of violence and oppression of various kinds, I argue that in the case of Palestinian women in the camps, this artistic "silent expression" is actually essential to the survival of the people. As Zahra states above, without those voices expressed artistically, subsequent generations would not be able to fully achieve the embodiment they currently utilize to continue resisting their erasure. In essence, creating becomes resistance, which in turn, is key to the survival of memory and identity. In reconceptualizing silence, Gust Yep and Susan Shimanoff (2013) offer that it's "not necessarily or exclusively oppressive or liberatory; it can be both depending on the discursive, material, historical, and geopolitical contexts in which it is deployed" (Yep & Shimanoff, p. 142, this volume). Embracing this alternate perspective allows us to see the embroideries that the Palestinian women create as silent speaking, a self-elected nonvocal form of expression of self-representation, identity, and collective memory.

It is significant to note that women are, by and large, the keepers of culture in most societies and that family lore and cultural traditions are always significant. What makes this point most salient, and the reason for the focus on women as the bearers of history, of testimony, of survival, and of resistance,[2] is that their voices are silenced on three significant levels. First, the women's work/narratives are not valued as important within the public arenas of their own communities; that value was and remains relegated to armed combatants and political players. Second, the work of women and their narratives are paid no heed on a geo-political level, even though their lives are hanging in the balance. Third, the Palestinian people in the camps in Lebanon have been virtually forgotten on a global scale since the massacres in the camps of *Sabra* and *Shatila* in 1982. The only Palestinian people receiving any recognition, albeit almost exclusively negative attention, are those living in the Occupied Territories. Keeping all of this in mind then, the fact that these women are managing to engage in these acts of artistic resistance/survival at all in the conditions under which they live is remarkable.

It is hard to describe effectively for readers the imagery of daily life in the camp: How each three room "home" has two or three more floors built by other family members, accommodating large extended families, despite a Lebanese government ban on permanent structures in the camps; how a family of eight is living in two rooms with no windows or ventilation; how more than fifty-eight percent of the inhabitants suffer from chronic respiratory illnesses from the damp and the fumes of cooking stoves; how rations doled out by the UN are dwindling yearly, despite the growing need during a prolonged period of massive unemployment; how the bombed-out structures prevalent through the camps cannot be repaired and serve as a constant reminder of their fragile existence; how the Israeli fighter jets frequently fly overhead sending people instinctively running for cover; how the children get half the education in UN schools, resorting to "shift classes," allowing them to crowd in fifty pupils to every teacher in unheated, unsanitary compounds. The injustice of their circumstances is imprinted in daily life, year after year, decade after decade.

As a feminist performer-scholar who is committed to human and civil rights, particularly those of women whose lives are so lacking in social justice and rights, I embarked on a two-year ethnographic research process starting in the spring of 2005. I spent many months in Lebanon at a time, building relationships with various women from all generations and backgrounds in the thirteen camps as well as a few unofficial "gatherings."[3]

While it may seem on the surface problematic to use traditionally female activities such as embroidery as the focus of the survival of history and/or identity, it is consistently at the heart of their narratives and viewed by these Palestinian women as a transgressive act. I argue that transnational feminist methodologies help us to highlight global conditions of women without losing the specificity of their local reality; in this case, their refugee status. This framework lays bare the deep roots of colonialism and the violent legacies that are inscribed on these stateless peoples. Just as home/space/place is gendered, so are the content of memories and how they are narrated. The impact on identity and the relationship to feelings of being vanquished, victimized and a sense of loss lead to a particular kind of remembering and a gendered style of breaking the silence around their experiences. But what is more salient is how they are marking their silence with action: a living history created through silent expression, wordlessly stitching together their lost past and their survival as a people for the future. Ignoring/silencing the fingers that weave the fabric of the narratives of their lives would be tantamount to a partial death of Palestinian culture.[3]

These embroiderers create literacy through the colored threads that bind them, albeit tenuously, to the spaces of "home" in the diaspora. They fill the absence of vocal expression with elaborate patterns from the specific locals they fled from during the *Nakba*. These patterns are one of the few elements of predictable physical reality that is still perpetuated in the camps. Cricket Keating (2013) reconceptualizes one form of resistance silence as "silence witness," asserting it is, "often—though it doesn't have to be—organized and collective and is often used as a marker of respect, of mourning, of protest, and of defiance" (Keating, p. 27, this volume). Traditional embroidery, or *tatreez*, is a silent expression, a narration of the politics of women's labor reconceptualized beyond the limits of gendered production in a Western feminist sense. It stands in the face of forced and multiple displacements, dispossession, extreme violence and loss of life, and an embodied "homelessness." These embroideries are not viewed by these women as "merely women's work," or self-representation . . . they are viewed as a deliberate refusal to stop living, to stop documenting their continued existence regardless of how fragile it may be.

Most of the women in the camps, especially in the South of Lebanon, are from rural agrarian towns in the north of Palestine and exist within tightly woven communities. These social groupings are replicated in the camps in the recreation of sectors that are named identically to the region in which they lived prior to the *Nakba*. Walking through the maze of tiny darkened alleys in the camp, each area is distinctly identified by the name of the town those residents originally lived in. My contact walked me to the Women's Centre, describing each sector's (village) name and the current status of both the camp people from that town and whether the town even exists anymore. When I pressed her for more detail, she stopped in front of an elderly woman sitting on a stool in front of her one-room "home" and asked her to tell me where she was from. The elderly woman stared at me fiercely—no longer drowsy or listless—and gave me a fifteen-minute lecture on her village, what they produced, and what embroidery patterns signified her people. She got very quiet then said much more softly, "we are all that remains. They destroyed it all. That is why we stay here in this hell together. We women are the ones to hold it all together here [pointing to her head] and in these threads [pointing to her embroidered *abbeyah*]." It is in this way that collective memory is also categorized by each group, making these particular gendered memories and their narratives all the more central to their survival.

The phenomenon of embroidery as the means of "holding it all together" is reproduced across generations of women. There are two major distinctions, however, between each generation's cultural/material work. First, the younger women are keeping the culture and history alive through teaching in the UN schools, in non-governmental organization (NGO) work throughout the camps, and through cultural activities such as traditional folkloric dance and song. Second, they are earning wages for their work outside of the home, often doing double duty, thus remaining intimately connected to their own children. Conversely, given the need to foster a sense of continuity of place, space, and land that they collectively lost, the elder women in these familial and regional groupings can't re-root for more practical reasons. The Lebanese government will not allow for land ownership, or building permanent homes in the camps. This is in addition to the constant violent turmoil in Lebanon. After multiple internal displacements, death, and dispossession, their need to remain grouped together remains very strong. This fact lends itself to the elder women taking on a more intentional localized role in terms of cultural, monetary, and social support.

In the same way that the refugees who survived the *Nakba* use embroidery to piece together the histories of individual and collective memory, the younger generations are increasingly embracing these tangible products to break silence in ways perhaps that are not traditionally considered "formal" labor. Women perform this work in part to preserve their dignity and humanity despite the conditions in which they live. At a time when male unemployment in the camps is up to fifty percent, this becomes far more than efficacious art: it becomes resistance/survival in everyday life. Additionally, women's collective work creates new forms of solidarity and support for one another in the absence of structural support in the camps. It is vital to acknowledge this work by its own merit as a definitive form of activism—one that actually has a firm hand in shaping the future history of stateless generations to come. Yet a narrow view of activism—one that privileges "women coming to voice"—renders these embroidered forms of activism invisible. Women in the camps seek nonviolent means to preserve history and the cultural markers of identity through organizations such as *Inaash* and *Najdeh*; organizations focusing on traditional embroidery in the way that Najla from *Rashidiye* narrates:

> [I]t's important to work here to show that this embroidery is ours, and from our culture. Many times because the Israelis put our clothes on and say it is theirs.... We say where each type of clothing is from and from which village. Even brides getting married, we try to match it up from the town they are originally from. We learn each region. We were taught since we were children. I teach my girls now, and they also learn a bit from school. We teach them embroidery from every town the girls are from but also from other places. My daughter just watches me and tries to do the same thing every day when she comes home from school.... I want them to help me, but they also realize the importance [of it] and of just spending time together.... I started learning from my neighbors and from home when I was a little girl, so then I decided to try it, and I started getting better, and now I have been working and doing this for over 15 years.

From Najla's narrative we understand the way that survival is embodied as an enactment that is sustained in everyday life. The importance of elevating the mundane becomes salient here when challenging the assumptions often made about women's everyday practices in/outside of the home, particularly those of Arab/third world women. This approach of reading silent acts of resistance offers the possibility of extrapolating to other forms of women's resistance in everyday life, without conflating their current or historical struggles into the object of the "other's" strategies. Reading their acts of silent resistance invites the reader to take the threads of these narratives and wrap them onto their own bobbins, creating new fabrics through which to see the silent and mundane patterned differently. And so, it is precisely through these artistically expressive, if silent, transmissions that these women are re-inventing their identities under harsh social, economic, and political constraints. The hubris toward the mundane is called into question as we view the ways in which these women accomplish, maintain, and weave their cultural lives and collective and individual histories in the absence of a state.

As I walk through a busy market on a main path, I see the signs of abject poverty abound. The alleys, more like warrens actually, darkened by two or more floors of unstable construction to accommodate three generations of families. The average amount of electricity per day rarely exceeds six to ten hours per day, constraining livelihoods, healthy air circulation, food storage, functioning schools, or adequate and safe heating. My contact, Bassima, points to a stooped elderly woman in black and tells me that she waits for the end of the market day to beg for the vegetables that will be discarded in the trash heap on the edge of the market. She has lost six of eight children and has no means of survival since she has so few living children to support her. I ask why she does not join the group of women we are going to meet. She tells us that her eyesight is almost gone and she cannot manage to create fine stitches anymore. When we settle into the bright room of a new center, built by donations from a Danish relief agency, women are sitting about in various stages of embroidery work. We are offered the first of many cups of tea and cigarettes. It seems like a haven from the harsh conditions below on the street. A woman emphasizes the communal effort and the benefits of joining together to do this cultural and historical work:

When this place opened, we all started working. We would get our supplies from *Inaash* and then we built this place. We sit here and enjoy each other's company. We stay up until 1 and 2 am working together. Sometimes when there is no electricity, we will just sit together and work even more! Before it used to be just one room, but now we have grown!.... We went to schools and told them we want to teach this. We believe that girls should know it especially, because we were taught as children. Also, if there is no one in the house to teach them, then this is where we come in...we go to as many schools as possible to teach as well. We try to go to other camps. We talk to principals and tell them how important it is for the girls to remember...we won't allow the Jews or anyone to tell us this isn't a part of our history. A girl can decide if she wants to do this, but the important thing is that people don't forget...people don't understand the situation in Lebanon and how long we have been in the camps here. People don't know about the homes that get demolished on top of someone, or how the electricity goes out, or the health situation. They don't know that people here have to work for so cheap, to get paid anything. They don't realize how people are working here and that Palestinian people can't even work outside [the camps], can't even get jobs...so we are trying to show that you [women] can work and get by with doing things like this.

The layers of resilience evidenced in this insistent rationale for passing on the art of embroidery are both born of necessity and an urgent strategy to avoid the erasure of historical and cultural belonging. It is not solely the women's intention to minimize their own sense of displacement and dispossession: they steadfastly pursue avenues of widening the art beyond their own intimate spheres. The significance is multifold. There are over sixty-five professions forbidden to Palestinians in Lebanon; the sociocultural mores are often unwelcoming to the notion of young women leaving the confines of the camps to work; the expense of education and transport needed to open the fullest range of employment possibilities is beyond most camp resident's means, and so on. But what is perhaps most salient here is that having lived through dispossession and displacement, sometimes multiply, the only tangible means of historical preservation are embroidery, dance, song, and oral histories. Within the women's milieu, the embroideries afford a way to narrate each specificity of the lands they lost, each unique pattern and color scheme offering a singular, if silent means of maintaining cultural identity—and on multiple levels—life.

We feel the urgency of these stories, the weaving one's self, community, history, and nation into existence. It is powerful and worthy of attention to honor the dailiness of these women's silent resistance that is so often unrecognizable in so many other narratives. This sense of urgency is what I get from the women who know only too well that there is a lot at stake. As Miriam Cooke asserts, "[W]omen improvise ways of participating that are unlike those of their male counterparts, ways that do not negate their identities as women. Their resistance becomes self-consciously feminine. They insist on this difference in activism while emphasizing the commonality of the goal" (p. 11). They are very clear about how horrific their circumstances are as well as the terror they have experienced on the ground within the camps and through multiple displacements, and yet, they are clear about how they must play a role in the survival of their families both culturally and financially, and thus, in their view, the survival of the Palestinian people in the diaspora. Further, they accept the shifts in gender roles, but for the most part are comfortable with accommodating these shifts without undermining the fabric of their social structure. They are very protective of their roles as mothers and often, as wives, and while they have clarity about their power dynamics within the family infrastructure, they do not want to make shifts that may be experienced as disruptive to their families. Despite the possibilities of taking advantage of the exigency that exists for these women in the camps, they are only interested in what already fits into their cultural and religious framework. The paradox is that they create change intentionally, and limit it with the same goal in mind: to help their people to survive.

The smell of open sewers is compounded by the oppressive humidity coming off the nearby sea, running in open channels in the center of alleys so narrow two people cannot pass without turning sideways. As I look up the sides of the cinderblock buildings, they seem to tilt in toward each other, laced together by a multitude of illegally strung electric lines. My contact, Im Nizar, explains that the United Nations Relief and Works Agency (UNRWA) has been promising a new sewage system as other camps have received, but that was a long time ago. As we enter another darkened building, a group of women are working at the Palestine Liberation Organization (PLO)-sponsored cultural center, chattering loudly and laughing over endless cups of tea while working away on their stitching. They are discussing how they cope with exigency in the following ways:

Woman 1: Since '77, I have been doing embroidery and my children have been helping me. I have been working for a very long time and I have done ok, Hamdullilah....I need to help my family because I have seven children and my husband is sick, so I need to work to pay the rent and help out as much as I can. What can we do, this is our life.

Woman 2: I also do embroidery. It doesn't pay for many things but we don't have much else, and it makes some money, as does being a seamstress. I learned from these women here.

Woman 3: We all live in the same building and help our mothers and each other because this is the only work we have.

Woman 4: The problem is if we don't teach each other and our children, then our traditions and embroidery will not continue, *and* there will be no work. You feel as if you are doing some good when you do embroidery; this needs to last, all types of Palestinian dress.

Woman 5: I would like to go and finish my school, but I work at home to support my family. We have many people in my family and I have to help take care of my sister's children so that I make a difference. And actually, with working [the women] and doing this, I meet other women, which is good because we are all doing the same thing. But with our history, Palestinians have to keep doing our embroidery, so people know what Palestinian culture is. We have to take care of ourselves and everything we learn, we have to teach each other so the tradition continues.

These women's voices are creating a living history that is, in fact, a material history which has both efficacious characteristics and culturally symbolic purpose. Both the second and third women articulate how embroidery is one of the few means available to them to contribute to the material well-being of their families. Equally important is the solidarity among the women to recognize and support each other through their difficult circumstances. Although mentioned only in passing, this solidarity extends to keeping each other (and their extended family members) alive in ways that feed more than mouths. The social aspects cannot be under-valued, particularly within a population of women who are trapped, as they are, within the confines of the camps. The focus on sustainability extends beyond their current circumstances—they are insuring an intergenerational legacy of substance *and* sustenance. The embodied (women's) memory is placed onto cloth, to be worn intergenerationally. Identity flows through the very threads of these pieces of embroidery. It may be useful to consider these intentional expressions and the ways in which they continue to shatter the silence surrounding their lives while returning to the notions of resistance in terms of reflexivity, agency, political dissent, and activism. In terms of these diasporic subjects, the deliberate decision to incorporate these intersections becomes an overt and intentional political tool as well as a teachable one. Those with little or no exposure to such conditions suddenly are offered an intimate view into diasporic life on the ground, made "real" in the flesh. These are silent expressions of the narratives of nation— essential to memory—that interweave silence, voice, and an embodied resistance.

Their narratives reveal how these women are using a form of silent expression to "break" the silences around their experience. As the youth carry on their embroidered histories, both personal and collective, they are sharing their narratives of dispossession and displacement (using artistic creativity) to communities across Europe and beyond. Once the narratives underlying these embroideries are elucidated, then we cannot ignore the generations of trauma and social injustice that this community of refugees has endured, nor the consequences on the younger generations. Their very existence is dependent on the continuation of these silent expressions. As one who employs a transnational feminist lens in her research, I cannot escape the fact that the women's insistence on continuing their silent voicing of their material reality is often the only voice they are afforded, both within the camps and beyond. As I leave the center, children dragging on my arm to take a photo of them, I thank the women for their immense generosity of sharing their narratives, embroidery, and tea. I realize what power resides in that room: for them subjugation is not an option. I am also conscious that I will be escorted to my car and have a privileged life to return to, papers to show the Lebanese army officers and again at the interior PLO checkpoint to guarantee my departure. I am humbled as I leave the barbed wire encampment, already missing the cacophony of camaraderie at the center.

I inscribe these women's narratives, as Miriam Cooke (1996) says, to "further a global movement of women's empowerment. Women who have had experiences that have changed their conceptions of who they are must [act] to inscribe their transformed consciousness. Women must fight to retain the authority to [act upon] experience[s] that they are supposed not to have had" (p. 5). These artistic forms may not be self-described as "feminist," or as mechanisms of survival or "legitimized" forms of breaking silence, but surely one can look to other cultural equivalents and find parallel silent witnessing. One need only look to the *arperilleristas* in Chile under the brutal dictatorship of Pinochet to see how efficacious these powerful expressions of witnessing play a significant role in the documentation of injustice. In Chile, hand-stitched pictorials, known as *arpilleras*, were created from fabric from the clothing of the tortured, disappeared, and dead family members. The scenes depicted similarly inscribed the place and details of their personal and cultural history through wordless creative expression. Bettina Aptheker (1989) considers quilts in a similar vein "both as the embodiment of dailiness and as a metaphor for the way in which we as women might piece the diversity of our experiences into meaningful and useful patterns" (p. 68). In all of these cases of women silently expressing both their life histories and the history of their people, women's labor gives meaning to their continued struggle for dignity and human rights.

But my resistance, perhaps especially in mainstream Western feminist locales, is to return to a word-based artistic resistance within transnational/global feminist practices based on my own silent witnessing. And so, by birthright and timing, and holding the privilege of dual-citizenship and diasporic subjectivity, my duty/desire is to portray these women's silent expressions of resistance and survival. I want to draw attention to space and place, that our understanding of gender can't be secondary to survival, but constituent to survival. My critical move is to highlight the geographic spaces of diasporic experience, both as inscribed in the mind, as written on the body, silently created with full hearts—and stitched into the fabric of Palestinian women's lives. As Aptheker reminds us, "life must be propelled in practical ways, every day. That propulsion is women's resistance" (1989, p. 228). There is no vision of a subjugated and abject diasporic subjectivity in these intricate silent expressions. Spoken word is contingent upon silent activities: that is where the stories get passed on. Nonverbal activities are stitched together, becoming the condition of possibility of the process of how the story gets exchanged in the fabric. We see a weaving of silence and voice. We have much to learn from these women's wordless tactics of survival in the absence of statehood.

Notes

1. There are many excellent sources on the conditions of Palestinian refugees—UNRWA and the Electronic Intifada website are two good over sources for further details.
2. For further discussion of how I conceptualize resistance and survival in everyday life, see the chapter "Shaping the World with Our Hands," in *Performing Autobiography* (Laila, 2003).
3. I conducted over 120 hours of interviews, utilizing focus groups as well as individual and family interviews. These will be forthcoming in a more comprehensive text on Palestinian women in the refugee camps in Lebanon. I was as intentionally random in meeting and engaging women as I was in conducting interviews. The process was truly organic, where neighbors would enter during an interview and then insist I come to see their daughter's dance troupe or talk to their eighty-five-year-old mother or aunt. I employed a similarly organic approach in the interviews themselves, asking only one initial question—"tell me how you and your people came here and how have you managed to survive?" The remainder of the interview would be led by the women, either individually, or in groups, according to what they felt important to narrate about their histories, the current life conditions on the ground, and how they were maintaining their national identity and cultural heritage. I interviewed women in their homes, places of work, at NGOs, and in cultural centers. As I am a fluent speaker of Arabic, I had access both linguistically as well as socially, in terms of gender segregated space based on cultural or strict Islamic practices.

References

Aptheker, Bettina (1989). *Tapestries of life: Women's work, women's consciousness, and the meaning of daily experience.* Amherst, MA: University of Massachusetts Press.

Cooke, Miriam (1996) *Women and the War Story*. Berkeley, CA: University of California Press.

Farah, Laila (2003) "Shaping the World with Our Hands," In Lynn Miller and Jacqueline Taylor (Eds), *Performing autobiography: Staging women's selves*. Madison, WI: University of Wisconsin Press, pp. 282–300.

Keating, Cricket (2013) "On resistant silences," In Sheena Malhotra and Aimee Carrillo Rowe (Eds), *Silence, feminism, power: Reflections at the edges of sound*. London: Palgrave Macmillan, pp. 25–33.

Yep, Gust A. and Shimanoff, Susan (2013). "The US day of silence: Sexualities, silences, and the will to unsay in the age of empire" In Sheena Malhotra and Aimee Carrillo Rowe (Eds), *Silence, feminism, power: Reflections at the edges of sound*. London: Palgrave Macmillan, pp. 139–156.

19

Sun Moon Silence

Aimee Carrillo Rowe

The river knows how to give to the sea. The rain and snow and glaciers know how to feed the river. The earth to give life. The sun knows to wake her to this gesture with each rising. The moon knows her own rhythm. This wisdom she offers as a gift to the dolphin, who exchanges the breath of life to the cadence of the tide.

This impulse rises in me. To be like the river, the rain, the snow and the glaciers. To become the earth, the sun, the moon. To exchange breath with the dolphin. To surrender my body to the cadence of the moon's pull. To dance, as the seaweed and the sweet grass do, to the rhythm that pulsates through their fibrous bodies.

The river doesn't need to think before she offers herself up to the sea. The gesture is entirely natural. The sun doesn't assess the terms of the exchange when it rises, bringing life and light to the earth. These gifts arise spontaneously at the interface between them. The moon need not count the days until she is full. Her path will weave, her positioning will shift, she will feel the pull of the earth and the sun holding her as she moves. Her cycle exists as a set of relations.

This impulse rises in me. To give you something so profound and innocent and natural. To offer you the rhythm of the moon, the waters of my river, the touch of the sun—penetrating your skin, generating life in the dark soil of your body.

When in your life did you stop dancing? At what point did the fairy tale fail to enchant you? When did you come to believe you couldn't—couldn't dream, couldn't flourish, couldn't fly? At what point did the shadow cast by fear and doubt begin to cast its long pattern over the shining path of your dreams?

How do I locate those moments in my path that have pulled me from my orbit?

These are the questions that led me to this writing. They are questions inspired as much by the mind as by the body and the spirit. They circulate in an alternate register from the main of academic knowledge production, what Diana Taylor might describe as the "repertoire" of embodied performance. The repertoire is significant because it works to dislodge the often-unspoken hegemony of the archive. As a repository of written history, data, maps, documents, literary texts, letters—archival memory stands in as "fact" to legitimate Western knowledge itself. Fact: immutable, objective, solid, resistant to change. Fact somehow reassures us, even though, or perhaps *because*, its irrefutability lies outside of our fallible capacity to grasp it. The hegemony of the archive elides the ways we know through the body and through the spirit, Taylor writes, making it difficult to "think about embodied practice within the epistemic systems developed in Western thought, where writing has become the guarantor of existence itself" (2005, p. xix). Thus, the dynamic tension between the archive and the repertoire is metonymic of the Western subject's being-in-the-world as ontology itself is "guaranteed"—somehow affirmed as certainty—through a faith in the written word and the facticity it ascribes with alleged transparency.

The archive hangs the hat of its legitimacy on the written word: logos. The written word gains its authority through its capacity to transcend space and time. We can read old letters or manuscripts or reports to gain access into lives far away, removed from us by time. The repertoire, on the other hand, "enacts embodied memory: performances, gestures, orality, movement, dance, singing—in short, all those acts usually thought of as ephemeral, nonreproducible knowledge. The repertoire requires presence: people participate in the production and reproduction of knowledge by 'being there,' being a part of the transmission" (Taylor, 2005, p. 20). The repertoire is the performative expression of our fullest being—still always partial, fleeting, ephemeral. Performance is staged so that others might witness our most intimate moments. It is the "being there" that is the condition of possibility for the repertoire to speak, yet such modes of being are often etched in silence.

My hands trace the contours of this dark cave. I long to create from the void.

For four days I lie in this desert. The sky moves over me, the earth moves under me, and I dance as I am held between them. My body is a vast horizon.

For four days I dance to the rhythm of the great heartbeat. It resonates from the wood and hide of tightly strung drums, a heartbeat pounded out with the rhythmic bounce of the drummers' palms, popping back against the drum's perfect surface. My heart rises with the low and high reverberations of the well-worn chants the drummers release as a prayer. Like an infant splayed out face down on the great mother, her pulse filling me with life, I wrap myself around vibration, manifesting heart. At last there is no separation. My body is the beat and I dance to its timing. My feet pop back against the desert floor, up and down they move in unison with the popping hands of the drummers, with the heart of the mother. I move. The rhythm moves me. I am it. We are. We.

In the late 1990s the Sun Moon Dance was given to the people by Grandfather Joseph Rael, "Beautiful Painted Arrow" (Tiwa). Rael envisioned dancers moving back and forth from their place on a circle to a tree in the center. He saw us moving in and out of dancing, a masculine form of prayer that symbolizes manifestation, and sleeping and dreaming, a feminine form of prayer that symbolizes receiving visions. Back and forth without words, for four days, dancers would dance, fast, and dream. Since Rael's vision, Sun Moon Dances have inspired countless people. Dances are held every year, all over the country and all over the world.

I learned about the Sun Moon Dance when I attended a New Year's Sweat Lodge in Yucca Valley, California, about ten years ago. After working with Medicine Cards and doing sacred ceremonies with my friends for many years, I'd been longing to be part of something more formal and communal. After years of experimenting with various extremes, from sports to bad relationships, I longed to fill a hole, to sit in ceremony and to learn from spiritual teachers and elders. "The Sun Moon Dance is the graduate school of spiritual work," a middle-aged Chicano with a long brown ponytail told me as we chatted, hovering near the fire that heated the rocks for the sweat. That was it: graduate school. I was in graduate school at the time, so the challenge held within his description thrilled me. Extreme spirituality. I knew I had to dance.

I wanted that something, that intense, transformative *something*. When fall rolled around, I showed up for the dance. I took my place in the arbor. I danced and fasted and struggled with the incessant clamor of judgment, fear, and an unquiet mind until finally, two days into the four-day dance, I surrendered to the force of the Dance and let it do its work on me. I've been dancing ever since.

In the Dance I receive visions. I await their unfolding without words.

For six months I keep the silence. The visions move through me: a flash, an image, a dream, a memory. One time it was a stink bug who visited me, reminding me of my childhood. How I played with bugs, feeding rolly-polly bugs to wolf spiders. Other times it's a light that radiates above my head as I lie in bed watching the ceiling. The light is a red reverberation that pulsates like heat waves off of the pavement. It radiates around me as I lie sleepless, charging with Life Force. I see the heat waves in the dark. For days after the dance the room reverberates the drums that have since fallen silent. Sometimes the Force is so thick I feel the whole room pulsating. I glance at my lover, sleeping like a gray stone beside me. Does she feel that? Is it in me or around me? Am I separate? Are we separate? I wonder, but don't voice these questions.

For six months I walk with this silence. I occupy it and it occupies me. During these winter months it feels so natural. "The space between snowflakes absorbs sound," she tells me one crystal morning. We ski down the path that was sprinkled with fireflies in another season. We follow it down to the frozen lake. Blinking into the morning sun, sparkling off ice hanging from leafless trees in shards, tiny beams or rainbows. The ice-covered trees hang low on each side of the path that winds down to the lake. The vista opens out onto the wide expanse of the frozen lake covered with snow. The path always feels like a birth canal to me.

Silence is the slow stretch of the birth canal as it prepares for the push of life. Bit by bit my mouth opens, stretches beyond its capacity, reforming the contours of my face. It takes time to rework me, to make my face, to open my soul to its gifts.

Silence is my invitation. Silence is my respect. Silence is the receiving posture. I recline into this silence and wait for you.

The Dance teaches many things. Rules and customs help dancers to integrate its lessons. Fasting allows us to sacrifice our bodies, to become pure spirit. By forgoing water, we learn that water is sacred. We learn the importance of silence. During the debriefing after the Dance, Valerie, the Chief, always warns the dancers not to speak of the visions they've received for six months. "Holding the silence allows the dreams and visions to manifest," she intones to the circle of dancers gathered around her. Speaking the visions robs them of their power. The power of silence is an aspect of the Void, that space of creation from which all new life emerges.

The Dance has many secrets, sacred secrets—things that I still don't understand after a decade of dancing, studying the teachings of Grandfather Joseph, and serving the Dance in various roles. This essay works between voice and silence, between performance and sacred secrets, in an effort to express and share a glimpse of the repertoire of the Sun Moon Dance. It offers not so much an argument as a sketch of the experience of being in the Dance. I strive to generate words and images to convey the repertoire of the Dance.

The silence of the Dance profoundly holds the dancer as the dancer holds silence: for four days, for six months, sometimes for a lifetime. This writing thus blurs the line between silence and voice, between archive and repertoire. It shares a glimpse of the vast array of sensations I have undergone during and around the Dance. I hope that the healing I have experienced might reach beyond the two dimensions of this page to envelop the reader: to convey the healing potential of silence.

I've never known the sun so bare. Hot white, it burns. Hot white, it burrows into my marrow. Hot white, it penetrates my protective layers: skin, flesh and bone. Hot white it burrows into the vulnerable dark brown core of the self. The heat gets all the way inside. Nowhere to hide. Intimacy and terror spiral, dust-devils in my marrow. I am stripped. Bare. The sun has turned me inside out, sucking the marrow from my bones like we did when we got to the core of the lamb chop when we were little. In relation to the sun, I've never been so bare.

Never mind that I grew up one hundred miles from here, no stranger to one hundred plus degrees. My skin is thick and brown, more reptilian than mammal. My eyes rove left and right beneath their lids, like those of madmen and dreamers.

In this state between states I surrender. I ask you to drink for me. Quench my thirst. I wonder what you are eating. I entreat you and my hunger, my thirst dissipate like heat waves into thin air.

I wake from dreaming with a start. Was something scratching my back? A stick? Claws? Someone waking me? Startled by the unexpected touch, I flip onto my side in time to glimpse the lizard scrambling out from under my shirt. She scampers only about a foot from my reclining body before she stops and turns back to face me. I see her little sides pulsating in and out. She is panting. I notice that I am panting too. I guess I scared her as much as she scared me. We size each other up. Up and down the lizard pushes on tiny arms to get a better look, sizing me up. The lizard looks not once or twice, but from up and then down. The lizard brings blessings of the dreamer, who delves into the shadow where she previews the future behind roving eyelids.

For four days I lie between earth and sky, between day and night, between sun and moon. For four days I surrender to the movement of the sun, to the passing of my thirst and hunger, to the roving of my eyes. For four days dreaming the lizard's dream.

Cherríe Moraga sees writing, especially writing for theater, as a "ceremony of remembering." Memory, return, and recovery are recurring themes in her recent writing, *A Xicana Codex of Changing Consciousness* (2011). She challenges herself, and by extension, her reader, to engage in acts of writing and performance to *re-member* who we were prior to conquest. "Our preconquest imaginations offer strategies for building self-sustaining societies today [...] that can disrupt the mass suicide of global consumption, engineered by the empire of the United States" (2011, p. 81). Moraga writes, for instance, of her experience working with seven- and eight-year-old children to develop a Cinco de Mayo play. In playing the roles of Columbus and his crew, an Arawak chief and his tribe, and slaves on an auction block, the children displayed a kind of embodied knowledge of colonial encounters that *skipped* a generation, or several.

A pre-conquest knowledge seemed to animate the bodies of the performing children with a wisdom that "re-members" against the grain of the myth of American Democracy—a myth, Moraga argues, that makes us stupid. When Columbus and his crew raised their rifles to shoot the indigenous people, the Arawak actors "drop dead en masse. They hadn't been directed to do so. This was improvisation, which ended our rehearsal for the day and began our first lesson in colonization" (2011, p. 38). In the reenactment of the slave trade, Moraga directs two African American children playing slaves to show " 'great loss, great sadness.' And somehow these children, who are not actors, knew how to enact this story, for there was an ageless, an old knowledge, in their bearing that indicated to all of us that they remembered slavery on a visceral (genetic?) level. Nicole and Dion are their ancestors incarnate. Nicole and Dion are slave children being separated from their mothers" (2011, p. 38).

I wonder a lot about my ancestors. We are mestizos, shorthand for the blending of indigenous, Spanish, African blood. But what is the long hand? What is the repertoire that accompanies this archive? The great-grandmother, Malintzín, reminds us of the story of bodies and fluids co-mingling to produce a people—indigenous and Spanish, Malintzín and Cortes. Bernadette Calafell writes of her pilgrimage to Mexico City and her longing to "return to a home [she does] not know but that continues to define [her]" (2005, p. 45). During her trip, she begins to dream in lush colors of a "Preconquest past that is somehow mine and yet not mine. I am dreaming of her face. Her plain wide face, her full lips and her long dark hair have come to me in visions time and time again yet now they are so blaringly clear that I can no longer ignore them" (2005, p. 46). In her vision, Calafell *tastes* Malintzín's tears as a cross-generational queer desire—what Elizabeth Freeman would call erotohistoriography[1]—bridges the distance and the difference that separates Calafell from her lost origins. These bodies that could not, within a Western frame, *touch* find their way to each other through dreams and visions, through travel and silence, through a deep desire to know those from whom we come.

I often wonder about those cross-cut relationships that give rise to mestizos. Were/are they forged in various forms of violence and rape? Did/do people manage to build loving inter-connections? I wonder about Malintzín and the many grandmothers who came after her. What made her laugh? Did she find inspiration in the beauty of a stream or a mountain? Did she dance? How long have my ancestors been dancing?

When in your life did you start dancing? At what point did you find that the magic is everywhere? When did you come to realize you could—could dream, could en-vision, could fly? At what point did the love well up in your heart and overflow without a second thought, giving itself like the river to the sea, like the glacier to the river, like the sun to the earth or the dolphin to the moon? At what point will you stop counting and realize there is enough?

In Chapter 8 in this volume, "*Inila*: An Account of Opening to Sacred Knowing," Amira De la Garza writes of the centrality of silences to maintaining the dignity of the people. "These things are not meant to be recorded," she writes.

lots of words, but not what you meant

to share... what you could say by listening... by waiting.

De la Garza describes the importance of her ancestry to her research as qualities, desires, and a deep sense of longing that animates her identity, and her body: her grandfather's love of the land; her grandmother's "supernatural sensibilities"; De la Garza's own gait as she carries a bucket of water. "You walk like an Apache," someone calls out. In such moments we are hailed by a different form of power from that imagined by Louis Althusser (1988) in his parable of the police officer, who shouts, "Hey, you there!" and we turn, knowing we are called. Althusser's notion of interpellation—this turning to the police officer's hailing—indicates that we are subjects, that we know our place in the social world, that we have been schooled in discourse and power sufficiently to recognize ourselves in the hailing. Chela Sandoval (2000) *reverses* the terms of this hailing, inviting us to consider how we might respond to oppositional forms of power. I have argued for the *multiple* forms of interpellation that constitute our belongings (Carrillo Rowe, 2008). And how might such hailings—in which we *know* it is we who are called—be possible *across* temporal boundaries? De la Garza is hailed by her ancestors, as she is hailed by the observer of her gait when she carries water. Carrying water and cutting wood. The most basic, yet life-sustaining tasks; within their mindful execution, we might find the secrets carried in our DNA.

My home in Iowa was a cabin by the lake. When it snowed, I'd find myself stranded for days—solitary, with the sparse company of a dog and a cat and a pair of cross-country skis. The sound of snowfall. The long nights. The wood burning stove. The depth of winter, the season of the bear that teaches us to hibernate, dream, and integrate the teachings. Inila. I enter the silence. Still, the silence. I wait for my ancestors to speak, for the visions to come, for the dust to settle.

Raven passes over the arbor with her mate. Raven mates for life. Raven is blue black, neither blue nor black, both blue and black. Raven—messenger from the void, magic. She bridges worlds, carries new designs in her beak, grasps unseen visions in her talons, holds unknown truths between her feathers. Raven and her mate paint the vast blue sky with triangular paintbrush tails. Their bodies dip and merge, then gracefully part. But their paths are distinctly joined. Raven and her mate create a new dialect of intimacy with their dance.

With every encounter I know another arrival. Another layer of meaning. There are no accidents. Raven, what is your message? If I could just hear you. If I could learn to listen. Straining toward the sky, I hear a faint 'wooph' of your wings as you pass. I hear your resonant call, throaty, it reverberates through me like the voices of the drummers. Like the drum, animating my heart.

In his reading of Native American literature and debates over the politics of sharing indigenous cultural practices, David Moore invites his (non-Native) reader into an alternate conceptual framework—one that gestures "toward a silence off the page where song and dance, tumbleweed, buffalo, and spirit overlap" (1997, p. 633). He calls it "rough knowledge": a relational space in which "readers and writers share the common sense that there are certain experiential levels of context that no one from outside can understand, except only roughly" (1997, p. 636). His insightful readings of Native texts draw out the silences infused in the texts—the spaces between text and context, the sacred and the profane, knower and known, signifier and signified, language and the dancer's step or the tumbleweed or the buffalo or the eyes of a coyote. It is in this space *between,* especially the *relational* space between (non-Native) reader and (Native) writer that Moore wittingly points to, but fails to excavate. He points to a space beyond the binaries imposed by logocentrism and dialectics, a place where we might meet on the other side of "this versus that," wherein the "sacred sign [...] points to but does not name a powerful referent that splits time and space into meaning" (p. 641). It is this slippage between signifier and signified that creates space for the sacred to breathe. We can no longer, if we ever could, place absolute faith in the word. The sacred evades signification, even as it "points to" *something.* The Western investment in certainty is compelled to capture, driven by a desire for language to make that pointing gesture depict a complete and accurate representation, "but a sacred sign often forces language to resort to silence" (p. 641).

The repertoire resonates in those sacred and embodied places of silence. It takes time for visions to manifest. They may make their way into the archive, but sometimes at a tremendous cost. The place between voice and silence is a *relational* space that recognizes the impossibility of knowing the other. This relationality is based in rough knowledge, in the possibility of *not* knowing. Gayatri Spivak calls this relational space "the secret."[2] For Moore it is the linguistic turns of the Native text that plays with a dynamic of revealing and concealing cultural knowledge in silence. This dynamic creates and arises from nothing short of a radically *different* way of knowing and being from that which we take for granted in the West/North. It is expressed through a pointing gesture toward a signified that is best apprehended through the heart, through the sideways glance, through the body-in-motion.

It's October. Soon it will be time to Dance again. My sixth Dance, the South of my South. The place of the child. I pray to restore the Innocence. So much has been lost.

Today I started to detox. No coffee. I feel mushy, heavy, no bones in my body, my mind slow sludge. I'm not sharp, clever, or confident. I lie in bed and begin the surrender. No need to judge it or try to get it all done or make things challenging with my chatter. OK. It's all OK.

Today I started to detox and somehow I finished this writing I've been holding for years.

Embodied performance allows us to express those sliding moments that dwell within the silence of memory. In the Lodge Circle we call it *tiy-oweh*. It means we learn to enter the silence and listen to the inner voice, small and divine. To enter the silence we must take time to allow the monkey mind to play its tricks, to push past the endless noise, to recognize that there are infinite layers to silence. Silence can be so loud. But on the other side of noise, we might settle into the feminine aspect, ready to receive visions and insights. Our history, our ancestry, the recollection that we can fly. Things we don't know that we know because we forgot. In the stillness I can recall the scent of my grandmother. The sandpaper of my father's cheek pressed against mine. Even those

I haven't "met" in this lifetime. The silence is a meeting ground of the generations.

Even though we could have no "real" account of them, these memories from before our own individual lifetimes are held in the visceral body, in our DNA. These memories are the building blocks of decolonial knowledge, because they come from a time prior to colonization. How might they be leveraged to remind us of what it *really* means to be free?

For six months after Dance we do not speak of those dreams and visions we've received. My mom always asks me, "What happened in the Dance?" Then reminds me, or herself, "I know, you can't tell me." She knows that some things are too sacred to speak, or that to speak them too quickly would steal their energy. Funny, by the time I can speak them, I don't remember what they are. They are visions that need no words. Dreams that lose their power through chatter. Transformations that occur under ground, deep within, somewhere in the marrow. The heartbeat of the Earth, the drumbeat of the Dance, fills me, as I empty myself of my body and become energy, light.

Then somewhere in the silence the visions become me. Making me anew from the inside out.

Notes

1. By this Freeman (2010) underscores the importance of embodiments of queer pleasure, especially those across time, as a vehicle for excavating queer historiographies that might exceed the limits of homonormative queer politics in the present.
2. "We all know that when we engage profoundly with one person, the responses come from both sides: this is responsibility and accountability. We also know that in such engagements we want to reveal and reveal, conceal nothing. Yet on both sides there is always a sense that something has not got across" (Spivak in Davis, 2002, p. 154).

References

Althusser, Louis (1998). "Ideology and the ideological state apparatuses." In John Storey (Ed.), *Cultural Theory and Popular Culture: A Reader*, Athens, GA: University of Georgia.

Calafell, Bernadette. 2005. "Pro(re-)claiming Loss: A Performance Pilgrimage in Search of Malintzín Tenépal." *Text and Performance Quarterly*, vol. 25, no. 1, January: 43–56.

Carrillo Rowe, Aimee. 2008. *Power Lines: On the Subject of Feminist Alliances.* Durham, NC: Duke University Press.

Davis, Dawn Rae. 2002. "(Love Is) the Ability of Not Knowing: Feminist Experience of the Impossible in Ethical Singularity." *Hypatia*, vol. 17, no. 2: 145–161.

De la Garza, Sarah Amira (2012). "*Inila*: An account of opening to sacred knowing." In Sheena Malhotra and Aimee Carrillo Rowe (Eds), *Silence, Feminism, Power: Reflections at the Edges of Sound*, London: Palgrave Macmillan, pp. 101–113.

Freeman, Elizabeth. 2010. *Time Binds: Queer Temporalities, Queer Histories.* Durham, NC: Duke University Press.

Kamala (1994). *Fictions of Feminist Ethnography.* Minneapolis: University of Minnesota Press.

Moore, David L. 1997. "Rough knowledge and radical understanding: Sacred Silence in American Indian Literatures." *American Indian Quarterly/Fall 1997*, vol. 21, no. 4: 633–662.

Moraga, Cherríe L. 2011. *A Xicana Codex of Changing Consciousness: Writings, 2000–2010.* Durham, NC: Duke University Press.

Sandoval, Chela. 2000. *Methodology of the Oppressed.* Minneapolis, MN: University of Minnesota Press.

Taylor, Diana. 2005. *The Archive and the Repertoire: Performing Cultural Memory in the Americas.* Durham, NC: Duke University Press.

Index

CPSIA information can be obtained at www.ICGtesting.com
Printed in the USA
LVOW10*1500021213

363566LV00011B/476/P